# RACE
## BECOMES
### TOMORROW

GERALD M. SIDER

# RACE
# BECOMES
# TOMORROW

North Carolina and the
Shadow of Civil Rights

DUKE UNIVERSITY PRESS    DURHAM AND LONDON    2015

Designed by Heather Hensley
Typeset in Quadraat Pro and Trade Gothic Condensed by
Westchester Publishing Services

Library of Congress Cataloging-in-Publication Data
Sider, Gerald M., author.
Race becomes tomorrow : North Carolina and the shadow
of civil rights / Gerald M. Sider.
pages cm
Includes bibliographical references and index.
ISBN 978-0-8223-5976-0 (hardcover : alk. paper)
ISBN 978-0-8223-6008-7 (pbk. : alk. paper)
ISBN 978-0-8223-7504-3 (e-book)
1. African Americans—Civil rights—North Carolina—
History—20th century. 2. North Carolina—Race relations—
History—20th century. 3. Racism—Political aspects—North
Carolina. I. Title.
E185.93.N6S54 2015
305.896'07307560904—dc23
2015017939

All photographs were taken by the author in 2014.
Cover art: Main Street, Maxton, NC. Photo by Gerald Sider.

FOR MY SONS, MY MENTORS
BYRON, HUGH, NOAH

FOR ROBIN S
Who found and helped me see the center

FOR FRANCINE
My guardian spirit
Thanks

AND FOR THE
One African American
who is shot by police,
a security guard,
or a White vigilante
every twenty-eight hours
Each
one among many
Each
America's history lesson
And now . . .

**We dies in harness. That's what it is to be colored.**

Elderly and very ill African American man,
fellow restaurant dishwasher, whom I urged
to go home to take care of his health, 1956

**Ever since the colored got civil rights, we had
to get rid of them. That's not what colored
means. We got rid of them and got Mexicans.**

Senior southern county official, describing
the changing labor demands of the new meat-
and poultry-packing industries, 2006

**For the master's tools will never dismantle the
master's house. They may allow us to temporarily
beat him at his own game, but they will never
enable us to bring about genuine change.**

Audre Lorde

# CONTENTS

*A gallery appears after page 70*

## ACKNOWLEDGMENTS

This is the second of two books to come from a deeply appreciated, and surprisingly difficult pair of exploratory research grants from the National Science Foundation. The first grant from the NSF was joined by supplemental grants from the faculty union and my university (the Professional Staff Congress and the City University of New York) and from the Institute of Social and Economic Research of Memorial University of Newfoundland. These grants supported a decade of work on Native health and well-being in Labrador, where I sought to understand, in useful ways, the epidemics of substance abuse, youth suicide, and domestic violence among the Inuit and Innu (Northern Cree), and the interweaving of health and stress in and against increasingly difficult situations both imposed upon and developing within Native communities. The book that resulted from that work is *Skin for Skin: Death and Life for Inuit and Innu* (Duke University Press, 2014). I pursued these issues further, in a context that focused more on potentially useful confrontations with domination, by examining a similar situation among indigenous Australians: "Making and Breaking the Aboriginal Remote: Realities, Languages, Tomorrows (A Commentary)," *Oceania* 84, no. 2 (July 2014): 158–68.

As the first decade of research was ending, I became interested in the differences between the deepening and intensifying health crises among northern peoples and the comparatively somewhat better, or at least very different, situation of Native American and African American peoples in coastal and central North and South Carolina. These southeastern peoples have had a similar history of severe oppression and collective and personal domination by the larger society and its state as have the northern Native peoples, but they have not engaged as much in communal/collective self-destruction. Simultaneously, the southern peoples have suffered more directly—not more, just more directly—from what has been done to them by the dominant society and state.

A subsequent NSF exploratory grant made it possible for me to look comparatively at stress and the rapidly changing and, for the poorer people, increasingly difficult circumstances of Native Americans and African Americans in coastal and central North and South Carolina that have developed simultaneously with the gains and victories of the civil rights struggles. After some substantial work on this contradictory situation, I decided to first focus on the changing situation of African Americans in this region. This book takes up that focus, starting with my experiences in the civil rights struggles in Robeson County, North Carolina, on the coastal plain border with South Carolina, where I had worked for sixteen months in 1967–68.

Taken together, these two books are a developing argument about the changing situation of vulnerable peoples as many become not just vulnerable but disposable. Taken together, these two books seek to also address issues of how to usefully grasp—to engage as partisans—such situations, with some understanding. The question of what constitutes a useful social "science," for the struggles and celebrations—in sum, the lives—of particularly vulnerable people drives this work.

In addition to the NSF, and Deborah Wilson, Head of the Cultural Anthropology Section, and Anna Kertula de Echeve, Head of Arctic Social Sciences, I owe many thanks to the American Museum of Natural History, Department of Anthropology, which through the kindness of Laurel Kendall and Peter Whiteley has given me a continuing research appointment, which provides access to its fine research library. Tom Baione, Director of the library, and Mai Reitmeyer, Senior Research Services Librarian, have been particularly helpful.

The libraries in Newfoundland and Labrador, particularly the Legislative Library of the Province of Newfoundland and Labrador, were crucial to the northern portion of this comparative work. Kimberly Hammond, Director; Andrea Hyde, Reference Librarian; Kim Puddister, Internet specialist; and Allison Stamp made this library a scholar's dream. Robert Sweeny, a historian of Canada, provided crucial conceptual advice for both these projects, as over the years have Valerie Burton, Rex Clark, August Carbonella, Heather Wareham, and Elizabeth Malichewski, with special support coming from Sharon Roseman, Robin Whitaker, and Mark Tate.

In the forty-six years I have worked in the South, I have had more help from more people than is easy to acknowledge. And because the world is made as it was and is, many of the people who helped me are now deceased, although many were much younger than I now am. Their survivors have mostly turned away from the struggles I shared with their parent or spouse, so to thank them now would not be noticed. Among the still living, very fortunately, are my Lumbee Indian mentors Ruth Bullard Locklear, John Albert Locklear and Ms. Phoede Locklear, John Locklear Jr. and Ms. Clair Locklear, Bruce Jones, former head of the North Carolina Indian Commission, Rod Locklear, Barto and Ms. Geraldine Clark, Dr. Martin L. Brooks, and Woodrow Dial. They are joined, in memory, by the Reverend Joy Johnson, Julian Pierce, Derek Lowry, and Thadis Oxendine. To all of them I can say not only that I would not know what I know without them, but more: I would not be who I am had I not known them.

In Maxton, Mayor Sally McLean and James McEachon went beyond helpful. Chief Leon Locklear of the Tuscarora Indians of Robeson County and his activist son, Mitchell Locklear, shared their struggles and their knowledge. For general insightful Robeson County advice, the Reverend Mac Legerton was irreplaceable. In South Carolina, Chief Ralph Oxendine of the Sumter County Cheraw, Second Chief Mandy Chapman Oxendine, Ms. Claudia Gainey, and the Indian spiritualist Claude Chavis were my guides. For my historical work the librarians of Pembroke State University, plus Melinda Maynor Lowry and Karen Blu, were specially helpful. Theresa Rubin helped with health statistics for the larger project. And for helping me formulate and develop my understanding of everyday life history, very special thanks are due to the two leaders in that field, Alf Luedtke and Hans Medick, who led the Everyday Life History section of the Max-Planck-Institut für Geschichte, in Göttingen, Germany. My two decades of work with them have shaped the way I think.

Kirk Dombrowski, Avram Bornstein, Christopher Lawrence, Anthony Marcus, Charles Menzies, Ellyn Rosenthal, and Elizabeth TenDyke, when we were all at the CUNY Graduate Center together, asked me questions and "gave" me comments (to put it gently) that still ring through my work. I would like to express appreciation to the Schoff Fund at the University Seminars at Columbia University for their help in publication. The ideas presented have benefited from discussions in the University Seminars on Culture, Power, and Boundaries, Content and Methods in the Social Sciences, and Memory and Slavery. Similarly, the book benefited from comments during presentations at the Department of Anthropology, Memorial University of Newfoundland. And the two prepublication readers of the manuscript gave suggestions that have made the work more clear and focused. Thanks all. And may I say, as part of my commitment to collective thinking, that I hope they enjoy being partly responsible for all that follows?

I owe a very special thanks to Gisela Fosado, editor at Duke University Press. She works with a wonderfully productive mixture of solid and welcome support and trenchant critique. This is the most useful possible combination, and I am truly appreciative. Her editorial assistant, Lorien Olive, and project editor Liz Smith were both helpful and encouraging, and Susan Ecklund, who excellently copyedited my linguistic fantasies, has also earned special thanks. Heather Hensley, designer, has a very fine and helpful eye, and Celia Braves had the difficult and much appreciated task of indexing the book.

No acknowledgment would be complete without thanks to the most insightful search-and-discover librarian ever, Francine Egger-Sider, who beyond helping the research has the further virtue—and pays the further price—of living with, encouraging, and advising the worker and the work.

## Introduction  Past History

This book is about the changing ways race is lived, primarily in the south-eastern United States and in New York City. It is also about how and why race cannot be lived. We cannot be what society at large, and the dominant society in particular, tries with some success to make us be. The history of race—the history of how race is continually made, unmade, and remade—emerges in good part from the paradox that race simultaneously can and cannot be lived. The point is not to play with the paradoxes of life but to use them to get our hands on what is and has been happening, so that we can help make more livable lives.

More: race thrives on yesterday, while tomorrow intrudes. That provides a further fundamental tension in our lives. This book is about both these tensions: between a race making that both must be and cannot be lived by its victims (who are not just African Americans) and a changing history that will not either let go of yesterday or fully deny tomorrow. This book is about the struggles that emerge within and against these tensions.

Race can at times, often many times, be lived gladly, as people find joy, comfort, satisfaction, and much more in their identities. It can also be lived as a lurking danger, collective and personal, as race gets woven into racism. And this is a continually changing mixture. The focus here will be from the 1960s to the present—the ways that past and still current struggles against racism and especially against the surprising consequences both of racism and of our victories against it have been and are now being shaped since the civil rights victories of the 1960s.

An old friend, a single woman, White, adopted an African American daughter. When the daughter was about six, one of her playmates asked her, "How come your mother is White?" and the child answered, within her mother's hearing, "Because she was born that way."

People are born with different colored skin and different looks, but race is made. This is a book about the making of race *from* the lives of the victims of that process, those made more vulnerable by the making. This includes not just Black and White but also a range of Latino/a and Native American peoples who think of themselves, and in a few ways are, in between Black and White.

Note that the perspective of this book is not "for" the vulnerable, or "about" the vulnerable, but *from*. It is a book about how life at the far end of inequality is lived within, against, and apart from the making of race, and it includes those who dance with the fantasy that we are above all that. To write from the perspective of the vulnerable is not just to write about how race is and is not lived but also to address the inescapable questions in such lives: What can be done? What can we do?

Making race is always, of course, making races: race, like class, is meaningless if there is only one. And there is more to the process than making races to make race. Race turns out to be made twice, simultaneously: between and within each race. And the issue before us is not just making race but living race. Living race also must be done twice: between and within. But the relation of "between and within" changes dramatically over time, and some of the changes are more than surprising.

At the center of this work are, first, what seem to be stories, and then, what seem to be either the open wounds of our world or the not yet resolvable, or perhaps irresolvable, struggles. Yet the focus of the book goes well beyond these, first into what the stories actually tell, and how, and then to the problems of making new struggles in a world whose changes are both constantly surprising and constantly predictable.

To introduce both story and struggle:

1. Robert Piglia, in discussing the logic of stories, wrote:

In one of his notebooks, Chekhov recorded the following anecdote: "a man in Monte Carlo goes to the casino, wins a million, returns home, commits suicide." The classic form of the short story is condensed within the nucleus of that future, unwritten story. Contrary to the predictable and conventional (gamble-lose-commits suicide), the intrigue is presented as a paradox. The anecdote disconnects the story of the gambling and the story of the suicide. That rupture is the key to defining the double character of the story's form. First thesis: a . . . story always tells two stories. . . .

Each of the two stories is told in a different manner. Working with two stories means working with two different systems of causality. The same events enter simultaneously into two antagonistic . . . logics. . . . The points where they intersect are the foundations of the story's construction. (2011, 63)

Start there, but go further, for we will be dealing not just with stories that are told or written but with what is lived, and what can be lived. It is not always clear that what Piglia calls "the antagonistic logics" within a story, or more simply the parts in our lives that don't quite fit together, ever "intersect," ever connect in ways that form a coherent whole. Sometimes, and in important ways, the point of a story about lives that are actually lived is that things do not come together: nothing fits together, nothing works. That, as we shall see, may be part of our strength.

More: the (at least) two stories in any real story often take place not simply at the same time but in the not quite past and in the impending tomorrow. The stories that people live are often happening in a past that will not stay past, and simultaneously in a future that struggles to be born. Among the many tasks of the stories that follow is to show what the struggles for rights have been and are now, and how complex, how contradictory, how chaotic, how uncivil, and eventually how wonderful are the struggles for a different and a better tomorrow, while yesterday is still thrown in our faces or evades our attempts to hold on to it.

2. A story whose echoes I still live with, here partly to introduce what starts out as a simple and obvious point: that we do not choose, or we are not allowed to choose, all the struggles we must engage, though surely we do choose some. The complexities will develop as we continue.

In the late 1950s I went to college in Philadelphia and mostly supported myself by washing dishes at night in a coffeehouse restaurant. Weekday nights I was alone at this task; weekends I was joined by an elderly Black man.

One Friday evening he came to work clearly sick and hurting. He was pale, and he leaned hard against a sink while he worked, ignoring the water that splashed down his front. I urged him to go home and rest, telling him that for an evening or two I could work fast enough and hard enough to cover for him. He just shook his head no. When I repeated my urging, he looked at me and just said, "We dies in harness. That's what it is to be colored."

Not that's what it means, but that's what it is.

That named one of his struggles, and also ours. Both his and our struggles, as we shall see, necessarily change even faster than our situations, for otherwise domination defines us. To put it more simply and directly, but only here by way of introduction: the struggles we cannot avoid are not always, and never fully, defined by the situations imposed upon us.

Two further stories will begin to highlight the struggles of race as they become shaped by the uncertain connections between yesterday and tomorrow. These stories come from my work in Robeson County, North Carolina, which began with civil rights organizing for a year and a half in 1967–68 and has continued, for an expanding variety of purposes, episodically but continually, since.

First: On the evening of April 5, 1968, the day after the Reverend Martin Luther King Jr. was murdered, there was a memorial march along the main street of Lumberton, North Carolina. Lumberton is the county seat of Robeson County, on the North Carolina–South Carolina border: the old, then still openly violent, coastal plantation country. The march went north up Elm Street, then the town's main shopping street, starting at the northern end of the Black neighborhood on the swampy southeast of Lumberton, and ending in front of the county courthouse, with its Civil War memorial statue on a tall pedestal in front, to go back to the churches in the Black neighborhood.

It was a very scary march. On top of the two-story, flat-roofed stores were police—state troopers, town cops, and sheriff's deputies—with shotguns and searchlights pointing at us, and walking alongside us were more police, also with shotguns and pistols in open holsters. The march was sorrow-soaked and utterly peaceful. People were crying, and saying prayers, and quietly singing hymns, and mostly consoling and holding one another. There were, I would guess, several hundred African Americans, perhaps five to six hundred or more, and a few Whites and Native Americans.

While the marchers were mostly crying, the police looked mostly scared and were trying to look aggressive. They were in any case very scary: a frightened cop is a dangerous creature. Despite the cops in our faces, and despite the planned and controlled march route, the sorrow and the sense of loss emerging from the parade were close to, or beyond, overwhelming.

At the western edge of Lumberton, a town of about fifteen thousand people in the 1960s, is the main East Coast north–south interstate highway, I-95. And Lumberton has long had both east–west and north–south railroads. So the town has had a fairly viable economy since the mid-nineteenth century, first on the basis of agricultural and forest products shipped out of the county, and then with manufacturing that depends on highway and railroad access, plus more recently a lot of transient tourist dollars, for Lumberton is about halfway between New York City and the winter beaches of Miami, Fort Lauderdale, and Palm Beach.

Twenty-five miles west of Lumberton and Interstate 95 is the small town of Maxton, North Carolina. Since the transformations that ended southern small-scale agriculture, which culminated in the 1960s, the old market towns like Maxton are often economically finished. Small-scale local-supply markets and local-sale market agriculture were replaced by large, highly mechanized corporate farming. These corporate farms did not buy their major supplies or equipment from small-town dealers, did not sell their produce to local warehouses, and did not hire much local labor of the sort that had to shop locally year-round. What labor they hired, beyond the few skilled equipment drivers, was largely seasonal, and very substantially composed of undocumented workers who disappeared after harvest. A great many small market towns have been increasingly doomed by the disappearance of small-scale farming. If these old market towns were close to an interstate highway, and had the resources and skills to offer the kinds of incentives that attracted new industries, they managed to do reasonably well. But Maxton was twenty-five miles west of I-95, beyond what the newer industries consider acceptable, and so it started, by the late 1960s, on a relentless downward economic slide that, with Whites fleeing, turned it into a predominantly African American town. That had several advantages and several costs for those who remained.

All this, and more important its consequences for local "race relations," will soon be discussed in detail. For the moment, all that needs to be said is that in just twenty-five years since the spring of 1968, when Dr. King was murdered, Maxton shifted from a totally White-dominated, mildly prosperous town to an economically struggling town with a Black mayor and town council. Fueling this transition was a substantial population shift, as a great many Whites moved away from the seriously declining economy. In addition to all the social and cultural gains that Black control of the town brought to Black people and neighborhoods, which had their physical infrastructure significantly improved, Maxton became a place where it was very much harder for many, perhaps most, African Americans to earn a living, and very much harder for tax revenues to sustain the current town costs.

The second story: Thirty-five years after I marched with that heart-clawing parade in Lumberton to mark the murder of our dear Rev. Dr. King, grown even dearer and closer to many since his death, I walked in a commemorative parade down the main street of Maxton, on Martin Luther King, Jr. Day, 2003. The march went down Dr. Martin Luther King Jr. Drive, as the street had been renamed. It was previously State Highway 74, until Maxton was bypassed by a new highway. Several of the African American town policemen marched with us, talking with us, not to control the march but to join it, and also to stop traffic for us at the crossroads. So did the African American mayor, several African American town councillors and ministers, a hundred or so local Black people, a White minister, and the White leader of the local Boy Scouts. It was a quiet and short march, following some predictable and gentle speeches in the gym of the local elementary school. There could not have been a more different march from what had happened in Lumberton.

The starting question is what was hiding underneath these two marches, for in both cases there was indeed an incredibly powerful, almost invisible underground. In the 1968 march, with all the guns pointed directly at us, some right in our faces by the cops walking alongside us, the social relations that the theater and reality of White against Black violence were designed to produce were almost dead. That was the last gasp, as we shall see, of the world of domination that made, and tried increasingly unsuccessfully to still make, a category and a people they called "niggers."

To write about the production of race in the United States, it is, unfortunately, necessary to write about the production of "niggers," and the production of the kinds of "Whites" that went with this. Slavery, lynching, segregated schools, and the current Supreme Court–endorsed restrictions on African American voting rights were not used to produce "the N-word." Chapter 6 directly addresses what the current, more polite language of racism and sexism avoids, what it conceals, and how this newly "polite" language constructs what W. E. B. Du Bois so insightfully called, in the title of one of his very special books, *Darkwater: Voices from Within the Veil* ([1920] 2007). Not behind, within. The voice is the veil, in many cases, despite the fact that it is now far less insulting, far less demeaning, far less hurtful. What is veiled, above all, is not just the continuing abuse hidden within the newly polite language, but in both cases—the hard words and the more polite words—the social and cultural practices the words point toward and also conceal.

The names—labels, categories, hurts—given to oppressed and exploited people are never just names; much more important, they are never just insults, although they are intended to be, and are, deeply insulting. The names take on their cultural, social, and political force because they also point toward what was done and will be done to a people so categorized.

In this book, in some restricted instances, the word "nigger" is used. It is used in the context of a direct quote or an attribution. It is, in particular, used to name a social process designed to produce both a useful and a disposable people. The South, when it needed the least expensive possible labor, with the fewest possible rights, did not try to produce "N-words," so to use that euphemism or any other to discuss what was and has been happening is to conceal and minimize the brutality and the violence of the processes making inequality. It is also thus to minimize the strength and the resources of the opposition among the victims of this process and their allies.

Hopefully, by the end of the book, those who rightly find such direct language shocking and upsetting, which it truly is, will also find the concealment of what is now happening behind a language of politeness and pretend constitutionalism equally scary, and equally offensive. Chapter 6 deals with this issue in detail.


The central point of this process was both to make a kind of people to use for their labor in mostly hard and unrewarding ways, and also to make people who during and after these hard and poorly paid uses could be more or less readily controlled. The inner strengths and resourcefulness that it took to sustain being used so hard continually undermined the continuing attempts at control. Making Blacks largely in this way was also making Whites—not only as a different identity but also as differently uncontrollable, in their often violent relations to Blacks. Despite and against clear laws to the contrary, attempts by the state to suppress White violence against Blacks have been few and far between. Contradictions emerge at both ends of the processes creating difference, and in both cases these contradictions give shape and substance to what is and is not happening.

The mechanical cotton picker and the mechanization of other crops made ultra-low-cost hand labor almost useless. The world that needed to produce masses of such workers, readily available for one of the most grueling jobs in the world, was gone. All that physical and cultural violence increasingly, but never yet finally, became almost yesterday, became a past that is unfortunately very far from actually being past, despite the speeches, the new names for roads and streets, and even the holiday in dear Dr. King's name.

Farm labor is still rather brutally organized, but as we shall see in chapter 2, soon after African Americans got some civil rights they were replaced, as farm labor, with the peoples called "Mexicans," mostly undocumented and thus without rights. Even the "foreign" farmworkers who are officially recruited with government and state programs have very few rights, and the people here without documents have even fewer.

The best idea I can provide of the logic that drove what I am calling "quiet" violence can be grasped from two facts: Robeson County, in the mid-twentieth century, was by reputation the second-wealthiest, or more precisely, second-highest wealth-producing, rural county in the U.S. South based on the value of the agricultural produce shipped from it; at the same time, it was usually said that it was one of the fifty poorest counties in the United States by per capita income. It is still the poorest county in North Carolina. Lumberton was both the county seat, as the administrative center is often called, and the seat of those who administered and sought to maintain that spread—a spread that did not just happen but had to be made. It was, and still is, being made rather quietly and systematically, which does not make it much, if any, easier to oppose.

As the labor needs changed profoundly with mechanization and with the demise of small-scale farming, a whole new way of making different kinds of lives, tied to different kinds of labor needs, became increasingly necessary. A gun pointed directly at you is an act of intense violence, whether or not the trigger is pulled. The old ways of producing vulnerable people were no longer either needed or wanted by the new elites who ran the new factories, and they made it stop. That was part of the transformation in Maxton in 2003, turning very much away from the whole display of potential and actual state violence against our march in Lumberton, and putting in its place, even in a community where the elected officials were African American, a different kind of attempted control, one that increasingly produced disposable, rather than useful, people at the bottom.

We were witnessing, in this 1968 march in Lumberton, the end times of a long-lasting way of making specific kinds of inequalities, though we were mostly too scared, or more likely too upset by the guns in our faces and the death of our dear Rev. Dr. King, to realize that underneath the theater of total violence against us, and control over us, were the death spasms of a social order. Taking the place of these old ways of producing particularly vulnerable African Americans have been new practices and policies, as we shall see, with somewhat different goals and methods, and with results that include intensifying differentiation within African American communities.

Underneath the very different parade in Maxton, in 2003, was another, less hidden but still uncertain new world, a world struggling to be born but not quite making it. New kinds of suffering and unmet needs were emerging, shaping new kinds of failures in the midst of both new kinds of successes and new kinds of recognized or just barely acknowledged dignity. It is more difficult to describe, or even to point toward, this world that was then and still is not quite born, as opposed to the more easy task of naming a world that is not quite dead, so the discussion of the emerging history half hiding beneath this quiet parade in Maxton will have to wait a bit.


This book examines how race is both socially constructed and lived. It does so in the context of developing a new perspective on the familiar topic of transitions. I am particularly concerned with the transition from yesterday to tomorrow in the often unavoidable struggles that occur in the everyday lives of ordinary people.

The transition from yesterday to tomorrow often is, or seems, deeply chaotic. People all too frequently must be concerned with the "what-ifs" that impinge on their lives: What if the factory does close as the managers threaten it will? What if my flexible job schedules me for hours when I need to pick up my child from school? What if my kid needs to go to the doctor and I am already behind on my rent/mortgage? What if? What if? Then what?

We are entering a terrain of stress, doubt, and uncertainty that I will call the problem of tomorrow. All forms of inequality—race, class, gender, locality, and more—raise the problem of tomorrow with special intensity for those on the more vulnerable end of the continuum. Much of this is intentional, rather than accidental, for all these forms of inequality "work," as it were, in part by limiting and reshaping the possibilities for tomorrow, and by making tomorrow increasingly uncertain for people at or near the bottom, as they shift from being useful because of their position near the bottom to being disposable—some both useful and disposable, others increasingly not at all wanted, but just disposable.

At the same time, people caught in these confining nets that limit their possible tomorrows also actively and expressively can claim their own tomorrows within, against, and beyond socially constructed and imposed limitations—the constrained futures that so powerfully and painfully shape the now. All three usually come together, as people seek to claim their own lives within, against, and beyond the all too real constraints that are so central to making and continually remaking inequalities.

Here the special focus will be on race, for race is the inequality that is politically and socially still constructed with the most directly applied state violence. After decades in which the left and progressives have focused on "the economy," we need to pay equal attention to what we might, just to get us started, call "the state."

Gender violence may well be equally severe and equally pervasive, and equally usually granted impunity to continue by the state. But unless some prominent person is caught as perpetrator or seen as victim, it does not usually get the same media attention as does the violence that continually makes race, so race can seem, more than other forms of inequality except perhaps locality, that what is done to you is done on purpose. No pedestals, no pretense that it is unacceptably wrong, no jail time for the perpetrators, especially when they are employed by the state.

The violence that produces and sustains the inequalities of locality—differential schooling, housing, health care (including toxic waste locations and untreated rodent infestations), transportation, and community services just to begin—is scarcely mentioned or publicly opposed in any sustained ways at all. So the production of inequalities between, as well as within, localities is not widely seen as being a product of state and state violence, to the extent that it actually is. All those just-mentioned expressions of state making, of making unequal neighborhoods and communities, and making state at the same time, in the same way, are instances of what I am calling quiet violence. Violence, of course, is just one part of these processes, and not necessarily the most encompassing. But it is and has been a particularly compelling component of the continual, and only in some ways continually changing, production of race.

Race is a concept like class or gender: its lived reality lies in the fact that there is always more than one. "Making race" is actually always making races—the very same violence that makes some people "Black" or "illegal aliens" (for differential citizenship, as we shall see, has deep similarities to race) makes others "White" or "citizens." And the opposite just as much: the very same privileges that have made some people White and citizen make others Black and not quite citizen, not quite within the equal protection of the law and state bureaucracies. Race is, necessarily, races; inequality is, necessarily, inequalities: always multiple in the same location, always multiple among the same people.

However, when race is used in the generalizing singular, for example, when a college administrator says, "We need to reconsider how we admit students on the basis of race," or when a real estate company dealing in both rentals and purchases says to its agents, "We need to be more careful how we code race in the applicant's file," the word "race" here most directly refers to Blacks, and now probably also Hispanics. "Race," as used in the context of its continual making and remaking, almost always refers to categorizing people at the most vulnerable end of the changing ways inequality is organized, at any given moment, and the changing ways differential treatment is meted out.

The gains, losses, and major reversals in the United States, since the civil rights victories of the 1960s, along with fundamental changes in the economy, particularly with deindustrialization; the massive rise in unlivable-wage service sector jobs combined with massive nationwide declines in the availability of affordable low-income housing that has a modicum of services; the mechanization and chemicalization of agriculture; the increasing desire for seasonal workers, such as harvest labor, to go away after they are needed, and not make demands on local schools or health care or code-level housing; the proliferation of high-injury jobs such as poultry processing and meatpacking, where people with even fewer rights than Blacks now have employment priority; and a political process that once again specifically marginalizes Blacks and poor people with both increasing obstacles to voting and the gerrymandering that makes minority votes, in particular, not matter: all this and more provide the social and historical context for an analysis of the continuing struggles for the problem of tomorrow. Such struggles are historically specific, as the transition from yesterday to tomorrow changes.

The special focus here is on the changes that have occurred, often with very surprising consequences, since the "civil rights" victories of the 1960s.

To examine how race is lived in the transition from yesterday to tomorrow, we must necessarily broaden our perspective in two ways. First, when people invoke the usual mantra of inequality—now almost its holy trinity—class, race, and gender, they usually leave out locality. Yet locality is a major arena for the social construction of inequality and for its contestation. All four and more will be addressed here. Second, the task before us is not just to understand how race is made and lived by those made vulnerable, but also how its limitations and impositions are, and can be, contested while its pleasures and rewards are celebrated.

Focusing on what race does rather than starting with an attempt to say what it is, for what it does is what it is, permits us to center on a key manifestation of its continuing social history: race names specific kinds of unavoidable struggle. This is not at all to claim or pretend that struggle is the center of making and living race, nor all there is that is important to consider. Not at all. It is just a useful place to start when our fundamental concern is with the everyday lives of ordinary people.

Keep "with" in mind, for it shapes what follows in this book and in the daily lives of the people who are at stake here. With as in "along with"; with as "within."

We will be dealing in this book with an issue that is very simple to think and often very difficult to live. What might have "worked" yesterday to make it to tomorrow, more or less intact, is not quite certain to work today, even as poorly as it did yesterday. The history of how race is continually made, unmade, and remade emerges in large part from the paradox that race simultaneously can and cannot be lived. Race can at times, often many times, be lived gladly as people find joy, comfort, satisfaction, and much more in their identities of race, class, gender, and locality. Simultaneously, each of these identities can be and is lived as lurking danger, collective and personal, particularly as race gets woven into racism, gender into the supposedly restricted context of "domestic violence"—would that it were only domestic—class becomes an unlivable minimum wage and the banks stealing your home with no restitution when they are discovered doing so, and locality among its other manifestations becomes trying to live in a neighborhood in Detroit where many people's water is turned off to prevent any further taxation of the wealthy and the corporations, and to enable the profitable sale of the city's water supply to a private (equals profit-making) corporation.

I think it is beyond obvious that giving police forces tanks, armored personnel carriers, military-grade rifles, stun grenades, whatever, not just will not but cannot solve the problem of tomorrow in the production of race for long—because it only seems to postpone tomorrow, it only seems to keep tomorrow the same as today, which in reality is an impossible task, even for states and for police. There are fundamental, unsolvable contradictions between making a people completely disposable, as many poor African Americans have been made to be, neither needed nor wanted, and trying to control their lives at the same time. Formerly they were both useful and disposable; when you become just disposable, the world has changed in fundamental ways. The same with the walls and fences and armed guards with their helicopters, searchlights, and cameras, and the volunteer militia allowed to roam freely with their guns along the border between the United States and Mexico: all designed to prevent the replacement Blacks from joining the economy that clamors to hire them in construction, meat-packing and poultry processing, farm labor, domestic service, and other locales where there is a strong demand for people now without many if any civil rights, people who themselves are not, for the moment, in a position to effectively make many of their own demands. There are again unsolvable contradictions between wanting to use such people in large numbers and wanting to get rid of them.

The central point about race becoming tomorrow is that from the go-nowhere unfolding of such contradictions the production of race, which is somewhat predictable in the short run, becomes unpredictable in any even slightly longer term. Race is now produced, lived, and contested in that unpredictability. This is not a conclusion, but only an opening to what will follow.

With the issue of contradictions in mind—at its core the impossibility of both producing and either controlling or containing race, or "illegal aliens," another product of state—we can give a few more only introductory words about the changing worlds of Lumberton and Maxton, of race as it was and is made in the not quite yesterday and the not yet tomorrow.

The sorrow for Dr. King in the march in Lumberton was not just for his death but for the fact that he had helped to bring all of us a better tomorrow than we have had, and he held the promise of more. His murder raised the specter that tomorrow would no longer be somewhat better, and that tragedy, that probable intention of his murder at the moment when he decisively expanded his reach to labor organizing, was a full part of our grief.

The celebration in Maxton, thirty-five years later, had a more complex dynamic. The murder of Dr. King was fading somewhat into the background, with his flamboyant wisdom and power being contained in the names of streets and parks and other fixed material items, plus a holiday that somehow was less holy as the years passed. When racist-governed Arizona refused to accept Martin Luther King, Jr. Day as a holiday, as a holy day, shortly after it was declared nationally, we could tell that the day was still real, that it still mattered, but thirty-five years later it was slipping into ordinary.

How far the confrontations Dr. King helped to orchestrate and to win have slipped into the ordinary, and increasingly into a past that is indeed past, was thrown against our faces in the recent fifty-year commemorative gathering of his "I Have a Dream" speech and rally in Washington, DC, on August 28, 2013. I was shocked and dismayed by the fact that there were scarcely any police present at our demonstration, our commemoration. A few police to direct traffic, a small handful of military police behind the chain-link fence around some monuments, and that was all I saw. In the sixties, Washington was crawling with cops when we came. They were everywhere with their nightsticks, their tear gas spray cans, their walkie-talkies, and their Suzuki motorcycles. Now in 2013 there were almost no cops. I found this profoundly upsetting, and in some ways even more scary than cops with guns in our faces. They are not in the slightest afraid of us anymore. We and our protests have been fully domesticated. We have become the ho-hum. We can either invent something very new very soon, to make changes for a more just tomorrow, or lie down and shovel the dirt over ourselves.

To begin to think about what might be new, both in our situation and in what we might do about it, to confront our changing situation more assertively, we can note that there were fundamental and profound tensions within, or underneath, this quiet, more sparsely attended and more gentle parade in Maxton in 2003. Black Maxton, as we shall see, was in some ways also dying Maxton, dying economically for lack of state life support, for lack of tomorrow. Underneath the march in Maxton commemorating what from the past still lives with us today there was the widespread worry about how Maxton will live tomorrow. That worry can be a gift, a gift that we can pass on, for it may lead us to develop new kinds of struggles, new kinds of encounters with the new pressures against a more just world.

We cannot usefully struggle against the problems of today, nor can we invent an anthropology or a history that can create useful understandings of how to struggle, how to win against the problems coming tomorrow without grasping not only the changing and continuing violence of the not-yet-past but the fragments of tomorrow in the ruptures of today. This is a book about that task of struggle and confrontation, based on an expanded sense of history. This is not history in the abstract, not history as the study of yesterday. It is the history that we live, or try to live within and against, as we try to deal with, make, remake, or avoid—or all this together—our unclear, rapidly changing circumstances.

The histories we live are both the history others think we have and the histories that we claim. To say that one is more real than the other is to profoundly misunderstand our struggles.

At first this book will look like a memoir—a range of stories, many of which I either participated in or witnessed. It is, however, very much not a memoir. The difference emerges from some clarity about the work that stories do in this text, and the work they do, as they are lived, in shaping and reshaping our situations, putting both things and us both together and apart.

In most of my writings, which usually are rooted in stories, I invoke the poet, author, and art historian John Berger. He once wrote, and constantly used, the point that "if every event which occurred could be given a name, there would be no need for stories" ([1983] 2011: 74). And he also wrote that stories "testify to the always slightly surprising range of the possible" ([1985] 2011: 15).

Stories constructed and invoked in the perspective suggested by Berger are pathways into the complexities of situations that cannot be fully grasped. Where I continue on from that point is to suggest that we might not always want to fully grasp what the stories point toward, what they lead us into. To pretend that we fully understand a situation, and more—that we can grasp it: get our minds and our hands around it—is to separate ourselves, often in ways that make a lot of distance, whatever our sympathies and concerns, from the people living both in and against the stories of their lives. For they quite often, and quite realistically, do not fully grasp what is happening, or why. And they must seek to live in and beyond an impending tomorrow without fully knowing what might be happening. As all of us do, of course, but when you are fifty-something years old, and the factory you have worked at for a decade or three closes and moves far away, tomorrow can loom both exceedingly large and infinitely small.

Here I should also add that stories, of the kind we are most familiar with, have beginnings, middles, and ends. Many of the stories invoked here are not so linear, not so coherently organized. They may seem coherent as they are told, but not so much as they are lived.

People in such situations as these stories seek to describe often very clearly and powerfully know some of what and why, for they are living it and experiencing it, moment after moment, from yesterday to the coming and often crashing tomorrow, but a good story takes us both there and beyond, into what is not yet if ever knowable. Children get stories about "why"; we adults usually know that as an act of love, of sheltering them from the world by making it seem explainable when it often is neither fully explainable nor fully livable. The good and useful stories we might well tell each other, in our adult lives, take on their importance by the way they do not fully even pretend to grasp the why of the world. Maybe if we fully understood the why, we might lack the courage and the energy to confront it.

Not all the stories that follow are in this sense good stories, but I think some are, for they still wake up both me and the other participants in the middle of the night. Or so I have been told, and so I am telling these stories to you. They are waking stories not at all because they are scary, although a few are, but because they are so damn inconclusive. And that is hopefully their useful purpose, to make, or just to suggest, new openings.

I have been asked, in order to clarify all this, to provide a story about how race "works" through the uncertain connections between yesterday and tomorrow. Will do. But the best story I know on this topic, the one that taught me to worry about race in what for me then were very new ways, is one that I have told before (Sider 2003b).

One morning in late July or early August 1967, I was downstairs in the basement of the old county courthouse in Lumberton, trying to get some sense of Indian land loss, and former Indian landholdings, from early deed books. It was hot and airless, and so sometime between ten and ten thirty, I went to the courthouse lobby to get a drink of water and some fresher air. There were about four or five courtrooms, for tax matters, for civil issues, for criminal cases, and so forth, and at this moment they were all in recess. So the lobby was relatively full, with various people milling about—lawyers dressed like lawyers, a few judges, court officials and police, people waiting to be heard or to be with someone who needed to be there, whatever. This old courthouse, subsequently replaced by a modern building, had several "old" features, from the slow-turning, large ceiling fans that moved the air a bit, to six bathrooms and three water fountains. There were separate bathrooms not just for men and women but for Whites, Blacks, and Indians. And there were three water fountains, one for each "race." Behind each water fountain was a sign, black letters on a white board, that once said "White," "Negro," "Indian." The federal civil rights laws about public buildings had made this illegal, so the signs had been covered with a thin layer of whitewash, so it was still possible, without looking all that closely, to see what they once said.

I saw an elderly Black man, on this very hot and muggy day, dressed in a shiny gabardine suit, with unmatched jacket and trousers—the Sunday clothes of someone quite poor—walk up to the water fountains, look at those half-erased signs, and walk away without taking a drink.

He had enough troubles in this world without my going to ask him any questions, so I can only guess. In that theater of power, with who knew who was watching, he did not want to drink from the fountain that said "Negro," and it very probably was or seemed too dangerous to drink from the one that said "White." It was impossible for him—or us—to know how past was the past, and how uncertain was the future within that today in that place. That is the remaking of race within its supposed unmaking. That tension, that uncertain today between perhaps yesterday and maybe tomorrow, is a central part of the continuing making and remaking of race.


One further introductory point, to clarify what may both cause concern and be somewhat confusing. Occasionally in this book I use "we" or "our" to refer to both myself and the African Americans and Native Americans with whom I worked, with whom I engaged in civil rights struggles. Because the point is both important to the book and a bit peculiar, it requires clarification and explanation, some here and some at the end of this book, when the impetus for this usage has been developed.

The problem of my occasional usage of "we" and "us" does not start or remain simply with the fact that I am White and a northerner. It has other roots. To begin, on marches like the one the day after Dr. King was murdered, I also had guns pointed in my face, and worse. I suffered a few of the same threats and fears as others, including being chased at one point on an election day by Whites with guns. So in that sense there really is something by way of a material and social basis for "us," if never fully.

Very much on the other hand, against my use of "us": One day in 1967, after I had been working with civil rights struggles there for about six months, a Native American in the same locale, facing similar problems and assaults as did African Americans, started a conversation with me by asking if I liked being there with them. I assured him I did, very much. He then told me that many people in his community liked me a lot, and that he would give me a half acre of his land, down by the road, and help me build a house, so I could just stay there. This was an extraordinarily generous offer, as he had only seventeen acres, barely enough for a useful bit of income. I asked him what I would do to earn a living, and his reply was "teach school." I reminded him that with my known political engagements I would last maybe one term before the White elite, who ran all the schools, Black, Indian, and White, got me fired. Then what would I do? He replied: "You scratch out a living, same as the rest of us."

I asked for some time to think about it, and the following week went back to thank him intensely for the offer, but to tell him that after another year I was going to go back to New York. At that point we both knew—had there been any previous doubts—that "we" and "us" was in large part a fantasy. But when a village policeman put a sawed-off shotgun in my face one night, with one hand on the trigger and the other on a long and heavy metal flashlight, and said, "Don't make no sudden moves," it was not a total fantasy. I just ask the reader to live awhile with that contradictory simultaneity in my occasional use of "us," until we see both what it produces and what it masks.

# PART I

---

## STORIES

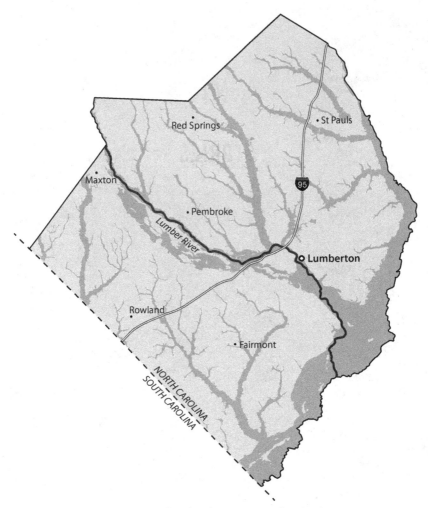

The towns of Robeson County, showing the swamps and wetlands.

—

# ONE

# Did the Conk Rag Lose?

## SWAMPS, ISLANDS, SOAKS

The coastal plain along the Carolinas is a strange region—multiple races making and contesting both each other and among themselves for places upon an unusual landscape. These two features, race and landscape, have for very long been related in ways that produce a dark, sunny, and violent land: both the classic South and a very different South. Our stories begin with the landscape.

If you stood at the shore of the Atlantic Ocean, at the Carolina coast where North and South Carolina meet, and looked inland, looked far inland, far past the near-shore golf courses and beach playgrounds, you would see a coastal plain, fifty to almost one hundred miles deep in the Carolinas. The Piedmont hills and the Appalachian Mountains west of the Piedmont give this coastal region a special and continuing history, from before then to beyond now.

From late spring through summer and into the fall, especially in summer, it rains briefly but intensely in the early afternoon, it seems almost every afternoon. The moisture-dense wind-pushed low clouds, blowing inland from the warm Atlantic, bang up against the Piedmont updrafts and empty onto the coastal plain. For just inland from the coastal plain is the Piedmont—the hard rock, bedrock, hilly uplands that begin 70 to 100 miles west of the ocean shore, and stretch 150 miles, more or less, westward from the coastal plain to the Appalachian Mountains. The updrafts from the

Piedmont hills block many of the summer rain clouds from being wind-pushed any farther west. Those rain clouds that make it past the Piedmont updrafts water the eastern slopes of the Appalachians. The rivers, rushing eastward from the Appalachians to the Atlantic crest over the eastern edge of the Piedmont, tumble down a fairly sharp boundary between the Piedmont and the coastal plain, a boundary called the fall line. Rushing down this steep decline, the rivers reach the flat and sandy coastal plain. When they reach the coastal plain, they join the rain-soaked lands there and slow down greatly. In recent years the rainfall patterns have been changing to an alternation between drought and deluge, but the consequences for the continuing formation of coastal swamps remain about the same, although farmers are facing more difficult and more costly problems.

The load of soil and silt a river can carry is directly related to how fast the water flows. When the western rivers drop over the fall line and reach the coastal plain and slow down, they deposit most of their soil burden. The rivers then spread out into increasingly shallow and broad soaks and swamps, often with a stream, or something like a stream, meandering somewhere between the middle and the margins of the swamp.

Then as the coastal plain edges toward the ocean, the land just before the ocean in many places rises slightly, holding back the swamp waters drifting toward the sea. So the coastal plain in the Carolinas is marked by two different kinds of swamps—the long and sometimes wide river swamps that wind and twist from the Piedmont edge toward the ocean, leaving dry islands scattered within them, and then, from place to place, episodically, great coastal swamps. It was not a very useful land for plantation farming, the kind of farming that depended upon river transport to the port and large plots of good land worked by gang labor. It was not useful for plantation farming unless and until: unless and until those who claimed intrusive ownership of the lands had their hands on a lot of labor, especially labor that could be whipped and driven, for the swamps were not just hot but also hotbeds of yellow fever, malaria, and a raft of other diseases.

These swamps were a very effective refuge for all the peoples for whom the expanding colonial plantation frontier was even more deadly difficult to survive. In these swamps lived poor Whites, running away from one issue or another, or just wanting to live more autonomous lives, and for very similar reasons runaway slaves and free Blacks, plus a wide variety of shattered Native American peoples, all of whom found the dry and farmable islands in the game- and fish-rich swamps, despite the disease risks, more safe and productive places to live than elsewhere in this violence-soaked, water-soaked land. As the plantations encroached by the early mid-nineteenth century, the formerly free people became harnessed to those intrusions.

Labor that could be controlled was used to ditch and drain the swamps, and then at the beginning of the twentieth century, when steam and then internal combustion engines were brought to the task, the drainage of the swamps was stunning. Back Swamp, for one example, was reduced from fifteen hundred feet wide just southwest of Maxton to an eight-foot channel, and the drained lands, rich with rotted vegetation, in those days before easily available chemical fertilizers, were very productive. But other people besides farmers wanted what grew on this fertile land.

Logging companies made vast profits at the beginning of the twentieth century, driving narrow-gauge rail tracks into the draining swamps and driving out the multicolored small-scale farmers—Indians, Blacks, poor Whites, and all the possible mixes—who had sheltered on the dry islands in the midst of these swamps. The lumber companies kept their promise to resell the land to local people when they were done logging the swamp-lands and pine forests they bought, but they sold their lands in large blocks, and local banks refused to loan the purchase price to non-Whites. Large-scale, primarily White- and corporate-owned farms were formed in this transition. In the midst of all this, Indians mostly stayed on the land, a large proportion as sharecroppers and in other forms of tenancy, another proportion doing the extraordinarily hard work of ditching and draining land they inherited or managed to purchase, mostly from each other, or just taking unwanted land. I describe this process and the rebellions it provoked in earlier works (Sider 2003a, 2003b).

The lumber companies did not want the smaller tracts of land, where the costs came close to or exceeded the returns, so there were several areas where small "dry islands" in the swamps were left out of this transformation. The people who took up these dry island lands worked beyond hard to make the land more farmable, selling off small tracts of pine forests that covered the more sandy soils, and then trying to manure and fertilize and drain the sand enough to make it productive. To support a family took somewhere between ten and fifteen acres of land: in most places and for most ways of living both in and from the larger economy, it took more like fifteen acres than ten. This was a lot of land to clear and to drain.

Blacks, too poor and too hard-pressed to get and clear much land, mostly moved into the small towns, starting in the early twentieth century and accelerating until midcentury, when the migration to local towns was largely completed. Living in the towns, the men were brought out to the farms as day laborers when needed for farmwork and the women used for what many Whites seemed to regard, from within their brutal codes of deference, use, and abuse, as both domestic and domesticating service.

The Whites who took more extensive control of this now drained and very productive former swampland seem to have wanted to make up for lost time, for the inequalities they developed were both severe and severely enforced. Indian farmers were hard run; still in the 1960s I was told many different stories of how the "supply companies," which sold seed, fertilizer, and tools to the farmers, would cut the fertilizer for Indian farms with sand, so the companies could buy the farm when it failed. By that point there were comparatively few Black farmers; almost all Blacks had been in towns since the early twentieth century. The ones who continued farming were also very poorly treated not just by the local White elite but also by the federal government's farm bureaus that were supposed to provide all farmers helpful advice and support and such services as soil testing, and very much did not. (For more on this, Daniel's [2013] account is crucial; Downs [2012] provides the long historical perspective.)

When Blacks moved into the towns, there were two features of this move that illuminate the severity of domination: first, the mostly swampy and unhealthy places in the towns where they were settled, and second, the way that African American town neighborhoods were politically constructed, to deny the people in these neighborhoods even minimal town services.

Most Blacks, by the early mid-twentieth century were living in what seemed to be a town—what I will call the "visible town"—but they were not actually living in the legal town. This mattered greatly, and in multiple ways. The legal town boundaries were specifically drawn to put most Blacks outside the town. Further compounding their problems, Blacks were also settled in places that I call "soaks." Soaks, along with town boundaries, shape life expectancy in major ways—even though on a dry day soaks are very hard to see, unless you know the area well, for the contour intervals are small and far apart.

A brief explanation of the mapping feature called "contour intervals" will help to just begin to understand the appalling infant mortality rate that characterized most African American communities in this region of North Carolina—a rate that was widely replicated, throughout the rural South, as racism, and also the poverty it created, destroyed health in one way or another. In Robeson County geography played an important role, but throughout the United States African American people were either settled in difficult locales, as here, or provided scant services necessary for maintaining health. So the geography of Robeson County, while locally specific, introduces much more general issues.

When the U.S. Geological Survey maps a local area, it does so quite differently than in the creation of an ordinary road map. The scale is much larger, often one inch on the map to a mile. The maps show what is on the land and the contours—the slope, or rise and fall—of the land itself. These maps usually use twenty-foot contour intervals—thin brown lines that show where the land elevation changes by twenty feet. Where it is very hilly, they use one-hundred-foot contour intervals, and in many maps with either kind of interval, the lines in some places are just about next to each other. In Robeson County and adjacent areas of the Carolina coastal plain borderlands, the contour intervals mark five-foot differences in elevation, and the lines are very far apart on the map.

All it takes is a very slight dip in the land surface, which is mostly sandy soils, combined with a slight rise in the mostly level subsoil clay, which holds much of the water above it, and you have a soak.

Out in the county people talk openly and frequently about swamps. Indeed, if you ask a country person for directions, particularly an older person, they are likely to tell you "go down that road across two swamps and then turn . . ." Nowadays these can be hard directions to follow, with many of the smaller swamps channeled and cars going upward of fifty miles per hour on paved roads. Sixty years ago these directions were clear and easy to follow.

It is a different story in the towns, where no one talks about the soaks, no one at all almost ever, except the Black folks who live in them, and no one with the power to do anything about it listened to them until very recently. Now that Black mayors and town councillors might well listen, they can often scarcely afford to do anything about it.

Soaks flood or just get completely waterlogged in heavy rains. In some towns they also flood as rising river levels wash over their banks. Once waterlogged, they can take quite a while to drain. This becomes particularly significant, as we shall see with the description of Maxton, when the homes in the African American neighborhoods have their water source from a hand-dug well in the front yard and also have an outhouse—a pit latrine—behind their home, as they did until recently. This did not begin to change until the late 1970s.

There is another much more widely used name for these areas that I am calling "soaks," a name that points toward social relations instead of geology. These soaks are what was called, until a few years ago, "colored neighborhoods." In reality the color of these so-called colored neighborhoods was unfortunately often found among the children who took on the pale coloration of high fevers, for the African American infant mortality rate, in and somewhat past the mid-twentieth century, was just about three times the White infant mortality rate. Now, in the orgy of progress having its way with the people, they are called African American, not colored, neighborhoods. The infant death rate for African Americans in North Carolina is now "only" double the infant death rate of Whites, and probably still substantially higher in the many towns like Maxton, where the home births are not fully recorded.

Not only are soaks difficult to see, unless you know the area well, but so are town boundaries, and both together turn out to have murderous consequences. These consequences, which are of course racist in origin, change in very surprising ways when African Americans take political control of their small towns.

Now that many of these small rural towns have no economic future, and most of the younger Whites have fled, leaving the towns to Blacks and to Black political control, many of these soaks are being drained. The local tax revenues to do this are substantially declining, as are the subsidies from state governments. As the small rural towns crumble, along with the small-scale agriculture that had sustained them, the increasing presence of Republicans in southern governments substantially diminishes subsidies, particularly to the small African American towns. So the infants (and children) are no longer dying quite as often, as local Black control tries to improve much of their situation, but the town is dying, which severely limits what can be done.

We will come back to that story—for it contains many surprises, along with many new developments, such as the return to flamboyant racist destruction of civil rights, particularly voting and school finance, under the new Republican political control of North Carolina (and similar if not yet as intense developments elsewhere in the South), that unfortunately are no surprise whatsoever.

By the early twentieth century many of the rural swamps were drained and cleared for farming. By then it was no longer considered appropriate, by those who get to define appropriate for the rest of us (while they appropriate what was ours), to kill or violently "remove" the people they called Indians, or to destroy the Maroon communities scattered through the swamps and byways of the Carolinas. These communities were widely found in places that were sparsely settled and not effectively governed, such as the border area between North Carolina and South Carolina before the Civil War, swampy regions, and the more inaccessible hill country. With a much different logic and history, these Maroon communities are also found in areas where there was, in the eighteenth and nineteenth centuries, a substantial naval stores industry—primarily producing turpentine and pine tar for building and maintaining ships. The most desirable workers for this labor-intensive forest work were neither slaves, nor Indians, nor Whites, but the wide range of people who fit none of these standard categories. Slaves could not reliably be sent into the woods with a bucket and an ax, Indians were not wanted that close to settlements, and Whites were too expensive to use.

Maroon is not a color; it is a contraction of the Spanish term *cimarroon* (wild, untamed) first used to refer to "runaway" slave communities. The term meant people who are uncontrollable by the dominant. Most people who lived in such autonomous communities necessarily sought to live as quietly and peacefully as possible, so they would attract little or no notice, except when they had to defend themselves against assault or encroachment, or take some necessary equipment from a nearby plantation (Sider 2003a, esp. pt. 4).


By the early twentieth century the dominant could not destroy or easily remove whole communities of Indians and Blacks directly. Those who got defined as Negroes, to use the then polite term, were still flogged and lynched throughout and beyond "the South," well into the mid-twentieth century, forced into submission, and just as destructively, in terms of the lives distorted and taken, forced to live in deeply unhealthy conditions (Daniel [1972] 1990; Tolnay and Beck 1995; Litwack 1999; Christensen 2010). In the midst of all this, many managed to build healthy and productive lives for themselves and for each other with each other—to build churches, to support and improve schools, to take care of one another, and to develop and demonstrate their pride and the dignity of their own identity. That story comes later, for it too has a history. The Native Americans in this region did not need such brutally direct control, for most were sharecroppers, and the poverty and dependency of that situation—somewhat both salved and isolated from constant supervision by the day-to-day autonomy in running the farm—were control enough. Besides, the Indians had an earned reputation for using the shelter of the rural swamps to develop and shield a counterviolence that kept direct White violence at a bit of a distance from them (Blu 1980; Sider 2003b; Lowery 2010).

But the situation of control-use-take, as imposed on Blacks and Native Americans, fell apart in the last third of the twentieth century, both from its increasingly unfit connections to the larger national society and from increasingly trenchant and popular protests from within its clutches. In the decline of this older form of domination and control, a new social, economic, and political dynamic emerged on this coastal plain, one whose paradoxes and contradictions can be seen in ways that illuminate the impending and contradictory tomorrows of race in the United States.

The next two sections of this chapter center on two stories. The first is about imposed deference and is called the sidewalks of power. The second is about what seems at first to be chosen deference and focuses on the "conk rag," used to straighten hair. But the point of the two stories together is that the second is not at all what it seems to be. To make that point will require, in each case, several "background" stories.

## THE SIDEWALKS OF POWER

The larger issues, which the following stories will begin to illuminate, are the transformations during the last third of the twentieth century on the Carolina borderlands—the coastal plain lands along both sides of the border between North Carolina and South Carolina. These transformations were in some ways very stark, very obvious, and in some ways deeply hidden within the recesses of a changing economy and within so-called civil rights.

Why do I say "so-called civil rights"? The underlying term, naming the context within which civil rights were supposed to be claimed, is "civil society." This more basic term emerged in English language political discourse from a problematic, but widely accepted, translation of Hegel's originating German term, *bürgerliche Gesellschaft*. This expression was used by Hegel, and then by Marx and many Marxists, as well as Hegelians, to refer to all aspects of society that are not readily reducible to either state or the business economy—such as religion, education, the media, recreation, and so on. But *bürgerliche Gesellschaft* can also be translated not as civil society but as bourgeois society—the social relations controlled and disciplined by the bourgeoisie. In that sense "civil rights," however wonderful they are to acquire, and however huge the continuing costs to get these rights, are rights not particularly challenging or threatening to the continuing domination of the elite. When it usually takes millions of dollars to run even a successful state-level or large urban primary campaign for the opportunity to be on the ballot, to give us the right to vote for one of them is not exactly what we need, even though it is very far better than not being able to vote, and it can sometimes keep some of the more blatant sexist and racist people out of direct power. You can even sit on juries so long as you have no influence over the Supreme Court, and so long as no judge ever tells you that a jury has the right to reject the law under which someone is convicted, or more precisely railroaded: for example, a mother (or father, eh?) put in jail for years for small-scale possession, by means of laws that one imagines some on juries would refuse to invoke if they knew they had that opportunity.

*Bürgerliche Gesellschaft*, as bourgeois society or with even more historical specificity, is the society controlled by "burghers," the town and urban elites who in late medieval and early modern Europe controlled the walled cities and towns very much to their own benefit. In this historical perspective, civil rights, for all the wonderful gains for people who previously had none, were rights that did not seriously challenge the benefits and the supposedly orderly domination of the elite. Civil rights, in addition to the benefits they brought to the people who won them, also have worked very much to benefit the elite.

It has never been, however, a win-win situation, with both "sides" gaining, for civil rights have very much constrained the gains that could be made by those who were far from the elite. For ordinary people, for African Americans in the South, it is a gain beyond measure not to be treated as a second-class person, to be able to live as a citizen who votes, who attends local schools, sits on juries, rides in the front of the bus, and much more. At the same time, it remains a loss beyond wider recognition to try to raise a family on what is permitted—indeed encouraged—as the minimum wage, on food stamps for lack of a job-creation program; to live in housing that is clearly maintained by city and state governments to be substandard; to go to public schools that are also specifically funded and organized to be substandard, and much more. Civil rights for the folks who were long denied them turned out to be minimal rights when they were obtained.

Do not for a moment dismiss this provision of substandard housing and substandard schools (and health care, and, and . . . ) by thinking of it as the product of a "conspiracy." It is right out there in the open, part of how the world was made to work. In North Carolina, "Negro" schools were funded at much lower levels than White schools, up until school integration. After integration a variety of policies and practices continue to make sure that most predominantly African American schools are not quality schools, however hard teachers, parents, and even the students try. And so-called public housing, while often far more sound and serviceable than the poverty-devastated homes it replaced, was still built and especially still maintained to deeply inadequate standards. "Conspiracy" implies a secret agreement. This is worse: it is right out in the open, it is intentional, and it is well known that it is intentional. (Christensen [2010] is excellent on this.)

Further, and quite significantly, what have been called civil rights, while granted to socially constructed categories of people: African Americans, Native Americans, some immigrants, women, gay people, and so forth—are basically individual rights. The fact that many individuals in each category can access at least some of these rights does little if anything for communities.

Thus I prefer the more fundamental term "rights," which includes collective as well as individual rights, and rights to a living, to the more usual term "civil rights." A great many people in the struggles for civil rights knew and know this, and have sought to break out of the limitations of "civil rights," but that has remained the politically dominant term. Civil rights, as we shall see, have turned out to be quite limited rights, and the whole political, legal, economic, and social organization of inequality works toward keeping it that way.

An alternative term to "rights" would be "justice," which in some ways strongly conveys what is at issue. But I hesitate to often use it. The struggles for rights have been, and continue to be, so intense, so powerful and powerfully opposed, and so crucial to what has happened that I think we have become relatively clear that rights are not given but must be won. Justice is a more complex concept. It has some absolute meanings, rooted in our fundamental moral sensibilities. In this perspective, courts have made, in the past, some fine moves toward social justice, along with many decisions that have been aggressively destructive. So "justice" seems as if it comes, when it does, from "above," from the state. This can be a dangerous perspective, insofar as it can encourage little more than a hopeful passivity.

So I somewhat prefer "rights," as the product of struggle, to "justice," insofar as justice can seem the gift of state, produced by negotiations with our lawyers and their judges and bureaucrats—often after our direct action, or their failed ability to control, or their changing needs for us, led to a willingness to negotiate.

Rights, not just civil rights, have their own complexities and contradictions, in large part rooted in struggles that both seek to challenge the rules and play by them. These contradictions are usually well concealed. To begin to grasp what was revealed and what has remained concealed in the struggles for rights and for civil rights, we will start with the politics that sought to keep things as they were—to keep Blacks "in their place" (and thus, more silently but still equally, Whites in their place)—while the world was changing irrevocably. Especially for some on the bottom, in the midst of all the changes, things were staying as they were, or getting worse.

The focus to illustrate this will be on 1967–68, and an election for school board in May 1968 in Robeson County—a county that then was, just before a large proportion of the Whites fled, approximately one-third Indian, one-third Black, and one-third White. Because African Americans and Native Americans had, in general, more children than did most Whites, the voting-age population was slightly more than half combined Indian and Black, but Whites, with only slightly less than half the voting-age population, had much higher turnout and voting rates—the result of policies and practices that kept Blacks and Indians from registering to vote. That's just a bit of the background; the passions on both sides of the struggles over civil rights made a different backdrop for what happened.

To help explain what happened in that 1968 election in Robeson County, I want to first skip ahead two decades, to a story from 1988 that reveals one small part of the violence reexpressed as deference and "good manners" in a long-lasting history.

To introduce this crucial story, about the sidewalks of power, I will tell the two stories that led into it. The first of these stories is brought forward here for two purposes: most obviously to introduce a subsequent discussion of violence within African American and Native American communities, which the White elite was seriously committed to keeping there, as we found out.

The best illustration of how that violence within and against dominated communities was produced and channeled comes from two of our attempts to lessen it. The scariest demonstration in Lumberton in the late 1960s was not really a demonstration—just a small group of mostly African American people who went to talk to the White elite people who shaped what the courts did. We were making a novel request to deal with a familiar situation.

Blacks who committed a property crime (robbery, snatch and grab, etc.) against Whites got extremely stiff sentences, as did Indians. Blacks and Indians who did the same to others in their own communities got a slap on the wrist. That made a situation where elderly and vulnerable Blacks and Indians were the primary victims of property crimes. Although Native Americans were in much the same situation as African Americans, this protest, or request for change, was an African American engagement with domination.

All that was asked was that the punishment for crimes by African Americans against African Americans be the same as for crimes by African Americans against Whites. We did not yet dare mention crimes by Whites against Blacks, although this was a significant problem. We only asked for equal punishment for equivalent property crimes.

It was made extremely clear to us, very quickly and unmistakably, that our request crossed the line—the chasm, actually—that organized social life. We were left to guess how difficult and how dangerous it would be to try to change this, and it was not hard to guess what power was working to teach us. They did not make us stop trying, but they did make us try other ways to deal with the issue, particularly with roundabout sermons in a few churches about respecting one another. Meanwhile, Black-on-Black and Indian-on-Indian violence festered, as it was supposed to. Do not forget that it was the violence of the dominant that made and maintained this localized violence, for that matters in what follows.

We were also continually taught what the rules were for crimes by Whites against either Blacks or Indians, or even against those who openly sided with Black and Indian needs and concerns. One early evening in late 1967, a van carrying several Quaker civil rights activists, who were registering voters in Lumberton, was shot at and hit a few times. Very fortunately, no one was hurt at all. And very surprisingly, the man who did it was caught. The charges against him were continually reduced, from attempted murder to assault with a deadly weapon to aggravated assault, and at the end the judge fined him five hundred dollars.

The county newspaper reported the fine as five dollars. We were terrified that people would think that was the cost of shooting at us, and so a delegation went to see the editor of the newspaper, asking for a correction. He refused, saying it was not important. We offered to take out a paid advertisement about the actual fine, and the editor said he did not accept that kind of advertisement. All we could do was hope he enjoyed living in his yesterday, while we tried to figure out how, in such circumstances, to get to tomorrow, while domination was trying to make all too clear to us how very yesterday they wanted our tomorrows to be.

Now the second background story. In the spring of 1988 my dear and close friend Julian Pierce was shot and killed. Julian was a Lumbee Indian who started his adult life as a chemist, working in a shipyard in Newport News, Virginia. There he invented a process for chemically diminishing the dangerousness of decommissioned nuclear reactors. After that he went to law school, and then worked in Washington, DC. Then, growing to realize his special combination of brilliance and an intensifying commitment to social justice, he returned "home"—as the Lumbee Indians call Robeson County, wherever they are from—and founded and directed Lumbee River Legal Services, a poverty and social justice legal center, working for vastly less income than he had made in Washington but serving the legal needs of poor people, and the Lumbee Indians as a community. I worked for him and with him, episodically, from 1981 to 1988, doing historical and anthropological research for developing a petition to the Bureau of Indian Affairs for full federal recognition of the Lumbee Indians, who were fully "recognized" as an Indian people by the State of North Carolina but not by the federal government. (Note that while the usual term is "Native American," the Lumbee from the 1960s through the 1990s usually referred to themselves as "Indian," and I mostly follow their own usage.)

At the end of the overwhelmingly horrible day that Julian Pierce was murdered, I went back to the motel where I stayed to try to sleep. Toward morning I woke myself up, shouting into the night and the empty room. In my sleep I realized who most likely killed him, for Julian and I had talked days earlier about an order of protection he had obtained against a young Native American man, on behalf of a young woman who was being intensely harassed. At that point I had the feeling that I had to leave the county, not at all from any feeling that I too was in danger but because staying there in that destructively violent place was too unsettling.

I just got in my car and started driving south, because the border with South Carolina was the closest place that was not Robeson County, that was not North Carolina, with its appalling mixture of civility and violence. I spent much of the day driving slowly around, on the back roads, village after village, farm by farm. By midafternoon I wound up in the town of Clio, South Carolina. I knew this because the town's name was painted, in very large letters, on the water tower tank at the edge of town. In this flat land the water is pumped up to a large tank on stilts, where it flows down with enough pressure to service at least the White houses in the village.

Clio is the muse of history, according to Greek mythology—the religion of ancient Greece that we call mythology because we believe in something different. Walking around this village, thinking about the muse of history, I started to feel a very tiny bit of inner peace that let me start the work of grief and mourning. So Clio stayed in my mind as the site for the beginning of grief. The next summer, in August, when I was back in Robeson County, I took part of an afternoon to be by myself and went back to Clio, just to walk around, to think about and grieve for my lost friend.

Clio in August can be painfully hot, particularly on a day when it does not rain. I got there in the early afternoon, about two o'clock, on a very hot day, with the sun shining relentlessly, almost inescapably. The town—more like a village—had a broad sidewalk, running down Main Street, and another broad sidewalk at an intersection, where Society Street starts south from Main. I was walking slowly east down Main Street, away from Society—the metaphor seemed important—on this broad sidewalk that in the intense heat was completely deserted. Anyone who could be was indoors in the air-conditioning or near a fan.

I noticed two middle-aged African American men walking toward me. They caught my eye and my mind first because both were startlingly thin and then, most of all, because they were both swaddled in layers of wool. One had a wool knit "watch cap," the other an army surplus winter cap. Both were wearing heavy wool sweaters and ancient wool army surplus jackets, open so they showed the sweaters underneath. One man was wearing two sweaters under his jacket, the inner sweater sticking out and visible below the outer. I was stunned, wondering what was happening, until in a moment I realized this was the Bedouin strategy—shield yourself in layers of wool against the hurtful power of the sun.

They were, or must be, I thought, field hands, worked from dawn to midday, given a couple of hours off in the worst of the heat, and worked again from four o'clock or so until dusk. As they came closer to me, I smiled at them and nodded hello, and both of them stepped off the sidewalk into the gutter to let me go by on this very broad and otherwise totally empty sidewalk.

That is the brutality of the rural South, hiding behind the façade of civility and imposed deference—all that is possible away from the glare of the media, the TV cameras, and the civil rights lawyers, all that was embedded in peoples' souls and actions, on both sides of the great divide, on both sides of all divides—and this was 1988.

That love-starved, rage-fueled, fear-making, self-aggrandizing rape we call required deference is also, both for us and for the people involved, the gift of knowledge about how elections worked.

Do not forget or forgive one drop of this routine and totally ordinary violence, making both Black and White, making the world seem black and white, while we turn now to discuss an election for school board that took place twenty years earlier, and about twenty miles north, in Robeson County, North Carolina. And do not forget that for all its brutality, for all the routine deference, the world this violence created turned out to be very fragile, very breakable, especially by the claims and confrontations of the African American people themselves—all that came to life in the midst of deference to a brutal and increasingly fragile domination.

The struggles were not easy, nor did they often turn out well, yet sometimes they worked surprisingly well. It will be neither easy nor simple to sort through both the routines and the fragility of such domination, and the swamp-like morass of collusion, cooperation, defiance, evasion, escape, confrontation, and more that mark the engagements with this fragile and severe domination. Our task very much includes the need to find and to take hold of the fragility of domination, in the midst of the literally stunning complexities of the responses it calls forth. We begin with these complexities.

## CONKING OUT

The U.S. Civil Rights Act was passed in 1964 and was substantially strengthened by the Voting Rights Act of 1965. In every county in the United States where less than 50 percent of the population voted in the 1960 presidential election there would be, supposedly at first and then actually, an enforced removal of all tests, fees, and obstacles to keeping people—mostly non-White people—from voting. Just about everywhere this meant African Americans now had more of a possibility of voting, with some few poor Whites and many Latino/as also tossed into this not-quite-citizen, not-quite-qualified-to-vote trash pile that keeps "democracy" mostly a pretense. In Robeson County this elite-constructed not-fully-citizen trash pile also included a very large proportion of the Lumbee and Tuscarora Indian people. As the obstacles to voting are now being reintroduced, with the permission if not encouragement of the Supreme Court, it is clear that some sorts of government depend on some sorts of people not being allowed to fully participate. Think about the phrase "White trash" that is applied to poor Whites. What it clearly means is that these folks are being included in a larger trash pile of democracy, the nation, and the productive economy that is normally imposed upon non-Whites. The persistence of such inhuman exclusions defines the illusions not just of democracy but of the supposed legitimacy of the state, the nation, and society itself.

John Berger made an even broader and more powerful point, for it brings a long-standing issue into the "modern" world: "The poverty of our century is unlike that of any other. It is not, as poverty was before, the result of natural scarcity, but of a set of priorities imposed upon the rest of the world by the rich. Consequently, the modern poor are not pitied . . . but written off as trash. The twentieth-century consumer economy has produced the first culture for which a beggar is a reminder of nothing" ([1991] 1992, 234).

There were numbers of Indian and Black voters who could be closely controlled by their locality leaders and thus be "delivered" (as it was locally called) to vote for the White elite candidates, so they voted—"early and often," as is said in Chicago—but most Indians did not vote, nor did most Blacks (Sider 2003b, chaps. 3, 4).

A bit of an aside for those too young to know how Chicago "early and often" voting worked. The people who ran that city would have their workers show up first thing when the polls opened—early—go in, get their paper ballot, and instead of putting it in the ballot box, come outside with their ballot. They would then mark it for who was supposed to win. As people came to the polls, they would be asked if they wanted to make a dollar or two. If they said yes, they were given this already marked ballot and told to go in, get another ballot, but put the marked one they had been given into the box. When they brought back a blank ballot, they would be paid for this blank. (The ballot-marker is the "often" of "early and often.")

It is a very different matter for the people who run the place to do something like this and, on the other side, for very vulnerable non-Whites to try to play games such as that, or even to assertively confront the people who do. What assures victory for the dominant assures jail for the vulnerable. When we started to oppose the way the White "power structure"—as it was locally called—"delivered" Indians and Blacks to the polls, we could never dare to try such a way of organizing elections but absolutely had to play by the rules, despite the fact that the rules were stacked against us: indeed, in the 1960s and beyond, the rules usually made it impossible for us to win.

But playing by the rules was the right thing to do, and that was the lesson that we civil rights organizers were taught by all the wonderful people who were teaching, both in their actions and in the beatings they took, the power of nonviolent, deeply moral protest. The White elites who "ran" us, as it was called, had their own rules, some official, some not. We had to play, and wanted to play, by the official rules. These rules worked in both surprising and not very surprising ways.

By 1966 two partly separate voter registration "drives" for Blacks and Indians were under way, and in the spring of 1967, when I started to work on this voter registration—as did several Quakers and Baptists, all of us joining effective and powerful Indian and Black "movements"—the voter registration was moving well along. It was hard, time-consuming, and wonder-filled work, talking to people about the importance of voting and overcoming serious and realistic fears about the all-too-possible consequences of voting against what the locals called "the White power structure." Some weekends we—my Indian mentor and I—drove three hundred miles, going out in this very large county to meet and talk with people, driving them to the voter registrar's house, where registration happened, or was supposed to happen, many times to find the registrar out, or someone in his family saying he was out, and a large and angry dog unleashed in the yard.

But little by little it worked. By the May 1968 Democratic primary—then the key election, for whoever was on the Democratic slate got elected— there were a few more than fourteen thousand combined Indians and Blacks registered to vote, an increase from about six thousand, and a bit fewer than fourteen thousand Whites. In our optimism and our joy at the success of our work, we could taste and feel the possibility of victory.

There were two crucial contests at stake in this Democratic primary— the race for a seat as a county commissioner and the election for the school board, both organized within the election districts of Robeson County.

The focus here is on the race—or more precisely the races in several election districts—to win a seat on the county school board.

At that time in 1968, years before school integration came to Robeson County, despite all the national laws, there were four separate school *systems* in Robeson County. Three were major, and one consisted of only one small school for the people called "Smilings," who were legally neither White nor Black nor Indian. (I address the details of their situation, including especially how there came to be four "races" in many rural southeastern places until the mid-twentieth century, in a work I am currently developing on class formation in the United States.)

The three major school systems were White, Black, and Indian, and they were completely separate. Separate buses took children from each "race," and only that one race, to a school that was just for that race. The schools were separate but vastly unequal. A first-grade teacher in an Indian school told me, in 1967, that her entire first-grade class was given, by the county school board, twenty-four dollars a year for all the supplies for the children: crayons, paper, pencils, chalk, whatever. More: there were no shades on the windows, in this extremely hot and sunny climate. When she wanted to show slides or a filmstrip, which the teachers had to drive to the county school board offices to get, the teachers had to put wet newspaper over the shadeless windows. The White schools had both shades and air conditioners. Indeed, when they built a new Indian high school, the building had air-conditioning ducts installed, but the central air-conditioning unit was not provided.

Robeson County, in 2013 North Carolina state data, is still by far the poorest county in the state, and this is particularly evident in school construction and financing (see the appendix). The major White schools in Lumberton, and one Indian central high school, were always quite fine—and finely furnished—places. That has historically been financed by very major differences between the schools that are well supported and those that are not. Within the "not" schools there are often good and useful things happening—dedicated teachers, parents who manage to donate significantly from their often meager resources, good and popular sports teams, and so forth. But the physical plant and the resources available for teaching in the predominantly African American and Native American schools were, until "integration" and a bit beyond, poor and scant. Race, in the sense of people who are supposed to be the particular victims of this form of producing inequality, never can be simply determined by domination, for the parents and teachers of these scantily supported schools often made the schools into wonderful places. But domination can set many of the terms of the struggle.

So we were trying to turn this situation of severe inequalities around, to make the schools more equal, and doing so by tapping into widespread and deep concerns on the part of parents. There were seven members on the county school board, all White, and the school board controlled all three major school systems, plus the one-room school for the fourth "race," the Smilings, who were not legally allowed to go to the White or Indian schools and would not go to the Black schools, even if they could.

The racism of one vulnerable people against a different vulnerable people is a very painful subject, for not only did the Smilings, a very small Native American grouping, refuse to be associated with African Americans, but when the Smiling school was closed—it was too small to teach effectively, not having a library or for the high school any labs or lab equipment—and integration was slowly forcing change, the children who had been going to the Smiling school were brought to primarily Lumbee Indian schools. There they suffered substantially from racist taunts and physical assault, as did African American students who were integrated from their closed Maxton high school into a predominantly Indian high school.

Racism is almost, but not quite necessarily, contagious among vulnerable peoples. The old notion of "divide and conquer," however, is far too simplistic, for some important divisions emerge not just *between* socially constructed "different" peoples but *within* vulnerable groups. I think that the racism that emerges between different vulnerable peoples has reached its most destructive presence in recent years in a very surprising way. As an economic and political elite emerges from within many formerly oppressed "minority" groups, a significant portion, but only a portion, of this emergent elite either turns away from or, worse, turns against the needs and problems of the more oppressed of "their own" to focus on their own needs and their own advancement.

For one important example: In the 1960s most rural and small-town African American and Native American churches were small and plain. Many of the Indian churches out in the county were simply built, wood framed, with clapboard siding, or cinder block, perhaps with a brick facing on the front. A brick facing is one brick thick, much less expensive to build than brick construction.

There were a lot of mostly simply built churches, and they drew quite local congregations. A very few were large brick structures, radiating prosperity, with large parking lots for their more dispersed, mostly quite middle-class congregants. In towns the African American churches were a mixture of small brick buildings, cooled by ceiling fans, and less expensively built cinder block structures, usually on the outer edge of town. These all were the churches, and their pastors, that were so important for mobilizing people for the civil rights struggles. The poorest churches often could not be very effective, for the congregants were usually too hard-pressed and the minister occasionally not well versed in nonbiblical social issues and trends. Moreover, it was exceedingly difficult to organize in a church that was too poor to have a mimeograph machine—in those days the primary rural way of making flyers and announcements. But as soon as you went just a small bit beyond such hardship, all of these churches, very much including their pastors, were the absolute center not just of the civil rights struggles but of the social concerns for each other that deeply fueled the fires of mobilization and struggle.

By the early twenty-first century the array of church buildings looked very different. There were by then many large brick buildings, some air-conditioned, all quite finely furnished on the inside—pews, pulpits, lighting, decorations, the lot. And there are a lot more storefront African American churches in the towns, filling many of the abandoned stores with serious religious commitments on the part of people a good percentage of whom have also been abandoned by the productive economy, as have their churches.

Several of the larger churches, both Black and Indian, still had in the late 1990s and a bit after pastors whom I worked with back in the 1960s, registering voters then in their churches, and holding meetings about the importance of elections. By 2000 they were mostly "senior pastors," with several assistants, but they were still quite active, both preaching and teaching, and clearly pleased with and proud of their new and very fine church buildings, as they told me multiple times. These churches were financed by the emergence of a better-paid number of workers for the state—teachers, social workers, and so forth—and by the proliferation of nongovernmental organizations, many with large and reasonably well-paid local staffs. Several African American businesses had been established and were doing well.

Within five years after the enactment of the North American Free Trade Agreement (NAFTA) in 1994, every single textile assembly factory in Robeson County had closed, leaving more than eight thousand people unemployed, mostly women, and mostly African American and Native American. (This will be discussed at length in chapter 8.) I was very concerned to find out what had happened to these women, so I visited all the ministers I had known from the 1960s who were still active; they all gave me warm greetings and welcomes when they saw me again, so I thought I would get both good and useful answers, and hopefully some discussion of what now might well be done.

Not a single pastor knew anything about what had happened to all these women who had lost their reasonably well-paying jobs—not one, even though I knew that several had congregants who had lost their mill jobs.

I don't know what makes useful sense to say about this situation. I think it is not rooted in contempt but "only" in distance, only the perhaps intensifying separations that come with intensifying inequalities. That is what I meant when I said that the emerging elite "turns away" from the problems of the becoming poorer. Some few turn against—I don't want to tell those stories, for it is too easy to identify specific people—but turning away seems to be the much more frequent response. This whole situation is, I think, best left as an open but socially significant question, and with more extensive work in the region, the storefront churches need to be brought into this discussion.

My sense, from watching this develop in some of the communities I have known for decades, is that this distance is a development-transformation of the same attitudes that fueled social distance and, in part, prejudice between different oppressed peoples. It is too large a topic to engage just yet. The point of raising it here is that in the 1960s, when the social changes that let a numerically more substantial elite begin to emerge within Native American and African American communities, the first political repercussions of this were also emerging, in the form of politically and actively conservative sectors of these elites, many of whom were in situations in which they had to cooperate with the White elite. In the 1960s and for a good part of the 1970s, these conservatives were swamped by progressive activism, but all the while they were growing and getting increasing support from conservative elements in the dominant society. Here, in the 1968 election, we can only have a foretaste of an impending problem, embedded in a politics that sought to hang on to yesterday's inequalities in a partly changed world.

In 1968, four of the seven county school board members were up for reelection. Our dream was that we would put up two Indian and two African American candidates, and the Indians would vote for both Blacks and Indians, and the Blacks would vote for both Indians and Blacks. In church basement or Sunday school classroom, in meeting after meeting, we explained this over and over, graphically illustrating how much was at stake for the precious children.

We had enormous difficulty finding a second Black candidate to run for office. We had soon found two Indians to run and one Black, but the problem was finding someone who both would go for it and who was, in the local vocabulary, untouchable. Untouchable meant the White power structure could not take the candidate's or his or her spouse's job away, could not foreclose a mortgage for one or two late payments, could not suspend a child from school for a minor infraction. We needed a person who was untouchable by the techniques that were widely in use after the 1950s to hurt people, often permanently, after lynching Blacks was finally stopped, until police reintroduced the practice of killing Blacks with what seems to be utter impunity. We worked for months, asking people, pleading with people, praying with people, hoping—for the whole strategy would collapse, and all the hard work of registering voters, if we could not wind up with two Black and two Indian candidates. Black people would rightly be suspicious of a three Indians and one Black deal, for many felt, with some justification, that the Indians would likely side with the Whites to secure their own gains, and do so against the interests and needs of Blacks. Many Indians still farmed their own land, or worked for other Indians, or owned their own small businesses. Thus many were in the contradictory position of being able both to somewhat defy the White power structure and to benefit both personally and a bit for their local community from cooperating with it. We either had a majority of the school board or we had little or nothing. Blacks were, and knew themselves to be, more vulnerable. So we could more easily find Indian than Black candidates, but Indians often thought that they had more to gain from "playing ball" with the White "power structure," as they called it, than joining forces with African Americans.

Then one weekday night in a rural church, which we drove to late at night, on an incredibly dark road with only our parking lights on, so we would not attract too much attention, an African American man said he would run. And he was a wonderful man—a very pleasant and appealing personality, clearly very smart, a fine reputation—a plumber whose trade was entirely within the African American community, and a sufficiently prosperous trade so that his wife did not have to work. He was the untouchable person we needed.

The joy was intense, for many people knew what was at stake, having registered to vote for the first time. People were praying, and hugging one another, and calling upon the Lord for thanks, and laughing, and hugging one another again, and giving thanks to the candidate. It was an incredibly special moment.

The next morning I drove out to see him to talk strategy, for I had been developing and keeping the statistics on how many were registered to vote in which neighborhood, and from all the conversations we had with people as part of voter registration, I had some idea in what neighborhoods the passions and probable support were most likely, where it would be most encouraging to start campaigning. I was intensely looking forward to that meeting and that discussion, for we had worked very hard to get to that point, and I was delighted that it was he, in particular, who would run.

When I got to his house, soon after nine the next morning, he already had a conk rag on.

A conk rag is part of a process whereby African Americans could, in those days, straighten their hair. The complex process entailed putting Vaseline around the edges of the hair, on one's head and neck, to keep from getting burned, and putting watered lye on the hair, sometimes cut with potatoes or egg, which took the kink out of what was called, by Blacks and Indians, "bad hair." The whole mess was held in place by a rag tied around the head for the time it took the lye to do its straightening work. The conk rag was used when, as people said, they wanted to make their "bad" hair look "good." Of course, they meant "good" by White standards of proper hair, which is straight.

I went home, after a short meeting with him, and cried—lay down on my bed and cried from exhaustion and upset. I had the unshakable sense that the election was lost, then and there, although it was still a couple of months away. It was not just his hair that he thought was not quite good enough for the school board, it was himself. By my standards he was a wonderful man: smart, decent, and brave, and the people then running the school board so unequally, so destructively for Black and Indian children, were—to put it gently—moral misfits. But they were White and he was not.

Nowadays people play with identity markers—for example, stars like Michael Jackson and Beyoncé—but it was a much more serious matter then. Kinky hair was called "bad hair" by African Americans, Native Americans, and Whites, and more: they meant what they said. If you wanted to play ball with Whites, mostly you fixed your hair by their standards. "Black Is Beautiful" was getting started; Aretha Franklin released her song "Respect" in

April 1967, while we were registering voters and just before our organizing for this election—local Blacks and Indians called the song "the Negro national anthem"—but in the small-town and village rural South, in places as deeply and pervasively controlled as Robeson County then was, "Black Is Beautiful" could seem like, and also be, dangerous defiance, particularly for a middle-aged family man.

Maybe it was the conk rag, and maybe it was the muscle put on us, and maybe it was both, for we did lose, although we kept fighting as hard as we could. I will never know what part in the loss the conk rag played, and neither will you, because in this situation it is unknowable, however potentially significant it might be. All I know is that we are standing at the doorway to race in the United States, and we need to go in and, as the people say, "mess around with"—fuck over, to use a very special, complex, and as we shall see, deeply ambiguous term—domination, instead of our hair and ourselves. Would that this were an easy, or a clearly defined, task.

When we come back to looking closely at that very special and complex term, a term of strong emphasis that is deeply sexist, domineering, and intensely intimate, we may be able to get a clearer sense of the task at hand.

A "clearer sense" in this context is scarcely ever a clear sense. It turns out, as we found out some weeks later, that the White "power structure" knew all about that church meeting by early the next morning, and probably let the candidate know that they knew. We subsequently figured out who the informer was by keeping careful track of who came to what meeting that was quickly revealed to the Whites, for the Whites almost always let us know they knew, one way or another. With all the meetings it took only a few weeks to do this. I suggested to my Indian mentor—in the full flowering of a critique of anthropologists deluding themselves by thinking that their fieldwork is based on a totally innocent, do-not-take-sides "participant observation"—that several of us together pay a visit to the informer and very gently, peacefully, and forcefully explain to him that his own long-term well-being, and very much also the well-being of a great many Indian and African American schoolchildren, depended upon his never doing anything like that again, ever, not even once. My Indian mentor told me, "I know you're right, Gerry, that's what we should do, but he's my cousin." My further introduction to rural politics, slowly taking shape.

And in all this the conk rag took on a further, and crucial, dimension. Power can be very scary. This is very different from believing, as do so many followers of the bourgeois French political philosopher Michel Foucault, that we the subjects of regimes of power are created by power. If we were, power would not be so scary. The conk rag is not, or not only, our collusion with power but just as much our fear of power, a fear that marks our separation and distance from attempted and actual domination. John Berger, as usual, recognized the larger issue, in a quote that is worth pondering for an extended time: "You can either be fearless or you can be free, you can't be both" (2005, 55).

And that fear we have—we have and we transcend in making our own identities—turns out to be our freedom, both our separation from domination and our autonomy. Power—in the form of the state, of popular racism, of elite sniffery, whatever—may hand us many of the struggles we are constrained to fight, but those who try to dominate us seem and probably are often surprised by the inventiveness of the struggles with which we confront them. And on the less positive side, I must emphasize that if power created us and our inner "governmentality," as Foucault would have it, we would not be so scared of them, nor they of us.

To be clear: the point here is not to argue against the notion that power and domination create and shape many of the social conditions through which and against which we struggle. The issue is the extent to which these conditions are created within us, as "governmentality"—which seems to mean our having the mentality to make us governable. Were that the case more than slightly, as we often try "to go along to get along," usually knowing that it is not fully in our best interest, but if it were any more than that, the cops would not shoot or beat so very many of us, nor the schools suspend us so frequently, nor, nor, nor. Our fear of them, as Berger so usefully insists, is our freedom. Even though it is not complete, it is still ours.

Advantage us, but in a match stacked against us.


There is one further, important dimension to all this, which has taken me a while to appreciate. In the production of race—and specifically the production of peoples at the bottom of racial hierarchies—it is very far from all pressure and diminishment. Even those who suffer the most oppression from an imposed identity can also claim this very identity as a source of dignity, of self-assertion and communal assertion, of what came to be called pride. To appreciate the complexities and simultaneously the wonders of all this, it is important to realize that "Black Pride" does not solely depend upon having, and perhaps flaunting, an "Afro"; it can also be claimed and asserted by straightening your hair, as part of doing what was locally called "looking fine." For way down deep, the issue goes even beyond the vast importance of Black Pride—pride in being Black—and is ultimately about Black dignity—the dignity of being Black. The candidate who straightened his hair was, as I finally came to see, a man of enormous personal dignity, and that is how he chose to express his dignity.

# TWO

# The Waters of Death and Life

## "THAT'S NOT WHAT COLORED MEANS"

You don't have to have a college education to know a lot about the word "culture." It is used to talk about "our ways"; about what either is beyond or is supposedly rooted in biology; what makes you and me different and special; what makes them foreigners or Blacks or Jews or Catholics or Mexicans not quite respectable, not quite fit to hold office, not quite fit to have full citizenship, or to join our clubs, or to live in our neighborhoods—not quite human, or just not quite us, not at all.

We all also know that culture is what fancy folks have, music and books and literature and such, and unfortunately we scarcely worry about whether or not these two different meanings of "culture"—one marking us from them and them from us, our ways and beliefs and values from theirs, and the other meaning of culture separating and elevating an elite, usually against the interests and needs of most of us—are in any socially significant ways connected. They are. And what connects them is muscle.

The supposed separation between the two different meanings of culture—our ways and values; high-priced art and music and theater—is not the most troubling of the thoughtless ways that "culture" is invoked. Culture in both senses is even, or especially, used by people with very fancy educations, including academic Marxists who are supposedly concerned with inequality and how it is made and remade. Even for all these academics the relation between culture and muscle—by muscle I mean the linkages of power and inequality in the domain of "culture"—remains largely unexamined.

Or unsuccessfully examined: For years African Americans and others begged President Franklin D. Roosevelt, who was supposedly deeply concerned with "the common man," despite his elite background, to invoke federal laws against the kidnap-torture-murder spectacle-festivals for lynching Negroes, and Roosevelt's reply was that he had to defer to "southern culture." It was both a brutal lie—he could have acted, just as he could have bombed the rail lines leading to the extermination camps in Germany and Poland—and it was also not completely a lie, for it was part of his deference to southern White senators and representatives, who controlled key congressional committees.

But even after that in-your-face invocation of anthropology's favorite innocence-making concept, not even anthropologists have been very likely to take the concept of culture apart. It can be a complex issue to express dignity within a larger culture that often denies even its possibility. We see peoples turning within their own communities, their own churches; simultaneously there is the dignity of being defiantly "bad."

What follows is just a start at revealing the realities hidden within and underneath the concept of culture.

Roosevelt used that deference to "southern culture" to get his social legislation, mostly for Whites, passed. In part II we will come back to the specific and surprising connections between what anthropologists and politicians call culture, and the knife in front of the plowshare that both draws the boundaries around a field and cuts apart the land within. There turn out to be some surprising connections between culture and the blade. For now we should just point out that it was this deference to "southern culture" that enabled Roosevelt to get Social Security legislation through Congress—legislation that simultaneously gave Whites some security in old age and against disability and also excluded farm labor and domestic service, the two largest categories of Black employment, from the benefits of, and inclusion within, Social Security support for old age and the disabled. "Culture" turns out to be more specifically inclusive and exclusive than usually realized.

There are only two issues at stake here, as an introduction to what will follow: the muscle on the bones of power and culture, and the flesh that conceals much of the muscle.

There was a lot of muscle put on the 1968 elections in Robeson County, for the county school board and the county commissioner contests in particular. One sort of muscle was fairly direct. It became manifest in the town of Maxton—whose current situation will be the focus of the last part of this chapter—where we had been working extremely hard on a registration drive among African Americans.

The way that population was distributed in Robeson County, Indians and Whites lived in the rural parts of the county, with sections of the county being either predominantly Indian or predominantly White. The towns were mostly Black and White, with very few Indians except in the one almost all-Indian town, Pembroke. So in and around Maxton voter registration focused on Black potential voters, and on issues important to Blacks. By the time of the primary election, in May 1968, the number of Blacks and Whites registered to vote was almost equal. The election would be decided by turnout, which for the Whites was usually quite low.

We thought that if a lot of African Americans came to vote, especially early in the day, the Whites would realize what was happening and quickly mobilize a larger turnout, for many African Americans who registered to vote were still afraid or unable to come to the polls. So what we did was to pack a church near where the voting took place. All day long, particularly in the afternoon, two or three Blacks would enter the church, and a bit later one or two would leave. By North Carolina law at that time, the polls closed at six o'clock (keeping domestic servants, field hands, etc., from reaching the polls before they closed), but anyone inside the polling place when the doors closed at six had to be allowed to vote. Current "voter ID laws" are the modern equivalent of this early closing, supposedly to "prevent fraud." To the contrary: such laws and practices ensure that the election and the "democracy" that such elections shape are fraud.

Between 5:35 and 5:50, we brought in well over a hundred African Americans from this church to vote. We were ecstatic. We had those SOBs who had been running the town and the county completely for their own self-interest, fair and square. They kept our people waiting to vote until almost ten o'clock, until the last person in line voted, marking a paper ballot, folding it in small pieces, and putting it in the ballot box. If you were registered with a middle initial and did not give it when you showed up to vote, you were challenged. Or you were challenged just because. But we had the numbers on our side, however much trouble they made for us, so we remained cheerful.

At ten o'clock, just after the last person voted, we were all thrown out of the polling place—not just the voters but the observers, including me—forced out by the three White "official" poll supervisors and the town policeman following their orders. Once outside we pounded on the door, we shouted at them, we threatened to call the FBI, we threatened to sue them. In a short bit we were let back in, the ballots were counted, and we lost.

The next day I went to see a White businessman, one of the power brokers and power breakers in the town, who talked to me, probably because he liked to brag about how much power he had, and how smart he thought he was, and partly because I was White, and so seemingly safe. I asked him how they did it—how they took the election from us. He answered that it was easy. He said all our ballots were on top in the ballot box. They put the box on the desk, threw us out, opened a bottom desk drawer and the ballot box, scooped up a couple of handfuls of ballots, dropped them in the drawer, kicked it shut, and let us back in while they counted the ballots that remained in the box. A year or more of work and planning and hope and dreams down the sewers that fertilize continuing inequality, and it never crossed any of our minds to compare the total number of votes counted to the total number of people voting. In our subsequent discussions of "could have should have," none of us knew that was even possible. As we understood voting, we put our ballots in the ballot box, they were counted, and the person with the most votes won. We thus mostly thought we had done something wrong, or that we had needed to do something more. Culture is itself muscle; muscle becomes culture.


All that is said about culture being shared values or ways of life is not simply wrong, it is simpleminded, for shared values and shared ways of life do exist, and can themselves be, or point toward, brutal and brutalizing struggles over who can, or may, share what, and at whose expense. What is called culture names struggles as pervasive and as powerful as does the word "class." The destructive insults called out to us—pick any dozen—accomplish much of their tasks because we all know, we share, what they mean, and why they are not only so mean but so consequential, and simultaneously we do not share how we belong to a world that gives us such names.

Culture is, necessarily and unavoidably, as violent as is class. Culture makes inequality just as much as does class or law. Class at least names the inequalities it creates. Culture and law often pretend to be about equality, and for a few they are.

The law worked particularly effectively in the county commissioners' races to take those elections from us. North Carolina had a law, in those days, against what they called "single-shot voting," applicable only to some counties—the ones with large numbers of actual or potential African American voters. It worked like this, to make a simplified but accurate example of a more complex district-specific process. Suppose there were, as there were in Robeson County in 1968, four of the seven county commissioners running for reelection. Suppose there were, as there were, about equal numbers of Whites and non-Whites—Indians and Blacks—registered to vote. The way the election was organized, there was a list of candidates, and you voted for four of these candidates—the same as the number of vacancies—or your vote was not counted. You were not allowed to "single shot"—to vote for one candidate, or two, and go home. You had to vote for the same number of candidates as there were vacancies.

The top four vote getters on the list, as there were four vacancies in this election, were elected. The Whites, using their routine elite control, made sure that no more than four or perhaps five Whites ran for office. The Indians put up one, in those days, and in some districts the Blacks put up one. The Whites almost all went and voted for their four White candidates and went home, assured of victory. The Indians and Blacks went, with real joy, and voted for "their own" candidate, but then, because single-shot ballots were not counted, had to vote for three more—that is, three of the four or five Whites, who then divided among themselves all the Indian and Black votes, making sure that only Whites had a chance to win.

How this violation of peoples' rights to free speech, to not have to vote for people they did not want to govern them, stood unchallenged for so long I leave to your imagination and to the manure-soaked pig pens of American political history, but with one comment from the perspective of a long lifetime in social justice struggles—and a perspective from outside the occasionally crucial court cases.

In those days of the 1960s, votes were bought for a dollar a vote. In a really intense election, the price was once raised, for the five hundred necessary votes to beat us by a good margin, to $5 a vote, and I was mocked by a local White businessman, the same one who taunted me about stealing the Maxton election, who said I had no idea how cheap $2,500 was for taking an election from us. I sure did not, when we were having trouble buying the gas to take people to register to vote, but $2,500 to win an election, even a local election, is indeed stunningly cheap by today's standards, and even by the standards then starting to develop. Since the 1960s, real money has come to reshape the electoral process, more money than ordinary people have available. So there is no longer any need for tricks like the anti-single-shot voting laws, which were struck down by the courts in 1984, and the United States could pretend to be more "democratic"—at least until what we now might call the Supremacist Court struck down the center of the Voting Rights Act and further undermined the pretense of democracy in favor of corporations and wealthy individuals being allowed unrestricted buying, more or less successfully, of elections. Laws often hide within the political arena, as politics hides within law, each showing only so much of its face as necessary, but sometimes sticking its tongue out at us, as the Roberts court just did.

So partly because direct muscle was then no longer "necessary" for the preservation of elite control, and partly because the economic basis and labor needs of Robeson County and the surrounding region were fundamentally transformed, "civil rights" came to Indians and Blacks by the mid-1970s. At the center of these rights were integrated schools, and for a few decades, now ending, not many problems with registering to vote or voting. With those changes came a bit of politeness in ordinary discourse, a politeness that both expressed and concealed a number of contradictory changes.

A brief review of the economic and social changes will show what made civil rights at first possible and then hollow.


What made civil rights possible? Peter Newcomer, a brilliant anthropologist who died too young from being unable to handle his own brilliance, or most of anything else, pointed out to me in the early 1960s—long before several articles were published, making the same point less cynically, articles that presented mechanical cause-effect analyses of the mechanical cotton harvester—that it was impossible to believe that after several centuries of our country brutalizing African Americans the governing elite woke up one day and said we should not do such things, or more precisely should not both permit and encourage such actions. Rather, Newcomer said, we should pay attention to the spread of the mechanical cotton picker. Segregated education, he claimed, was one central feature in the production of people who would sit in a cabin and starve for six months of the year for a chance to chop cotton the other six. When the mechanical cotton picker made that sort of labor much less necessary, it became obvious that segregated education does not produce people who are well enough educated and feel enough a part of the mainstream to be either effective soldiers or useful workers in modern factories. (See, for an example of this perspective, with citations, Holley 2003.)

Not being able to vote, or to send your children to decent schools, or to be treated with a modicum of respect, might well make people a bit less willing to send their children to die in wars against not-quite-White "foreigners." Of course the whole situation is much more complex than this, for sometimes people whose social weakness and vulnerability are constantly used against them want to join "the marines" or "the paratroopers" to show how tough they are.

Of course this perspective, this invocation of the mechanical cotton picker and the decline of small-scale agriculture, left African Americans, as they were formerly produced by segregated schools, severe poverty, and few rights, not very useful to a modern factory or to the military. Of course also they could never be reduced to these attempts to produce them as nothing but low-level workers, not at all—but that was what was attempted, and that was how most were unfortunately used. In World War II the navy only allowed African Americans to work in the kitchens or to load munitions on board ships, plus a few other similar tasks. That would not be possible now, and the point here is the ways that African Americans were treated, in those days, did not produce the kinds of people that were widely regarded as useful to current needs and tasks. The idea that the need for transformations in the making of race was introduced by the mechanical cotton picker and the decline of small farms has at least a grain or a cottonseed of truth.

So civil rights came to African American and Native American people in Robeson County in the 1970s, only a decade or so after the civil rights laws were passed, only two decades after the courts held segregated education to be unconstitutional. Underneath, or if you wish alongside, this change in schooling were basic changes in the economy. From the 1960 to the 1970 census, agricultural employment fell from a bit over thirteen thousand to around three thousand, and manufacturing employment rose from around three thousand to somewhat over thirteen thousand. The world of the old agrarian elite was literally turned upside down.

The new manufacturing elite, as they took political control of the county, got rid of the sheriff's deputies who wore two pairs of steel handcuffs on their belt, so they could handcuff you with one pair and whip you with the other, as was still done in 1967 and 1968, when we were registering people to vote and trying to organize demonstrations against the welfare department, for one instance. The Voting Rights Act of 1965 also made the election for sheriff—the head of the county police—somewhat more responsive to peoples' feelings and needs. The old agrarian elite were finished, and as they went out the back door of history, so did their enforcers. What the new manufacturing elite wanted to do—and did—as their equivalent to the two pairs of handcuffs, was to bring in a refrigerated tractor-trailer at Thanksgiving and again at Christmas and give all the low-waged workers, workers that a great deal of muscle, state laws, and corporate donations to the workers' churches kept nonunion, a free and quite large turkey. *Get one, become one* was the corporate elite's private motto, or so I thought.

That new social and political order scarcely lasted at all. By the 1970s the county was full of what the locals called "cut and stitch" factories, making everything from shirts to sheets and towels, plus athletic footwear in vast quantities. And these industries came, by the early 1990s, to pay very well by southern standards. An experienced woman sewing machine operator or an experienced machine mechanic could make twelve to fourteen dollars an hour—a take-home pay of a bit more than twenty thousand dollars a year, wonderful pay for non-White working people in this area of the South. But it did not last long, not at all.

Just about twenty years after the people got some effective civil rights, that era was finished in crucial ways. Starting in 1995 and accelerating very rapidly, the whole manufacturing edifice collapsed onto the heads of the workers, like a U.S. version of Bangladesh. In 1993 the North American Free Trade Agreement (NAFTA) was passed—which some have called the greatest transfer of wealth upward since the British conquest and looting of India—and this allowed two crucial movements. The first was the importation of goods from Mexico (and Canada, not relevant here) without duties or tariffs. The second was the importation of U.S.-subsidized corn into Mexico, also without duties or tariffs. The cut and stitch factories in Robeson County and the surrounding region all closed and moved south of the border. All of them, every single one.

Within a few years after 2000, the cut and stitch factories were replaced in Robeson County by hog, turkey, and chicken deconstruction factories.

These factories, which were huge, as were their supply farms, did not use local labor but primarily undocumented workers. At the same time that academics were talking to each other and mostly to themselves about "deconstruction," with no particular reference to what was happening in the real world, people were working in chicken deconstruction and packing plants where the belt moved at ninety-three birds an hour, forcing the workers to make one cut every thirty-nine seconds, creating—using only official government injury statistics—the highest-injury occupation in the United States, both wounds and repetitive-stress injuries. A very substantial further proportion of the actual injury rate was concealed by paying workers their usual pay, at some plants, to sit in the cafeteria with their bandaged hands and sometimes splinted wrists, all day for up to a week, until their wounds healed enough for them to go back on the line. This made it possible not to report the injury. Hog and turkey deconstruction and packing plants were just as difficult places in which to work.

As a result of the first construct, free importation of goods from Mexico, all—every one—of the cut and stitch factories closed within five years after NAFTA was enacted. They moved first to Mexico and then, a few years later, to China. More than eight thousand African American and Native American people just in Robeson County, mostly women, lost their jobs, with the few lucky ones getting jobs at or very near the unlivable minimum wage, $7.25 per hour, at Walmart or cleaning motel rooms. And as a result of the second imposition, the ability to export U.S.-subsidized corn to Mexico without tariffs or duties, U.S. corn could be sold there for well below the absolute minimum price at which a Mexican peasant, working with hoes and wearing homemade clothes and sandals—that is, people living at minimum subsistence cost levels—could sell corn and still afford to live. There was nothing to do but undergo the grueling and deadly dangerous attempt to get into the United States, where they could earn enough money to live and send the necessary supplement back home. As Linda Green has shown, many of the women who made this journey north took birth control pills before they started because they knew they would be raped on the way. And countless people died in the Arizona desert, on the way to becoming the without-rights replacements for African American workers. These replacements have been manufactured by a brutalization orchestrated by Democratic and Republican administrations alike (Green, 2009, 2011).

Why hire Blacks with civil rights when you can get such Mexicans? And keep in mind here that both the African American workers, when they had few if any rights, and their current replacements, the people called Mexicans, were manufactured by state laws and policies, and delivered to agriculture and industry as a subsidy-gift from the state, with what anthropologists have called culture as the wrapping on this gift.

Starting in the early 2000s, I became interested in the influx of undocumented workers—all called "illegal Mexicans," despite the fact that they were from a variety of places in addition to Mexico. I was particularly concerned with what the scale of this influx was doing to Black employment in Robeson County. What triggered this interest was being told, by a senior official of the county social services agency, that there were about fourteen thousand "Mexicans" in the county in the summer, mostly doing agricultural work. Some of them were what is called "H-2A" workers, named after a provision in the immigration code that lets farmers import workers from Mexico and work them under very abusive conditions, for the workers were not allowed to leave the farm where they were registered, whatever the farm owners and managers did to them or with them. At the end of the season the farm was supposed to ship them back to Mexico, but the vast majority of the noncitizen workers did not have H-2A papers and were completely without documents.

I was told, by a senior county official, that there were about seventy "Mexicans" living in a chicken coop near the north end of the county. He pointed to a spot on the large county map on his wall and suggested I go take a look. I drove up there early that evening, and indeed there were a large number of not very tall, mostly brown people in the yard around that former chicken coop. So much for housing codes, so much for health code enforcement, and more. It became instantly clear that the common phrase "illegal immigrant" had a crucial meaning: they could be treated with total legal impunity; "we" could do to "them" whatever we wanted to, with scarce regard for what is and is not legal, never mind what is and is not just. It was no surprise to the people who ran the county that there were farmworkers living in a chicken coop: they told me about it and looked slightly amused at the thought I might want to see this, which I guess to them was just part of the way the world worked. But not completely, for they were also trying to be helpful to me, and helpful to, or amused by, my struggles.

Such arrangements are clearly very profitable not just to the employers but also to the citizens of the county and the country, for labor has both a wage cost and a social cost, paid by taxes: housing with services, health care, and so forth, and all the Social Security payments that are deducted from these workers' wages, never to be paid out to people but used to support the fund's "eligible" workers and the employers who I was told pocket what they regard as their share. All these undocumented workers caused me to wonder what was happening to the people who once did the farm and factory work, also for both low wage and low tax cost. Did they move "up the ladder," as the American dream puts it, or did something else happen?

I went to see another senior county official, this one an Indian. I knew his parents, I knew his minister, I knew his people. He was not in a good position to paint what in a bad pun I might call whitewash over reality. All I did was to ask him what was happening in the way of economic development in the county. His answer burned into my core, and still burns.

He said, as close as I can remember his exact words: "Well, Gerry, it's like this. Ever since the colored got civil rights, we had to get rid of them. That's not what colored means. We got rid of them and got Mexicans."

All the suffering, all the struggles to win those rights, now trashed to clear the way for peoples with other suffering, other struggles, and most of all without those rights. But in the midst of this, new victories, or partial victories, were taking shape, at least for African Americans and Native Americans, if not yet very much at all for people made into undocumented workers.

## WATERING MAXTON

Using the 1960 U.S. Census, or any earlier one, it would be impossible to tell what was the population of the town of Maxton, for Maxton was in fact two towns. One was the legal entity, with specific boundaries marking out the town and a charter specifying how Maxton should be governed within these boundaries. The second was the actual town of Maxton, the one visible from above: a relatively compact area of settlement, surrounded by farm fields and swamps, bisected at its center by two main roads, one going north–south, the other, State Route 74, formerly a major highway connecting the metropolis of Charlotte to the coast, going east–west. The legal town was carved out within the actual town, by borders that curved and recurved to accomplish their purpose.

The actual town had a range of neighborhoods, richer and poorer, White and Black, plus the usual array of rural small-town stores. My guess was that this actual town had a population of more than three thousand by the 1960s, but the legal town was much smaller. We start to understand Maxton, and race as it was in this region in the mid-twentieth century, by asking why there were these two towns, and how it mattered to how people lived and died. Just to begin: The people who resided in the legal town got town services—piped water, sewerage, garbage collection, paved streets, sidewalks, all. The people who lived in the actual town, outside the legal town, were technically citizens of the county, not the town, and because they "belonged" to the county, they got absolutely none of these town services.

The legal town boundaries, viewed from above, looked like an irregular puddle of milk spilled on an uneven floor. But the boundaries were far from random, very far. In the mid-1960s, African American women were paid seven or sometimes eight dollars a day for housework, if they showed up to make breakfast and stayed to clean up after supper. Men were paid four or sometimes five dollars a day for work in the fields, on the days when they could get such work.

It was impossible to tax people being paid those kinds of wages enough to cover the costs of providing them water, sewerage, garbage collection, paved streets with sidewalks, and more. So the town boundaries were drawn to exclude most of the Blacks who lived in the actual town of Maxton, for the Whites who constituted the large majority of the legal town certainly were not going to "give" these services to their "colored neighbors." A fine set of photographs from 1904 and the years following, taken in the low country and midlands of South Carolina, illustrates—despite its invocation of stereotypes—how these African American neighborhoods looked at the beginning of the twentieth century, and still much so in the 1960s, with the roads now paved but few sidewalks, with the homes a bit bigger and the yards swept dirt or planted (Johnson and Root 2002).

The legal town of Maxton, not too far underneath its veneer of civility and what the local Whites would consider its southern charm, was still what was originally called "Mac's Town," a place for White Scots refugees from English brutality to come to and, as usual, reenact their history of brutalization by England, but with themselves on top.

Just as the French Canadians—the Québecois—after decades of strife with Canada, trying to gain some respect and local autonomy for their French language and for their educational practices, turned on the Cree Indians soon after they were granted this provincial control and denied them the right to teach in their own language, and denied much of the Cree Nations' autonomy. There are an appalling number of all-too-similar examples. When we ask the crucial question—what do people learn from history?—we must keep in our minds and in our struggles that the waters of the histories of inequality usually continue to flow downhill.

As different peoples clamber up the hills of inequality—rising up the social ladder as a people and simultaneously, for deeply connected reasons, seeing some of their own rise much faster and farther than others—a special feature of ethnic inequality emerges, with significant long-term consequences. The emergent elite within an ethnic group can—and often does—turn on its own, squeezing them economically and delivering them politically to a domination and exploitation situated within the larger society. Some of the emergent elite within an ethnic group act in very different and far more just ways. But the two very differently politicized ethnic elites, one defending and the other exploiting their own, to put the situation in oversimplified terms, while they engage in mutual name-calling, only very rarely see the more egalitarian actively confront those who live and grow by what some of the victims call "sticking it to their own."

This has been, and it remains, a very fluid situation. In the early days of the emergence of a modern non-White rural southern elite, in the 1960s and 1970s, large sectors of these elites were under much pressure to cooperate with White control. By doing so they not only helped to secure their own position but often won some quite limited benefits for their communities— some funds for the school band or sports teams, for example. As more assertive elites emerged in the 1990s, the economy was changing, so there has been less funding and less room for political maneuver, both as the economy changes in ways that undermine very many small towns and villages, and as state control in the South moves increasingly back into the hands of conservatives.

It will help to be much more specific about these downward-flowing waters of history: Robeson County in the mid-twentieth century, as I have noted, was by reputation both the second-wealthiest rural county in the South by value of the agricultural produce shipped from it, and at the same time one of the poorest counties in the United States by average per capita income. It is the poorest county in North Carolina (http://en.wikipedia.org/wiki/Robeson_County,_North_Carolina). The poverty of the people was socially created, actively created: it did not just happen.

*How this poverty could and could not be lived did not just happen either.*

If we looked at an ordinary street in an ordinary African American neighborhood in the actual town of Maxton as it was still in the 1960s, we would see a row of small wooden homes, many with tin roofs that were scorchingly hot in the summer, on plots that were thirty or so feet wide and about seventy-five to ninety feet deep. Behind every house was an outhouse—a pit toilet for those not familiar with this word—and in front of every home was a hand-dug well.

The ground was twelve to fourteen feet or so of sandy soil, sitting on a bed of clay that was largely impervious to water and kept the water table above the clay, making a hand-dug well possible. The distance between the row of outhouses behind the homes and the row of wells in front of the homes was usually about sixty or seventy feet—twenty meters. We are confronting, tragically, a different kind of recycling system than ecologists usually rave about. The nonwhite infant mortality rate here, as elsewhere, was about three times the White infant mortality rate. And these are the official statistics, not very useful at all, for they do not count many of the home births and the ensuing deaths, never officially recorded, with a far higher percentage of home births for Blacks than Whites. North Carolina, in 1961, counting just the official statistics, was one of the eleven states with the highest infant mortality rate, and one of the fourteen where this rate rose between 1955 and 1961.

Infant mortality is an absolutely crucial indicator of much broader issues in well-being. The court decisions and civil rights acts of 1963 through 1965 opened up hospitals to at least supposedly equal access to their facilities, and thus between 1965 and 1970 there was a substantial decline in infant mortality among African Americans in the rural South (Hunt and Goldstein 1964). But by 1980 African American infant mortality rates in the United States, but especially in the rural South, were very much on the rise. The following excerpts from an excellent study illuminate this:

> The United States overall infant mortality rate is high in comparison with other major industrialized nations. In 2004, the U.S. infant death rate ranked 29th against selected countries, including: Hong Kong, . . . Singapore, . . . Czech Republic, . . . Italy, N. Ireland . . . Ireland, England & Wales, Scotland, Canada, Israel, Greece, . . . and Cuba. The U.S. overall rate is at least 25 percentage points higher than that found in the European Union. Alarmingly, the overall U.S. infant death rate also increased between 2001 and 2002 while decreases in other years were minimal. More alarming still is the huge disparity between infant death rates for Blacks and Whites in this country. Nationwide, infant death rates are 2.5 times as high for African American babies than for white babies. This black/white disparity in infant death rates has either held steady or widened since 1980. In a number of states,

especially those in the Southeast, the gap between black and white infant death rates continues to widen. . . .

Some 44 percent of low-income African American women who become pregnant are anemic, a rate higher than for any other racial or ethnic group. . . . In one study of poor pregnant women in North Carolina, 37 percent of black women were food insecure [which means nutritionally adequate food was not available]. This compares to 19 percent of white women who were food insecure. Thus, poor black pregnant women in North Carolina were more than twice as likely to be food insecure as their white counterparts. (Joint Center's Health Policy Institute 2014)

*Some* of the material situations of African Americans in Maxton, and in many similar towns in the region, changed when they took political control of the town, but in surprising ways and with surprising results that lead us back to the peculiar consequences of civil rights. More precisely, the changes point us toward understanding—and perhaps getting our hands on—how the peculiar consequences of civil rights have been, and still are being, constructed.

My use of "peculiar" references both a widely known book about slavery, Kenneth Stampp's *The Peculiar Institution* (1956), and, more important, the point that slavery, in the South before the Civil War, was occasionally called "the peculiar institution." Several meanings of "peculiar" were being invoked. The first was a meaning that is scarcely used today: local—a locally specific practice. The second meaning of "peculiar" is strange, and considering the charter documents of the United States, slavery surely fit this meaning. The Constitution, along with the Declaration of Independence from colonial status with Great Britain, was based on the asserted equality of "all men," and slavery was based on the notion that some people were nothing more than property, who could be treated any way that the owner of the property desired, including the fact that the owner of property could destroy what he owned: beating a slave to death was not even murder in many slave states. From a rational perspective that was a strange exception to the declaration's assertion of universal equality and rights. Third, the whole phrase "the peculiar institution" was a euphemism, when the word "slavery" was being avoided in official and legislative discourse in the decades before the Civil War. My reference to the peculiar consequences of the civil rights struggles is designed, very specifically, to suggest that the consequences of civil rights victories are also peculiar (they are being constructed, at the local, regional, and national "levels," to limit the amount of freedom and autonomy that can be achieved) and that "civil rights" has turned out to be a euphemism—a not quite exact name—for something else, something that we will see is much more complex than the notion of "rights" conveys.

In 2004 a highway bypass around the town of Maxton was opened, and the substantial volume of east–west traffic, which often stopped for gas, meals, and groceries inside the town, was lost. Maxton is about twenty-five miles west of the major north–south highway—Interstate 95—and by now towns more than about ten miles away from major interstates usually have little in the way of a future, unless they can attract industries that need to hide because they are either serious polluters or serious abusers of their workforce, or both. At about the same time that the bypass was built, the largest employer in the vicinity of Maxton, Campbell Soup, which had been employing about five hundred people, I was told shifted many of its workers to "temporary" status—no benefits, no vacations, no sick leave, no pensions, nothing except the reality of a layoff every several months, then rehiring after a while, so the company can legally keep its workers' status "temporary" under the watchful eyes of a government that, like justice, wears a blindfold so it cannot see what is really happening.

Should we join our government to pretend, in our cost-no-object construction of a superficial democracy, that the government would desire to see and act to constrain situations like this, which both used and skirted the laws in ways that led to a major downturn in peoples' well-being? While some of the causes of human suffering do indeed get fixed, or partially fixed, the actual relationship between governments and peoples' needs is of course more complex. The following is not at all to specify these complexities, but to point toward a few of their features.

What happened as a result of all that happened to and in Maxton—from building the bypass without compensatory development to allowing Campbell Soup to do what it did, to the NAFTA-fueled closing of all the cut and stitch factories, to keeping the minimum wage at a completely unlivable $7.25 per hour, to a hundred other similar events—is not that anything intervened to make it better for local people, but that most of the Whites who could moved out, as did a substantial number of Blacks. Meanwhile, a significant number of Blacks fleeing the drugs and violence of the northern and western cities and the economic collapse of places like Detroit, Camden, and Oakland either sent their children back down south to live with grandparents or other relatives, or moved their whole families. Maxton, before 2000, was a Black majority town.

In more ways than many, this was wonderful. There was a Black mayor, as well as Black town councillors, an Indian police chief—and like the mayor, and just as special, the police chief now is a woman—and Black control of the town elementary school. There were new and larger brick churches with African American congregations. The dreams of the civil rights movement were coming true, at least here. But the peculiar legacy of civil rights was, at the same time, being born and nurtured. And it was happening in ways that did not completely maintain the old divides of Black and White. The Whites who moved out of town were mostly the younger, more modern-focused people, leaving the elderly, the former agrarian-elite widows and remnants, and a chunk of the White working class behind. One elderly White woman donated to the town the funds necessary to fix up main street—to clean and restore some old buildings, including what is now city hall, fix the old cast iron street lamps, make the center of the old town center look a bit charming. And she did this when the town became not just majority Black but Black governed. Even some of the old divides were changing.

What the town did, when it came under Black control, was to extend its boundaries, bit by bit, year by year, until well before the end of the first decade of this century just about every house in town, including all but a few very distant African American homes, was within the new town boundaries, with piped-in clean town water, sewer connections, garbage collection, and paved streets, mostly with sidewalks. Wonderful. The hopes for tomorrow here and now. But:

But the town managers who would work for such a small and poor and out-of-the-way village pretending it was a town, particularly a Black town like Maxton, were not particularly sophisticated in the ways of getting state grants and subsidies, whatever else their virtues were, and in some cases these virtues were many: many I knew were very decent, caring people, just not well versed in getting subsidies and grants for the town.

As the town came under increasing African American political control, the situation improved from what it had been when under White control, but many of the costs for improving and expanding the town's infrastructure were already incurred, and it is by now very difficult to get grants for maintenance or improvements or expansions of current infrastructure. Grants and subsidies to localities are, of course, based not just on need but also on connections: who you know and how and why you know them, and, as is now usual in politics, how much you and yours helped the political elite financially to get where and what they got. Say good-bye to the possibilities of state aid to poor Black towns. Such aid is not completely gone, but it is also not arriving by priority mail.

In late 1967, when the push for the 1968 elections was starting, a Republican in Lumberton, the county seat of Robeson, asked the county manager for a place to hold a meeting of Republicans, and the county manager offered him the telephone booth. We enjoyed hearing about that exchange immensely, but a bit more than a quarter century later the Republicans owned almost the entire state, and African Americans, who still usually vote Democratic, knew or were connected to few people who mattered for the process of getting grants and subsidies from the state.

So the not-well-subsidized piped town water that came to people's homes was expensive, particularly by local income standards. This in a context where a great many employed African Americans earned the minimum wage or slightly more—$7.25 an hour, or a take-home pay of about $260 a week, if you were lucky enough to get forty hours—which was not enough to be a living wage, considering that there was no medical or dental insurance, no sick pay, plus the costs of transportation to and from work and all the other costs of having and raising a family, especially where the schoolchildren come to care greatly about their appearance, as those who go to work must often also do, plus the costs of going to church and more: having a life. That's what the phrase "earning a living" points toward: the need and desire to have a life. And a thousand bucks a month, $12,000 a year, does not get you there, even when, as usual, someone else in the family is working part-time.

This is the context for understanding the new piped water. A family of four, using water quite carefully, could expect a monthly water bill of at least sixty or seventy dollars. If you missed more than one month's payment, your water was turned off, which was startlingly easy for the town to do—all it took was a turn of a locked valve. Then when you wanted your water back on, you had to first pay the entire back bill, plus a fifty-dollar turn-on or deposit fee.

As was said at the coronations of a new pope, from the fifteenth century to the mid-twentieth, but here with a rather different meaning, sic transit gloria mundi—so passes the glory of the world—from piped water to water that was difficult to afford. In Maxton something new was being crowned, something we might call, just for a start, modernity, with all its fleeting glories. Among the rapidly passing glories are now included the former social relations among vulnerable peoples, former relations that were very different from those upon which what we call modernity rests.

"Modernity" does not seem to rest from its task of continually transforming our lives, often not in good ways. Flush toilets, running water, and sewerage are good advertisements for modernity; the social production of minimum-waged people in rural areas with individual and high water bills, who cannot afford to keep up with these amenities, is not. Illustrating changing social relations that came with the piped water can be useful for getting our hands around the world that is being made over us and around us, if not within us.

In the days when, from a combination of poverty, occasionally contaminated well water, and a very fundamental lack of access to decent medical care, in the days, now almost past, when so many Black children died before their first birthday and then more before their fifth, there was a community that could help to partly, but significantly, ease the grief and the sorrow of loss. The minister of the church, in the midst of the community's tears and prayers and hugs, all the openly expressed love and concern for one another, could help to send the little angel's soul toward heaven and help guide the journey from the bosoms of the mother and father, the grandmother and grandfather, the brothers and sisters, the aunts and uncles— the journey from the bosom of family to the bosom of Jesus. And there was all the food, all the support, all the being-with of neighbors and kin. Now when your water is turned off, you are very much more alone.

Do not for one second think I am equating the tragedy and horror of the death of a child with the problems that follow having your water turned off. Not at all, and more, that is not at all the point that is at stake here. What is at stake is illuminating a changing world. Children still tragically die, not nearly as many: the African American infant mortality rate in North Carolina has declined from about three times the White infant mortality rate to "only" a bit more than twice the White infant mortality rate, more in rural areas. Children still die, tragically and as people partly know, unnecessarily, and church and kin and kith still turn out to help, and to be with and to comfort greatly those in need. For all the politically and morally crucial attention paid to African Americans killed by cops and vigilantes, vastly more African American infants die unnecessarily every day, and as James Baldwin urged us to know, they die in silence. This silence is not their cries, nor the cries and wailings of their families, but what the dominant society hears. Nothing. Silence.

When the new town water and sewer pipes were connected, the wells at the homes were capped with cement and made unusable. There is no going back to the old ways when your town water is shut. In this new context the neighbors can help with buckets and pots of water for cooking, for washing dishes, and so forth, but it is not possible to help each other with enough water to flush the toilet, take a shower, all that. Certainly not for long.

A story about all this, that also introduces crucial analytical issues: I knew, in the 1990s, an African American woman, working for not much more than minimum wage, with an unemployed husband and two children. Her water was turned off for failure to pay her water bill for about two months. She called the African American woman who was then the mayor of the town, and who had been her childhood playmate, as they were then neighbors. Calling the mayor by her first name, she asked for a bit of slack—she asked to have her water turned back on and promised to make good on the bill. She was turned down; the water stayed off.

This is what I am calling a "now what?" or, in a slightly different and more intense perspective, a "what now?" moment. The shock of moments like this, even though they can be expected, is the shock of not knowing what will happen next, or what to do next. *It is crucial to recognize how much of the struggles of the vulnerable for tomorrow take place in such contexts.* This is rather different from the optimistic, if brutally punished, former struggles for civil rights. And this suggests how important it will be, as our struggles against domination necessarily change and develop, to keep firmly in mind our relations to one another, and what we might usefully try to do with and for each other, for that is what such situations as the water costs in Maxton breaks apart. The point that when your water is turned off help from others is difficult for them to sustain is more generally the case than for just this situation.

This transformation in our relations to one another calls out to us for the kinds of work that might, bit by bit, turn this around.


The individualism that lies at the core of modernity, particularly in the brutal economic and social reality named "neoliberalism," using its teenage prostitute, "austerity," and the slightly older trickster, "structural adjustment," to take care of the hot-breath fantasies of the neoliberals—all this individualism is now central to modernity. Individualism becomes an inescapable part of the very structure of modernity when your water is turned off. Neoliberalism is not a choice about how to live; it is the road we have to travel, with a rough and isolating wall on either side. These walls keep us on a road that is impossible for many to travel, for it is the pathway to becoming disposable, unneeded, unwanted.

The name of this road that we increasingly realize goes nowhere, that is designed to lead us nowhere, that is built to get us nowhere, no matter how far and hard we travel on it, is tomorrow. For while we are trying to build pathways to a better tomorrow, other forces are making sure that for us tomorrow will be worse: the stuck minimum wage, the impending Trans-Pacific Partnership: NAFTA was the first steel handcuff on the policing belt of domination; these are the second, seeking to ensure that we continue to serve the interests of the elite, as we did when chopping cotton or the equivalent, whatever the continuing and reintroduced costs to our lives.

## HOW WE LOVE JESUS

In 2007 I went back to Robeson County to visit friends, to see what was happening, and to do research on some new topics. Even though I am not particularly religious, church communities were important in my civil rights work, and I respected and even loved some of the communities of people I met through those churches; thus, when I am back in the county, I often go to church to be with the people who are there.

On one Sunday morning I went to a service at an Indian Baptist church, where I had gone many times before, so I had friends in the congregation. During the service a young girl—I would guess her to be between twelve and fourteen—stood and said that she had accepted Jesus as her savior and was now saved. She thanked Jesus, and the congregation was overwhelmed by emotion. People were thanking the Lord, and many were crying—really crying, real tears. It was a very moving service. The next week I went to Maxton, and to a Black Baptist church. I had registered voters in both of these churches, as the older members of the congregations knew, and so I was easily welcomed as part of the congregation—nothing much special or different. In this church a young African American girl, also between twelve and fourteen years old, stood and told the congregation that she had found Jesus and had taken him as her savior. She thanked God for being saved, and the congregation exploded in joy—with people singing hymns, people laughing and thanking Jesus, an outburst of genuine happiness.

Early that week I went to see the leader of the Indian Baptist Church association, the Burnt Swamp Baptist Association, a pastor whom I have known for years, and with whom I have close and friendly relations. I described this stunning difference and asked him if it was usual. He assured me that when an Indian gets saved, it is usual for people to cry, in every one of the many congregations he knew, and added, "When Indians get saved, they think of Calvary"—the place outside the walls of Jerusalem where Jesus was crucified. The Black minister also told me, without amplifying his comment, that what I saw and heard was the usual response to finding and accepting Jesus. His attitude radiated an "of course" to the joy I saw.

Indians and Blacks, while both seriously abused and hurt peoples, have had significantly different histories. But I think it would be impossible, as anything more than "let's pretend," to develop an explanation that links the particular differences in the history of domination and imposed chaos and suffering to the particular differences in how those church communities reacted to one of their own being "saved." And one cannot just say "it's culture," for that explains nothing, understands nothing. A description is not an explanation. What we must do instead is recognize the surprises in how people live their continuing histories—including the capacity of dominated and exploited people to generate surprise. It will help if we also recognize that we must craft our struggles against domination in recognition of this capacity to surprise, so that something like the Occupy movement, which caught the state completely off guard, happens more frequently. Not necessarily in that form, for then the surprise will be lost, but in new and unusual ways. This is not a call for hippie politics, but remembering the Stonewall riots, when the people in a gay bar in Greenwich Village successfully fought the police, and how that shock to the dominant state changed so much, by people acting in ways it was thought that they were incapable of acting. Thus we need to cultivate our capacity to surprise, which unfortunately may be a bit of a problem for the more orthodox sectors of the left, who despite their very useful insights about what is wrong, often think they know almost all there is to know about what protest is and how to organize it.

That is for me, and hopefully for readers, the central lesson of this early chapter: There are no straight lines or clear connections between what is done to a people, or just to people not even together as a people, and how they engage their worlds. To help make change, to get our hands around the inequalities of skin color, gender, differential citizenship, locality, and class, we must appreciate both such surprises and the limits on our ability to understand or explain.

In this context a look at how poor Whites have handled their situation in the United States may deepen our perspectives on the production and transformation of race, for domination cannot produce Black without also and simultaneously producing White. One can never be the simple opposite of the other, or anything even close to that, yet both remain linked. So the complexities and peculiarities in the production of Whites will illuminate the production of both.

For several reasons I have not had much contact with poor Whites in this region of the South, so the scope and focus of this inquiry will get broadened. It will also be useful to move our discussion out of the South, at least for a while. For the discussion of Whites in the bottom half of the working class I need to shift my focus to New York City, where I grew up and where I taught many working-class people.

The Maxton town hall, restored as a gift to the town.

Main Street, Maxton: yesterday in today.

The home of an elite White.

A home in an African American neighborhood.

A "soak" on the edge of town. Maxton in the distance.

A wetland at the edge of an African American neighborhood in Maxton.

The former hardware store in Maxton.

Current farming, which helped to put that hardware store out of business and African Americans out of work. The truck is actually quite large.

A current African American church in Maxton.

Social housing in Maxton.

Main Street, Rowland, North Carolina. Similar to Maxton, and in the same county.

The N-Zone barber shop in "Historic Downtown Rowland."

# THREE

## Cockroach Racing

### PIE PLATES MAKE US A BETTER PEOPLE

When I was a child in the 1940s—a young child, for I was born in 1938—there were times when I had to get away from my parents, so I went and stayed with my grandfather and grandmother. They lived in an "old-law" tenement on the Lower East Side of New York City—Tenth and Avenue C, until recent gentrification a neighborhood of poor and ethnically mixed immigrants, then mostly from the Mediterranean and the ghettos of Eastern Europe, more recently from the Caribbean, Asia, and the Pacific Islands. Old-law tenements did not have to have a window in each very small room. They had lower ceilings than the current legal minimum, and old and usually inadequate plumbing and fixtures. My grandparents had an icebox, a wooden refrigerator, lined with galvanized tin, that had a compartment on the top where you put a block of ice, a large tray on the bottom to collect the water that dripped down, and a space in the middle where food would keep for a few days. In honor of my grandparents whom I loved, and the lives they struggled to live, I still call our modern electric refrigerator an icebox. That whole way of life still is part of a very living memory.

Going to the bathroom at night was quite scary. The tiny bathroom was on the far side of the kitchen from the living/dining room where I slept, and when I turned on the kitchen light to see my way to the bathroom, the walls, covered in what seemed to be a sheet of cockroaches, changed color as the roaches disappeared into the cracks and crevices, or hid beneath whatever. I would close my eyes and turn on the light, and count to ten or twenty before I opened them again to walk to the bathroom, hoping all the roaches were gone. It was the same when I got to the bathroom: turn on the light with my eyes closed, hoping there were no roaches on the switch, and wait a bit.

These old-law tenements were literally crawling with roaches and had lots of mice, and some—not my grandparents'—had rats. In my grandparents' apartment my grandfather had stood the legs of every table, the "easy" chair, the old sofa, and of course also the beds in a pie plate. In each plate he put water, and a bit of what he called "lamp oil"—kerosene, or paraffin as it is called in Europe—was floated on top of the water, to keep the roaches and mice from the table and chairs and beds.

And my grandfather would tell me, as I got older, how much better we Jews were than the *Schwartzers*—the Yiddish word for Blacks—because they were too cheap to use pie plates, but used old tin cans, which were too narrow to work well. I was in my twenties, after he died, when I realized that he had never been in a Black person's home, had no idea what they actually did or needed to do—this was all his fantasy of "racial" superiority. And in the midst of this fantasy of superiority, in the midst of his poverty, he lived like a cockroach, scurrying from one place to another, as quick as he could, to earn one crumb after another, worrying about getting squashed— and all that was on a good day. Living like a cockroach was probably part of his sense of how his way—and what he thought of as our way—of dealing with cockroaches made him and us superior. Meanwhile, he worked in a small factory, wiring lamps: screwing the wire to the plug on one end and the socket and switch on the other, and making so little money that he had to always be on the lookout for extra bits of handyman work here and there.

The key point here is not just his sense of superiority but his illusion, and the way race is founded on an utterly tangled mixture of illusion—pure or impure fantasy—and brutal reality. We can get a much deeper sense of the dynamics and the logic of these illusions, this need for superiority, when we leave the bloodied arena of race bigotry and look at similar, but far more hidden, illusions within the White working class.

## RACING MOTORCYCLES AND COCKROACHES

Nineteen seventy-three was a hard year, the start of hard times especially for the White working class in the United States, and in particular for the bottom part of the urban working class in the old neighborhoods of what was called "the Rust Belt." I am not sure if what I will describe is relevant to large sections of the White working class, but it helps us to see the rusty nails now used on the cross of domination.

An introductory story will make the object of this section a bit more clear, as will a subsequent brief look at the changing national economy in the 1970s. This story is just a prelude to the core of this section: racing dirt bikes on garbage dumps and racing cockroaches on your mother's dining room table, and what both reveal about the tensions within the changing fortunes of the White working class, changes that would undermine both the former sense that each generation would have it better than the one before, and the former sense that they could take for granted their continuing ethnic superiority. The stories will make all this more complex, less certain, and perhaps more useful.

In the 1990s my wife took me to the wedding ceremony of an old friend of hers, a woman who married a deeply religious man from Puerto Rico. In the context of the route to marriage my wife's friend had become deeply religious herself. The wedding ceremony was held in an Evangelical Protestant church in the middle of the Bronx, toward the bottom end of the stably employed working-class neighborhoods in New York City. The ceremony took hours, with prayer and hymn upon prayer and hymn. For distraction I started looking closely at the building itself, and then I noticed, over the cross behind the altar, a string of Hebrew letters very faintly still visible underneath the newer coat of paint. Looking even more closely I could see, behind the cross, the outlines of the ark, the enclosure where the Torah—the sacred handwritten scrolls of the first five books of the Bible—were kept. This was the synagogue I had gone to, occasionally, as a child. It had been sold to an Evangelical, mostly Puerto Rican church when the Jews decamped for the suburbs.

Looking around the Hispanic congregation, I realized these were the identical people of my childhood—the people who got up every morning and went to work, came home and ate supper their wives had to prepare, read the paper or listened to or now watched the news, week after week after week, with maybe two weeks' vacation a year—now often less. These were and still are my people, the people that are the focus of this chapter—then the bottom end of the regular working class, the working class that still had the dignity of regular work, of going to work regularly every weekday or more, a dignity that transcended, or almost transcended, the measly pay and especially the insecurities of work and life.

There are multiple ways that work, particularly regular work, work that once became an occupation that lasted for decades, was associated with the dignity of doing a job well, over and against the stress of constantly being supervised, constantly being judged, constantly being told what to do and how to do it. Increasingly now people are still glad to have a job.

Decades ago, sometime in the early 1970s, I saw an advertisement in a working-class newspaper left open to the help-wanted page on an empty seat in the subway. It was an ad for "porters" at Grand Central Station. The kind of porter that was wanted was not someone to help with luggage (those were called "redcaps") but one who swept and mopped the floors and cleaned the toilets. The ad ended with "Experience necessary." It was a stunning call for help, because I could quickly see, as could anyone going after such a job, that the experience called for was not cleaning shit, which could be quickly taught, but taking it—doing a job like that hour after hour, day after day, and not coming to work drunk or stoned or looking for trouble. And also "getting on" with the boss—showing a minimum of deference to those who told you what to do, and judged how you did it, while they stood "above" you.

The romantic left (in which I include myself) has had a notion that from workers' experience came their agency—the working-class commitment to change, to making a better society. The British historian Edward Thompson, whom I admired greatly both for his work and as a person, often emphasized that agency—active engagement with struggles for "progress" and betterment—came from experiences of work and life. The point in this advertisement was not to use "experience" to make a better society, as the left would wish, but to get someone else to do it, efficiently and without much complaint. It is still the point, of course, only who constitutes the someone else is changing.

What follows in the discussion of the illusions of the White working class, or some segments of it in the early 1970s, is about the kinds of people who were grateful there was someone else to do even worse work than they did. They worried they might be reduced to that if times got harder. Even though these worried White people were, as I just tried to show, almost exactly the same people as the ones they were trying to keep separate from and "above," their expressions of sympathy remained occasional.

Those ones "above" are the people who often had to deal with the indignity of having their first name sewn onto their work shirt when they went to work—more of an indignity for many than most who are not there realize.

And more: their wives or daughters had to both wash and iron these shirts, dripping with anger and resignation when they came out of the machine, because the job demanded that the workers "looked good," in both senses of that phrase. Above is only very slightly above, but it is nonetheless crucial. And more important, this "above" can no longer be directly defended or ensured. Jobs are now too contingent, too easily downsized. Instead, fantasies of being a bit "above" get wrapped into a whole range of fantasies and assertions of power and control, from playing computer games well, to using a credit card (not so innocently called a "MasterCard" or "Visa card," as if you were in charge, as if you were going somewhere besides into debt), to hitting your spouse or children, to driving aggressively—to what we now might productively consider.


In the 1970s I had a job teaching anthropology at Richmond College, which later became the College of Staten Island, a branch campus of City University of New York (CUNY). In the context of City University, then with its nineteen campuses and about 250,000 students, Richmond College was very unusual. Very. First, it was mostly White, in a City University that increasingly was not White any longer. Second, Richmond was an experimental college. It was just for the last two years of a regular college education—only for juniors and seniors. The idea was that we would specialize in taking students who had graduated from "community colleges"— two-year institutions that ordinarily serve mostly the bottom part of the working class and ethnics, and we would work them toward a bachelor of arts or a bachelor of science, called a "four-year degree." Like the "two-year" community colleges, the "four-year degree" named a situation and a time when people could afford to go straight through.

In 1969, CUNY, in response to very forceful student demonstrations, began a policy of "open admissions." Any applicant with a high school diploma would be admitted to one or another campus of City University. The students who did not have good grades in high school mostly were sent to the community colleges. Because the demonstrations that created open admissions were mostly led and populated by Black and Hispanic CUNY students, it was almost universally thought that the main beneficiaries of this open admissions policy were Blacks and Hispanics. Not at all. In fact the least academically qualified of the New York City high school population at the time were Italian Americans, who constituted the largest segment of those admitted to CUNY under the open admissions policy, at least in the early years of this policy.

Both the media and politicians usually portray non-Whites as the primary beneficiaries of social welfare or social justice policies when actually, as usual, White folks get most of the benefits, whether from the bottom, the middle, or especially the top of the government handouts. There are massive "welfare" benefits that middle-class Whites get, for example, from being able to deduct mortgage interest from the income they pay taxes on, and being able to not count employer health care benefits as taxable income, and the wealthier being able to pay taxes on capital gains at 15 percent. All such arrangements so greatly exceed the "welfare" benefits paid to poor Blacks and Hispanics, and paid in even larger amounts to poor Whites, who vastly outnumber all other ethnic categories of the poor, that the figures for who gets what can scarcely be compared. Race is a fantasy in more ways than can be easily counted. What we can count are some of the consequences of this fantasy: a non-White life expectancy, male and female combined, in the 1960s and early 1970s seven years shorter than White life expectancy. Race is also, in profoundly consequential ways, not in the slightest a fantasy. When that small portion of state aid and subsidies that went to the poor, the portion that was called "welfare," was expanded under President Jimmy Carter, in the late 1970s, so that African Americans began to get some substantial aid, that was exactly when the generosity of those benefits began to be increasingly severely restricted.

This double presence of race, as fantasy and as reality, has a range of manifestations among the White working class. For all the obvious expressions of racism and sexism, everywhere among Whites—and not at all just among the working classes—much is also half hidden and very broadly influential. To explore this we return to CUNY's Richmond College (now the College of Staten Island).

Richmond College, as a result of open admissions, was packed with Italian Americans, Irish Americans—each about a third of most of my classes—and a variety of other White ethnics, many of whom thought they were better off than they actually were. I liked these students greatly, and appreciated the opportunity to teach them, but it was not easy work, for a substantial portion of them were both intellectually lazy and very ill prepared. They thought the world belonged to them, so they had no need to work hard, and many believed their relatives would get them a job through "connections" when they were ready for one. The recession of 1972–73 and the draft that sent folks like them to, and brought them often visibly broken in one way or another back from, Vietnam substantially eroded their confidence. One Vietnam vet, for an example, regularly came to my early afternoon winter class completely drunk and often fell asleep on top of the radiator. This upset the whole class greatly, particularly when he resisted our multiple attempts to help him. Yet the self-assurance characteristic of large segments of the White working class had not yet been replaced by specific and focused concerns.

Fortunately, the college was explicitly experimental, which meant that it was easy to develop and teach different kinds of courses that I kept hoping might reach these students. I taught a course once a year, from 1971 to about 1976, called the Anthropology of Our Everyday Lives. The idea behind this course was simple. I would try to get across some of the more complex anthropological concepts by using utterly familiar data from my students' own lives—and simultaneously teach the students how to look with a bit of a critical eye (even if appreciatively critical) at the world around them, the social relations from which they came and into which they were mostly destined to remain as they matured into jobs and their own families.

One day two young men in this class, who had taken two other courses with me, came to see me after class. They had seen me ride my underpowered, tame motorcycle to school and wanted to talk with me about it, and of course about many other things. After some small talk they told me that they had spent a lot of time and work trying to learn the world I was showing them, and now they wanted to show me their world. They had a wonderful perspective on our relationship; it did indeed need to be more equal for either of us to "reach" the other. They said that I should bring some old clothes to school next week and join them after class. I did as asked.

They took me with them, with me following their larger and much more powerful off-road dirt bikes, all across the island, to the Staten Island garbage dump. This facility, which collected all of New York City's garbage for decades, was a mound of garbage, more than two miles wide at its base, the largest mound of garbage and the largest construction in the United States. There were layers of dirt spread over the garbage as it grew. By the late 1960s this mound of garbage was the highest hill alongside the Atlantic coast. It was more than four hundred feet high, just passing the next highest hill, Cadillac Mountain, the charmingly forested, ocean-view, appropriately named hill at the Rockefeller preserve on Mount Desert Island in Maine.

They took me to a hidden break in the chain-link fence, where we could get our motorcycles into the dump, on a late afternoon when most of the workers had gone home. What they did, which I did not have the skill to imitate very well at all, was to race their dirt bikes up a short stretch of the hill, or horizontally along the side of the hill near the base, spin their bikes around in a sharp skid-turn, and ride back through the cloud of dirt and garbage dust they themselves had stirred up, breathing it, getting it in their eyes and ears and mouth. After several passes back and forth, with one of them loaning me his powerful dirt bike so I could try, so I could enjoy with them the experience of riding through the shit that I myself had stirred up, we went and had a beer at a local tavern.

They had successfully put me in the same situation as I regularly put them, showing me a somewhat different world that hopefully would have some influence on how I thought and what I did.

The whole experience of riding through the dust of garbage that we ourselves had stirred up was a metaphor, I thought, but I did not know of what or for what, beyond the obvious point that it was about what class is, and how it works, and how it can be lived by people who still have their youth and their energy and their skills at their disposal—riding through the garbage you yourself had stirred up, breathing it and eating it, instead of breathing and eating someone else's shit that had been handed to you or shoveled over you. Or maybe it was about something else. I will have more to say about this and my grandfather's pie plates, and their political implications, after the next story.

A bit later in the semester, on a rainy day, I asked the students in my Everyday Lives class, many of whom came from Brooklyn, what they did when they were younger, in high school, to pass the time on a rainy day. After a bit of mumbling and snickering, one young man said, "We had cockroach races." In the midst of several young ladies in the class going "yecch," which of course egged the young men on, several of the young men in the class started making excited and happy comments about cockroach racing. So I asked them to describe what it was and how they did it.

They told me that everyone—the boys visiting each other—went around the apartment or down in the basement and caught a cockroach. When they had several, each put his roach down in the center of the dining room table—their fathers and mothers being out—and they all pounded their fists or the flat of their hand under the table. Cockroaches usually look quite different from one another, so you can tell which roach belonged to which person. The first roach over the edge of the table won, and the other roaches got squashed on the table by being smacked, flat handed, if they could be so caught.

We are in some ways back with my grandfather, but far more optimistically and less strategically. The losers in the world of these young men did get squashed, squashed on their own dark-wood dining tables that were the mothers' pride and a major expense. These were men who then both had and did not have a future, if they could make it through college, if they could get what was called a paying job afterward, if they did not get some young woman pregnant while both were still young, if they did not come back from one war or another, as several of the Vietnam veterans in the class so fully demonstrated, broken on the inside or the outside.

We have to appreciate the lighthearted way they made pleasure within apartments where everyone could quickly catch their own roach, but we also have to realize that cockroach racing is most widely known as a game that prisoners play. Vulnerable people often have this double life, optimistic and occasionally joyful in their strength, and at the same time trapped, confined by a variety of pressures and imposed limitations to jobs that do not pay quite enough, or last quite long enough, to relationships riven with strains, but a life that still can be permeated by times of real pleasure. It is, or can be, a double life that lasts at least until things get really bad.

And it is this double life—optimistic and trapped—that will come to define the possibilities for those imprisoned in the inequalities and the homes of race, class, gender, locality, and differential citizenship. Race, for everyone—Black, White, whatever—can be both a source of strength and pleasure, a framework for self-assertion and collective assertion, and simultaneously also a trap. These young cockroach racers were at the same time desecrating their mothers' precious dining room tables in acts of macho sexism, defying the world of order and cleanliness and care and polish that formed a substantial part of the self-image of their mothers and their mothers' friends and relatives. More: they were also defying, by playing with, the world that gave them easily caught roaches to race.

For the moment, at this moment in their lives, they were the ones doing the smashing. This is, in that way, the identical story as racing motorcycles on the garbage dump, yourself creating, with your skill and your daring, the shit-cloud of dust through which you ride back and forth. And the thoughtlessness—perhaps, perhaps not—of desecrating a mother's precious dining room table, the theater of her holiday and Sunday magnificence, prefigures the way they will be trapped and undermined by their sexist fantasies of male domination. Those are only some of the possibilities of the homebound; those imprisoned in their homes by the rain, and then by the increasing lack of a better future than their parents had.

They lived in a world, outside their homes and off their motorcycles, that did not give a shit for the shit they lived in, or breathed, or ate, nor the homes they shared with easily caught cockroaches. These were and are the homes made by race, by the production and use of White working-class workers, for these tough-ass, shy, proud, and embarrassed cockroach racers.

These are the young men who were both proud of their ability to make the girls in the class go "yecch" and anxious about their future from the difficulties many were having in college. They knew they had to be there, they knew that a college education "mattered," and they did not really know if it was their own limitations or the profoundly inadequate high schools they had gone to that were the source of their problem. In sum, they both did and did not have any real power. They had the power to race motorcycles, they had the power to catch roaches with their bare hands, then race and smash them, they had the power of being White, but they did not have the power to do college easily and well. In a complex and partly unspecifiable way, racing cockroaches and motorcycles, "bonding" together with your friends, was also making race or, more broadly, making identity.

What joins these races, in all senses of that word, are the contradictions they share, between assertion and acceptance. Both are perhaps necessary.

A prime contradiction also emerges between the sense of power or dignity—especially the dignity of hard-won skill—that comes from smashing cockroaches, racing motorcycles, preparing and serving great meals to large families, keeping your own family clean and well dressed and well fed and well loved, ironing well the shirt with your husband's or father's name sewn onto it, an advertisement that he has a regular job. But it is a job where he is told by his first name what to do with his skills, just like a kid who is also called by everyone by his or her first name. Beneath this is often the relentless grind of today, along with all the domination and manipulation and senses of inadequacy that permeate the relentless grind. And the reward for all the struggle to "stay on top" of it all—not meaning to be the best, but to have and keep some control over it all—is now increasingly held back by a deeply uncertain tomorrow.

Nowadays, when you telephone to a call center, most of the people there will call everyone by their first name, supposedly as a sign of "friendship" or "closeness"—as these sentiments, along with much else, are now being reborn in their debased meanings. Two or three decades ago, calling an adult you did not know by a first name had very different meanings, mostly about claims to inequality. Your first name on your shirt was not a source of respect, nor then a claim to friendliness: but the skill to do that job well, and the fact that the job lasted, were.

Those who think of themselves as on the White end of the world's continuum are now increasingly confronted, particularly in the past few decades as they watch their children grow up within and against the declining "American dream," by the realization that the world that makes increasing inequalities has increasingly little in store for them.

The progress in such worlds—and the progress was undeniable while the economy expanded—is from my grandfather living like a cockroach and proud that he could use pie plates to keep his cousins off the table and the beds, to these kids who were proud that they could themselves smash the cockroaches and, riding their powerful motorcycles, themselves create the clouds of shit they breathed and ate. This was real progress, and it was progress indeed, to put the matter both with ambiguous and ambivalent cynicism and simultaneously with recognition of all that my relatives, comrades, and colleagues in the working class have accomplished.

The contradictions implicit in the way this is posed are best realized if and when we ask how many of such folks became Republicans, and why, and how.

The answer, unfortunately, is rather obvious. Rosa Luxemburg named it when she said that the choices before us are socialism or barbarism. Between the drones and the waterboarding and the continuing and increasing cutbacks in food stamps, and the still privatized and fundamentally unregulated health care system, barbarism, at least on the state level, is clearly winning. All I am adding for now is that this choice is lived not just by states and nations but within homes, *and it is lived in ways that for ordinary working people often actively try to deny the specter of both socialism and barbarism.* To vote Republican is to be White, even for some Blacks, and orderly, and proper, and still part of the "great American dream," unlike all those others. It is also, as I see it, to somewhat aggressively flaunt your ignorance about who is actually getting what from "our" government's policies and practices. But that reality of who gets what is not how the choice is lived. It is, I think, primarily a choice to still try to be White, even if one's material well-being is collapsing, or because one's material well-being is collapsing, in a country where, especially for what was once the solid "middle class," that kind of Whiteness scarcely matters anymore, except to people who still believe, who still try to believe. And they get some real rewards from their identification with, and symbolic membership in, the dominant society, the society of the dominant. In Ulster County, New York, in the rural areas surrounding the ground-down city of Kingston, the largest American flags are clearly most often found on, or in, the very well-tended lawns of the trailer homes.

This denial of both socialism and barbarism, or more precisely what gets called socialism in the United States, particularly when it is not just nourished by ignorance, can also be the realization of the immanence of either one, or both. Barbarism is not that different from the underlying realities of today in the United States. You can volunteer to be waterboarded or drone-bombed or feed your children on minimum wage when unemployment insurance and food stamps are cut off, if you want to argue about the intensifying barbarism of the United States. Despite either the denial or the immanence of socialism or barbarism, any specter of what seems to be major change, especially change from our illusions about yesterday, can be very scary, particularly to people who live, despite the outward orderliness of their lives, on the edge of chaos.

So both what gets called "socialism" and, by admitting barbarism, the loss of the illusion that "we" are a "civilized and humanitarian democracy," a "beacon of light to the rest of the world," can be an extremely unsettling confrontation with how we survive the now. Even more, it can become a reinvigorated murderous racism that seeks to re-create what was always an illusory order. It was, of course, a social order so repressive that it had to be scary to the perpetrators and their silently willing witnesses. That scariness, that profoundly unsettling sense of the immanence of chaos, returns us to the issue of what lies beneath the three stories I have told about the White working class.

To understand what is at stake beneath these three stories—my grandfather putting pie plates under the beds and tables, racing motorcycles back and forth on the garbage dump, and racing cockroaches on the dining room table—you have to take very seriously my remark after the story about my grandfather. What I said, which may have seemed only a casual distancing from the racism of my grandfather's comment about Black people—it was more serious even than that—was that my grandfather lived like a cockroach, scurrying from place to place, always fearful of getting squashed, looking for crumbs and glad when he found them. That was the reality he was pressured to live by the fact that he grew up an orphan, coming to America desperately poor with little useful background save his wits and his skillful hands, no resources or relatives to draw on, and a wife who was often too sick to work at a waged job and contribute to the family income. Who else would then marry an impoverished orphan?

My grandfather was a "foundling," abandoned about 1870 on the steps of a synagogue in a rural village southeast of Vilnius, on the moving border between Belarus, Poland, and Lithuania. He was raised by the Jewish community, in a state of extreme poverty, and when he was about eighteen he became a tinker—a Jewish and mostly solitary gypsy—traveling from village to village, fixing things. When he came to America, he walked from Lithuania to get passage from Hamburg, Germany. That journey took him two years to make and to earn "steerage" passage, a journey of constant watchfulness, constant worry, because he was constantly walking into strange and unfamiliar villages where he always represented someone who could work, who it turned out could fix things, and yet someone who was an alien danger, a potential threat. He had a lot of experience at living the life of a cockroach, in the midst of their subsequent swarm throughout the tenement where my grandparents lived in New York City. So he did what he could to separate himself and his family from them—with his pie plates, water, and lamp oil. And to separate himself not just from the cockroaches but from others who led very similar lives. That is the point of his fantasy that Blacks use tin cans because they were too cheap to get pie plates. He was above all that, on the fifth-floor, small, back apartment of his walk-up tenement.

What all this says, beyond the racism and the arrogance of "we are better," is that we must not be what we are, what we have been made to be. We must deny it—deny the fact that we are living like cockroaches, not just living with them—and deny our affinity with superficially different others who do the same, for we are going to rise. We must deny our current lives and those who also live them to give ourselves the belief that we rise above it, especially by braving our way through it while we live in it.

The issue of bravery, of braving our way through the circumstances of our lives, of braving our way through the ways others try to treat us, can be crucial. In the 1960s, doing civil rights organizing in Lumberton's large Black neighborhood, I got close to a very tough Black man in his late twenties. He would say to me, and others, things like "They call me a badass nigger. I'm going to show them what a badass nigger can do." So he got into fights at bars on the weekend, got hauled off to the town jail for that and other confrontations, and then, much to my great sorrow and loss, died when his car hit a bridge abutment going, the state police estimated, about a hundred miles an hour.

Being what you are called, and being even more of what you are called, is not a fight that can often be won. The point of the names you are called is to make you lose, but sometimes it is important to openly confront, with your bravery and your skill and your wiles, these names, and the lives that go with these names. That is "take back the night" that is also take back the day.

That is also, more subtly but just as seriously, the bravery of the motorcycle riders on the garbage dump, going very fast on soft and uneven terrain, being very good at controlling unpredictable skids, while breathing and eating the shit they themselves have stirred up in their very impressive displays of power and speed and skill. That is the macho youths catching and smashing cockroaches on their mothers' tables, making a game on a playing field defined by the cockroaches and water beetles under the sink and in the basement laundry room, shall we say as one goalpost, the goalpost belonging to the opposition, and the other goalpost the dark wood, polished, working-class, elegant dining room tables of their mothers and most likely, in the 1970s, their future wives. Above all, that bravery, that arrogance, that claim to our joy or just to a bit of distance, impossible distance, from the circumstances of our lives, are our hope for the future, our ability to live both in and against the lives we have been handed.

It is about the same for women in circumstances where they have their lives diminished for reasons of gender. We all must, necessarily and inescapably, live against as well as within our circumstances. Our circumstances, for many people, are only marginally livable and deeply uncertain. The story of the pie plates, the motorcycle racing, the story of the clean and polished dining room table in a neat and orderly house with well-cooked meals, at least on the weekend, with a well-done hairdo, with well-ironed and clean work shirts, a well-cared for self and family, are all stories of the potential birth of a better tomorrow, or at least one not any worse.

The crucial lesson here is that struggle is only rarely directly against the sources of our problems. It is and it isn't. A lot of struggle is just to make our everyday lives in the midst of circumstances much out of our control, so our efforts to shape our everyday lives sometimes descend into trying to control our spouses, our children, our aging parents, our difficult siblings. Struggle is often very mixed, and our task as "progressives" is not at all to "teach" proper struggle but to work with and through what struggle really is in the real world of the vulnerable and unequal—the pie plates, the motorcycle and cockroach racing—in the hopes that a door or two may open, may be pushed open, in one surprising place or another.

One of the more serious mistakes the left made in the twentieth century—particularly the more orthodox segments of the left—was to think of itself as a "vanguard party," teaching truth and reality to the workers and the oppressed. There was a small bit of justification for this, rooted in Marx's understanding that the "reality" of commodities, and their prices, was illusory. What was in fact real, as he showed, were the social relations that produced commodities, including especially the social relations that made and kept labor a commodity. An actual and an explanatory revelation.

But a "vanguard party" attitude toward workers, the oppressed, and the exploited, an attitude that claims "we" have to teach "them," misses several crucial points, in addition to being arrogant and elitist, and often deaf to what is being said to the supposed vanguard party as well. One of the crucial things that vanguard party attitudes missed was the importance of the multiple and creative ways that the victims of domination and exploitation have created some spaces of order and satisfaction in their lives, within and against the chaos routinely imposed upon them. The victims of domination and exploitation also can and do act in harmful and destructive ways toward those who are even more vulnerable—but it rarely has helped to explain to those who do this that this is wrong, for it turns out that not only do they know this, but many live in a world where "being bad" is precisely why they do this. (Sider [2014b] directly addresses this situation, in the context of trying to deal with perpetrators of domestic violence.)

It is rarely easy or obvious to figure out where and how to go from such daily life engagements with inequality to something that reaches toward making social justice. But what I am saying is not to turn away from engagements such as these but to think about their potential, and act from that starting point. This is a very different approach from the usual approaches to class and civil rights struggles. What I am suggesting may be almost completely useless, but it has the advantage of starting with people who are usually largely left out, or take themselves out, of more direct struggles against domination and exploitation. The rapid current rise of protests against an unlivable minimum wage, against the conditions of work at McDonald's and Walmart, and the political rising of undocumented immigrants—all these struggles by extremely vulnerable people—show that what constitutes struggle is immensely fluid and rarely predictable.

What progressives and the left call class struggle has many similarities to shielding beds and tables from roaches, to racing motorcycles through dust clouds on garbage dumps, to smashing the losing roaches on the dining room table—with your own hand, and cleaning up the mess before mom comes home. Some of the key similarities lie in using one's own everyday life to try to make that everyday life more livable, more ready for tomorrow.

My sense, at this point, is that of all struggles about inequality, the sorts of struggles called civil rights are the most profoundly and most directly situated within people's everyday lives. That is not how such struggles are usually seen. But I want to suggest, for it has important implications, that the rooting of civil rights struggles in everyday life, rather than their confrontations with racism, is the absolute core of their energy and their commitments. It is where people get the strength to confront racist people and racist governments. Those confrontations with racism are crucial, even definitional, but the fire fueling such confrontations, as James Baldwin wrote about in his extraordinary book The Fire Next Time ([1963] 1995), comes from within our bellies—within our daily lives in our families and in our communities. Everyday life is our political as well as our social core.

This point is quite important, and perhaps unclear, so I will try to explain, by returning us to the political struggles in Robeson County, North Carolina. One evening in 1967, after I had spent the day doing voter registration with my Indian mentor, Thadis Oxendine, then a man in his fifties, we were sitting on his porch, exhausted from the strains of a difficult and at times potentially dangerous day, exhausted as much emotionally as physically. He started talking with me about what urged him on. He told me a story of driving with his family through the White section of Lumberton, when his wife had a sudden need for sanitary napkins. He left his wife and children in the car, which was not air-conditioned, on a very hot August day, to go into a drugstore by himself to get them for her, which in those days and in that place was embarrassing for him. He told me he did not want his wife and children to hear him called "boy" by some young White clerk, and he wanted to shield his wife from being called "Auntie," which did not happen when they could shop in the Indian community of Pembroke. And he was crying after he told me this story. This was a man who would face down aggressive dogs in the voter registrar's yards, who one night, when some people drove by his house and fired a couple of shots into his living room wall, below the window so probably intended as a warning, grabbed his rifle, ran across the road, lay down in the irrigation ditch on the far side of the road from his house, and when they came back fired three shots into the trunk of their car—his counterwarning. He told me he knew they would turn around up the road and drive back by his house to see what they had done. But when he talked about shielding his family from insult, or from hearing him being insulted, and said to me something like "a whole lifetime of doing this," that's when this brave and assertive man started crying. And that is why I say that the fires in the belly that drive the struggles come largely from everyday life.

Everyday life is also where a lot of the most vicious assaults against people who are claiming their rights and their dignity are focused. This becomes one of the several reasons that it has become an arena for pushback.

To illustrate, to illuminate: In the 1968 May Democratic primary, the election where we were trying to reshape the composition of the school board and also the county commissioners, in one decisive precinct that we needed to win, the sheriff was inside the voting place, handing out money to Indian and Black voters and telling them how he would like them to vote. I called the civil rights desk of the Department of Justice—a direct line number I was given by state-level African American civil rights lawyers—and my call was subsequently transferred to the Justice Department agent who had the adjoining office to the sheriff so suggestively twisting arms, necks, and futures, although I specifically asked to talk to an agent from outside the county. At one point when the sheriff was still handing out cash inside the polling place, a middle-aged African American man whom we were working with in this election got his old "Brownie" box camera from his car and took a couple of photographs of this. Shortly thereafter, his wife and preteen children started getting several phone calls in the early morning—before the children went to school—and in the evening, all saying what they would do to "that nigger" husband/father of theirs if he did not hand over the camera and the pictures. When he answered the phone, the caller hung up—they were calls directed at his family. The photos never came out; the camera was defective or would not work indoors, and he insisted, very firmly, that neither his family nor any of us "let it be known" that there were no pictures.

So I spent a lot of time with him and his family, the next few weeks, by way of their always having a witness, and one day, while we were riding in his car, he pulled out a very large pistol from under his car seat and told me that he took it off a dead North Korean soldier who he shot in the Korean War, and if he was good enough to risk his life for his country, he was good enough to risk his life for his family and his people.

So I think that it is within everyday life that the fires of struggle are lit, fueled, tended—and attacked by the reach of the long hoses of domination. I doubt that is the whole of those fires, it is just the part that I want to emphasize here, to make sure that we understand that everyday life is far more than just everyday.

# PART II

CULTURING WORDS

———

# FOUR

# Naming Troubles

## STATING CULTURE

In 1965, when I was young and innocent—I think more innocent than now, although reviewers and readers might well disagree—I got married in Maryland. Maryland, more of a racist and "southern" place than people who live elsewhere often realize, then had a law against miscegenation: against Whites and Blacks getting married, a law that required you to marry what the state and society thought was the same kind of person, except for gender, where you could not marry the same kind of person. When we went for the marriage license, the middle-aged White lady behind the raised counter, who filled out the form as you stood there and answered her questions, wrote "White" as my future wife's answer to the question on the form that asked her race. From what happened next, my future spouse for a brief while should have ended our relationship then and there.

When it was my turn at the counter, and the lady asked me, "Race?" my reply was "What do you mean?" I got a hard look and then a complex question-answer to my own question. She asked me: "Are you Negro?" Since I don't look like Negroes are supposed to look, her counterquestion was a way of saying to me that if I wanted to give her trouble, I must not be one of her sort of people—I must not be White. But I was not going to play her game, not at all, because I did not want to play by the rules of people or states that had laws against what they called "miscegenation." So I said to her, "You tell me what's a Negro and I will tell you whether or not I am one."

She quickly came back at me: "Were any of your parents or grandparents Negroes?" My reply sought to close down that familiar line of reasoning: "That just postpones answering my question. You tell me what a Negro is, and I'll tell you whether or not I am one, or any of my parents or grandparents were." I got another hard look, a pause, and then a faint smile, as she thought that now she had me. "Were any of your people from Africa?" she asked.

I was delighted with that question because my family thought of themselves as Jews, and thinking that she was the kind of person who took the Bible and the biblical story of the Jews in Egypt literally, and thinking that she likely thought that Jews were a race—once one, you were one forever—and with Egypt of course being part of Africa, my answer to her question of whether my people were from Africa was "Some of my people spent some time there a while back."

Bang. She slammed shut the binder with the question form in it and went into the back room to get her supervisor.

It took quite a while for her supervisor to come out, as they were probably discussing this situation and what they might do about it, for all I was doing was asking them to clarify their question. In that time I did a lot of thinking. First, I had the momentarily delightful fantasy of going to court and saying that because they could not define the terms "Negro" and "White" (having a Negro ancestor of course does not answer for a definition), I might get all the race laws struck down for lack of precision—a basic requirement of the law. Then I thought that the voting rights and civil rights acts had just been passed, and this was absolutely the wrong historical moment to rock that boat and challenge the definitions of racial categories. Moreover, I did not want to be beaten to a pulp by the tears and recriminations of my then future wife. So when the supervisor came out and very aggressively asked me, "Race?" I just said "White" and in a final flourish gave her a very nice smile. We have to score what points we can.

But—and this is both the crucial and the obvious but, the but that introduces this whole part of the book—while race is a social construction, having no definable biological meaning whatsoever, people who get called

Negro in the United States then, and for most still, had and have a much harder life: the fiction becomes all too real.


The reality of race is deeply interwoven with a very large variety of what I would call "naming troubles." These troubles pursue not just racists and the uncaring but also deeply caring and committed people. For just one instance, the fall 2013 issue of the *Crisis*, the magazine of the National Association for the Advancement of Colored People (NAACP), includes a review by Nisa Muhammad of a new book, *So Rich, So Poor: Ending Poverty in America*, by Peter Edelman. Edelman is a law professor at Georgetown University, an exceptionally decent man who in 1996 resigned, very publicly, from a senior policy position in the U.S. government's cabinet-level Department of Health and Human Services. His resignation was in protest of President Bill Clinton's so-called reform of welfare regulations—reforms that had the intended effect of making life very much harder for poor people and poor families. This was supposedly to drive them to work, but there was scant concern for those too ill or stressed in one way or another to be able to work.

Muhammad's review of Edelman's book points out that in the 2010 census "about 48.5 million people, or 15.9 percent of the U.S. population, had incomes below the [shockingly low] poverty level. More than one in five children [= 20 percent] . . . live in poverty. Nearly 40 percent of Black children and 32.3 percent of Hispanic youth are being raised in poor households."

And this, as Edelman points out in his book, is in the wealthiest country on earth. So the name for this situation is not just poverty but race and racism. To call it poverty names one aspect of this extraordinarily difficult-to-live situation, but I am suggesting that to name it racism and sexism—the continuing production of race and gender—is more adequately to name its causal force, its causal content. The hydraulic press squeezing the poor and the vulnerable also catches both citizen and undocumented Hispanics and others, and the so-called White trash, or trailer trash—all those who can't find a job, or can't live on minimum wage—in its thrust. But proportionately it seems to do what it was intended to do: put a full-scale squeeze on African Americans, already suffering from the kinds of discrimination that keep their schools deeply inadequate and, even when they are adequately prepared, keep the job market pressed against them.

As the reality of race making came back into mind, at that time as I thought about the struggles of what were called "interracial couples," I realized that the pleasure I had taunting the bureaucracy of power was blinding me to all that was at stake. The laughter within me was a mask over suffering, and mostly other people's suffering. I was doing little more than joking with myself or, in a more clear formulation, kidding myself with this taunt derived from knowing that race has no definable biological meaning whatsoever.

For those who may wonder about the statement that race "has no definable biological meaning whatsoever," a bit of an explanation may interest people into looking much further into this enormous complexity. If you take a map of the globe and sketch on it all the supposed criteria used to define what gets called race (skin color, hair form, nose width, proportions of blood types, etc.), you will find that none of the boundaries of difference— or more precisely the boundary regions, as one changes into another— overlap. There are no packages where all the differences that mark who gets called what come together. There are, of course locality-specific variations in internal biological processes such as lactose intolerance, or susceptibility to sickle-cell anemia, and malaria resistance, but even here there is no neat mapping. Not all the peoples who get called Negroes are lactose intolerant as adults, and many people who do not get called Negro are.

The key point here is that concepts such as race, nation, and culture may not refer to anything definable in the real world, but they nonetheless can have life-shaping real consequences.

It very well may be that their all-too-real consequences take on a good part of their force from the fact that they are ultimately undefinable—what they name cannot be specified clearly and unambiguously—or, in other words, these concepts are fluid enough to be readily bent to the task at hand. When people talk about "the arc of history," they may also be talking, at least in part, about concepts such as race and gender that can be bent around people's necks.

We need to grab hold of three concepts that, one after the other, have shaped the arc of recent history: race, nation, and culture. One comment before beginning the pursuit of these words through the alleyways of history they both have built and down which they run.

The concept of culture has attracted an enormous literature that has pointed out a lot and grasped only a little. What I am trying to do here has absolutely nothing to do with this. I am interested in only two aspects of two concepts of culture. First, the sequence that goes, in historical unfolding, from race to nation to culture. Each term in this sequence tried to deal with the unsolvable problems of the prior term—how reality both did and did not wiggle out from the term's embrace. Second, and more significantly, each of these terms does more than describe: each term names a process for producing inequality.

*Of the three concepts, race, nation, and culture, culture makes inequality in the most hidden and the most deceptive ways, and that as we shall see is the basis of the increasingly wide appeal of the concept of culture.*

We can confront and oppose people who focus on producing and reproducing their combination of race and inequality and call them racists; we can say of nationalists that "patriotism is the last refuge of a scoundrel" (Samuel Johnson)—while we pay our taxes and vote to support and encourage these scoundrels—but unfortunately no one calls anyone flaunting culture anything like the equivalent of racist or nationalist, such as a "culturalist."

Think of this, just to get oriented to the problem of the deep connections between the concept of culture and the concept of race. One of the more popular uses of culture nowadays is to talk about "hybridity," the people between two different cultures, merging elements of each. But for some people to be "hybrids," to have or to exhibit "hybridity," somewhere on each side of them there must be purity. Purity? Haven't we heard all this before with the Aryan race, or with concepts such as "mixed race," "mestizo," or, to take an example from some of the few survivors of the U.S. holocaust imposed on Native peoples, "half-breed"?

The concept of culture also references music, art, dance, and so forth— nice stuff on the one hand, but on the other doing its work separating people, making above and below, and making the supposed space between the two. While in some senses everyone supposedly "has" a culture, or at least a "subculture," as the elite once put it (as, very quietly, in "subhuman"), when they refer to "culture" in the context of "cultural events," the main reference, outside of the more democratic and more popular kinds of concerts, is to what the elite sponsors primarily for itself and its own interests. After Darwin's book on evolution (*On the Origin of Species* [1859]), flanked by two revolutionary events in Europe—the risings of 1848 and the Paris Commune of 1871—two elite Brits corresponded: A. Lane Fox wrote to Pitt-Rivers that they should build natural history museums to teach the masses the lessons of evolution as opposed to revolution. The British elite sure knew for what they wanted to use the "culture" of museums.

For a clear illustration of this double but hierarchically joined process of culture as elite manifestations and as popular values and beliefs and practices, we can look at the cultural critic Terry Eagleton, who wrote *The Idea of Culture* (2000). The book starts out, "'Culture' at first denoted a thoroughly material process [i.e., agriculture, cultivation of crops], which was then metaphorically transposed to affairs of the spirit. The word thus charts within its semantic unfolding humanity's own historic shift from a rural to an urban existence, pig-farming to Picasso, tilling the soil to splitting the atom" (1).

Wow. Ouch.

At the edge of Robeson County, Smithfield Hams has a pig-packing factory that kills about thirty thousand hogs a day. It employs about five thousand people, the vast majority of whom are undocumented workers from Central America. The lagoon of pig shit outside the factory, mostly from the holding pens, I was told, is a half-mile wide, though the area is fenced and patrolled, so I could not see it myself. This lagoon floods and spills into the local streams in heavy rainstorms, carrying with it also its load of antibiotics that cause a range of health problems for those exposed to this pollution. And the factory's demands for water have lowered the underground water table significantly, creating problems for surrounding homes and communities (e.g., Charles 2013). The mechanized large-scale corporate farms that produce penned animals, heavily injected with hormones and antibiotics, for this factory are another corporate assault on what we used to call the countryside.

So if we look at the development of agro-corporations, their increasing control, via purchase of so-called elected representatives, against the supposedly democratic political process, and their increasing penetration into what we used to call rural life, the old distinction between rural and urban has a vastly different meaning and basis now than it once did. We can see a transition in the twentieth century not just from pig farming to Picasso, as Eagleton would have it, but from Picasso to pig farming.

Not that Picasso represented a better world, just a different one. And Picasso's most intense and wonderful critique of the modern world, his huge painting *Guernica*—the one that shows a screaming horse along with multiple screaming and shattered people that marked and commemorated the supposed first aerial bombardment of a civilian population, in 1937, in the Spanish Civil War. The bombing was done by Nazi German pilots flying Fascist Italian airplanes, in a practice run for World War II. Zygmunt Bauman (1989) has argued that this and the Holocaust were our introduction to modernity in political life: an argument with some important validity.

Actually, this was not the first aerial bombardment of people, although that is what is always claimed: that honor, as it were, may go to the British, who had already napalmed a Sudanese African people, the Nuer, to force them to submit to British rule. But the Nuer are what was then called Negroes, not Europeans, so they have not even merited a charcoal sketch on a napkin, much less a museum painting. And even more hidden, more close to home, but a "private persons" project not directly a state project, although the state prosecuted no one for arson or murder, thus announcing its complicity: the first intentional bombing of an entirely civilian population was in Tulsa, Oklahoma, in 1921, when Whites in airplanes dropped firebombs and fired rifles into the Black neighborhood—a neighborhood that before it was burned to the ground, and so many murdered, was both the wealthiest Black neighborhood in America and the place the Ku Klux Klan called "Nigger Town." (Thanks to Peter Linebaugh and Robert Sweeny, personal communications, who alerted me to this murderous White riot.)

But the important point to keep in mind is much different. Eagleton is using the changing concept of "culture" to both name and explain his perspective—both left and elitist—on recent history, and in the instance just cited, masking, very seriously and very significantly, the increasingly brutal role of the state in fostering the destructive tendency of dominant corporations intruding into our everyday lives. Meanwhile, we are witnessing an only partly hidden alliance of corporations and the state that together are making and attempting to manage the now increasingly severe inequalities of our world. What does he think pig farming now is? A bunch of peasants in rubber-tire sandals or clogs, with buckets of slop in their hands? Or, similarly, a bunch of family farmers with rubber boots and a dozen piglets?

A brief clarification is in order here. The state has supported and aided, in the eighteenth and nineteenth centuries, an extremely vicious and brutal development of industrial and agricultural capitalism, from slavery to the fourteen-hour workday to the colonial devastations that sustained expansion. So it may not be either particularly clear or correct to say that the state's assistance in and direct production of inequality are *increasingly* brutal. But I think of Eric Hobsbawm's point in *The Age of Extremes: A History of the World, 1914–1991* (1994) that when the twentieth century opened, 90 percent of the victims of war were soldiers and 10 percent civilians; when that century ended, the figures were just about exactly reversed. More: Hobsbawm also there pointed out that by the time the twentieth century began, torture had almost disappeared as a tool of state; by the end of the century, it was once again in full flower—the flowers of evil, of course— by France in Algeria and Vietnam, by Germany in South-West Africa, by Belgium in the Congo, by America all over with its drones, its secret renditions, its cages in Iraq and Guantánamo, and its special "university," the School of the Americas, which trains Latin American military officers— often future politicians—in advanced torture techniques for their own countries (Gill 2004).

If you think of the School of the Americas as a clever cultural name, pretending to an innocence that was the opposite of what it did and why, we can come back to what we might well call the problem of culture.

The key point is that culture, in addition to all its other manifestations, is a mask the state both wants and needs, and that is the core of the issue here. Its current primary use for the U.S. state, I think, is rooted in the illusion that the United States is still a "democracy," still a beacon of light and "civilization" to the rest of the world. If things are ever to get any better, both these cultural productions, these illusions, must be seen for the concealing fantasies that they are. All the rest of my critique of Eagleton's elitism is actually irrelevant, it is just my anger against that highhanded stance, an anger that really has no place here except as a tribute to the farm families I have known and loved, and my dismay at the idea that splitting atoms, which has so far included splitting Hiroshima and Nagasaki, Chernobyl and Fukushima, and poisoning increasing areas of land with nuclear waste and nuclear "accidents" is supposedly vastly superior to what Eagleton calls "tilling the soil."

## THE ROAD TO DEMOCRACY

That is where the array of terms—race, nation, culture, and let's add democracy—takes on a different life force. The issue now becomes both simple and crucial. It has to do with the apparent or actual *stability*, or orderliness, of inequality. George Fredrickson, invoking the pro-slavery advocate James Henry Hammond, who wrote in South Carolina in the 1850s, noted:

> Class, according to . . . Hammond . . . , was an inevitable feature of human society; there always has to be a menial or "mudsill" element to do the hard, unpleasant, physical work. But a *stable* class hierarchy could only exist in the presence of inherent racial differences between leisured and laboring classes, such as those said to exist between black and white in the southern states. Attempts to have servile work done by biological equals, namely whites, was a prescription for class conflict and revolution. Hence the good society must be based simultaneously on racial differences and on a traditional order of unequal social classes. (1989, 11, emphasis added)

For those not familiar with southern metaphors, the sill is the raised ridge below the front door that keeps out rainwater and drafts. In the poorest cabins it can also refer to the raised dirt ridge that levels the walls. In the dirt floors or board floors of the very poorest people's cabins—their homes—the sills below the front door were earthen. This was the "mudsill" element.

The situation of racism making inequality more stable is clearly complex. It was not just ideas about inequality between Blacks and Whites but the literally staggering amount of state-sustained violence that it took to try to stabilize a social order that was actually far from orderly or stable. The elite desire or need for some substantial stability of inequalities, produced or attempted in both ideas and actions, indeed was and remains a crucial component of the actions of those who govern, or try to do so. Their attempts to make stability and order were so important because they were doomed to frequent, if not continual, failure. So it is often useful to think how a desired stability now continues to be sought as the state and capital create new, intense, and destructive kinds of inequalities that necessarily, unavoidably, and continually undermine whatever momentary stabilities emerge. This undermining of the bit of stability that people win against the chaos-producing social organization of imposed domination very much includes the stabilities that people often so admirably try to make in their own lives, in the midst of socially constructed poverty and all the stresses and disruptions that come with this.

There are actually two separate processes that underlay domination's attempts to produce stability—or that underlay what we might well call the struggle for stability. One process, rooted in both violence and culture, pits the victims of regimes of inequality against each other—those farther down the ladders pursued by those a bit better off in fact, or only a bit better off in their fantasies about race or gender or citizenship. The ensuing violence and systematic, enduring denials are designed to produce quiescence among the victims, a perhaps grumbling or prayerful "acceptance of their fate," or just an unwillingness or especially an inability to assault the people who seem responsible for it, if they can be identified, and if they can be "reached." The other process, which may in fact be deeply connected to this first one, is to produce indifference to what is happening in the general populace—including especially indifference among those who neither directly benefit nor suffer from what is being done to those at the bottom.

This indifference very much includes, and is masked by, attractive but ineffective remedies for the suffering of people at the bottom of the social hierarchies—remedies that may be attractive because they make people feel better about the suffering around them but do nothing to lessen the inequalities that produce this suffering.

An article in the *New York Times* offers a helpful example of producing both quiescence and indifference, both of which are rooted in a fake solution to an appalling social problem. The article, titled "New Ad Campaign Targets Childhood Hunger," shockingly found in the paper's business section, reports a truly dismaying level of hunger currently existing in the United States. It states, in part:

> According to data released on Wednesday by the Agriculture Department, almost 16 million children, or more than one in five, face hunger in the United States. This condition can affect their future physical and mental health, academic achievement and economic productivity.
>
> The department also found that close to 50 million Americans were living in "food insecure" households, or ones in which some family members lacked "consistent access throughout the year to adequate food." And it found that although the figures were unchanged since the economic downturn began in 2008, they were much higher than in the previous decade.
>
> The ad campaign is the latest initiative in a long collaboration between the Ad Council and Feeding America, which each year supplies

food to more than 37 million Americans through a network of some 200 local food banks. Those food banks, in turn, distribute food to 61,000 food pantries, soup kitchens, and shelters. . . .

The new ads are being released to coincide with Feeding America's Hunger Action Day, part of the organization's Hunger Action Month, held annually in September. They include TV, radio, print, outdoor and digital executions. . . .

Maura Daly, chief communication and development officer at Feeding America, said the new campaign was aimed at "adults who care" and could make financial contributions or volunteer at a food bank. . . .

Hunger experts in academia were generally critical of the new initiative.

Janet Poppendieck, emeritus professor of sociology at Hunter College at the City University of New York and director of public policy at Hunter's New York City Food Policy Center, said that by failing to mention the impending cuts to the federal food stamp program, the campaign "seems to imply that charity is the answer, that donations to your local food bank can solve the problem." Republicans in Congress are fighting to reduce federal expenditures on the food stamp program; these benefits will be cut in November, when a provision in the 2009 stimulus bill expires.

"We cannot end hunger in America with a canned goods drive," Ms. Poppendieck said. "We need to strengthen, not weaken the federal nutrition safety net, and we need full employment and a living wage." . . .

"People are hungry because they are poor." (Lavere 2013)

Both government inaction—or more precisely its actions, from the ending or funding decline of crucial programs—and such well-advertised corporate misdirection of problems and solutions produce both quiescence and indifference in the general populace. Inequalities are usually made, and often not just made but reinforced and manipulated, by states. Part of the process of making and manipulating inequalities very much includes the social production of indifference to their consequences. Racism (or classism, or gender bigotry) says the victims deserve it, or even more were we not so kind and generous. Indifference puts the whole process out of mind. What is being suggested here is that charity, however well intentioned at specific moments, can be part of the production of indifference—indifference both to the long-run well-being of the victims of inequality and especially to the causes and consequences of their plight.

What we call "class," especially since the mid-nineteenth century, was called in the Middle Ages in England and elsewhere in Europe people's "station" in life, or their "calling" from God to do what they are supposed to do. Race, in most ways, is the same as "station" and "calling," dressing people for the dance with a same tomorrow in a slightly more modern costume.

Significantly, "race" changes from a collective term for all humans—the human race—which it was from the 1500s on, to a term that differentiates humans into supposedly separate, and of course unequally different, races, a usage that became increasingly widespread by the late 1700s. Elsewhere I discuss the specificity of these dates, which come with the increasing intrusion of capitalism into both agriculture and manufacturing (Sider n.d.). The point at issue, all too briefly and schematically here, is that the modern state, making a transition from "subject" to supposedly equal "citizen," and the emergence of waged work, with supposed equality in who can claim an equal wage for equal work, used race and gender and locality and citizenship and . . . to restore such profitable and politically useful inequalities as came with subjects and serfs. Subjects have hopes and expectations and memories: in sum, customs. Citizens have rights, except for race and gender and locality and differential citizenship and . . . And our culture explains why.

But of course this early modern change in the meaning of "race"—from the human race to its divisions—does not work to explain the increasing inequalities and destructive varieties of suffering imposed within the White population, as people are forced from the land by enclosures and, after much suffering, into factories with fourteen-hour workdays at extremely inadequate rates of pay. For masking those inequalities, the state needed to also claim itself as representing the "nation." "Nation" has the same root as "natal" and "nativity"; it names people of supposedly common birth origins, as in "we Americans" fought the Civil War to end slavery, "we" fought to stop the spread of "communism" in Vietnam, and so forth. In the Civil War my ancestors were in ghettos on the Polish-Russian border; in the war on Vietnam some people went to war and came back emotionally shattered, or missing major body parts, or did not come back alive, while the people who owned and managed Halliburton made fortunes. One even became vice president. So much for the actual realities of "we" that coexist with a few more positive manifestations.

In my high school, financed substantially by property taxes, according to state law, which made the schools in wealthy suburbs vastly better than the one that I attended, there were thirty-five or forty pupils in many of the classrooms built for thirty, with thirty desks bolted to the floor. The five or ten extra kids had to share a desk, meaning that in some classes a third or more of the students in the classroom were doubled up. And you had to raise your hand to get permission to go to the dirty bathroom with much broken plumbing, to make what little children called a "wee," in a context where I was first learning to wonder about "we." Even then I knew what was happening, knew the differences between what some Americans got and what others had, for I was bicycle racing through fancy Long Island suburbs, and one summer even had a job mowing grass on an estate in one of the fanciest suburbs, an estate so big that its grass was mowed constantly, in those days before gas mowers.

I needed to make a point about this "we"—as in "we Americans," and all the required pledges to the flag, every school morning, that encouraged this mindless nationalism—because in 1952, a year or so before it was legislatively required by an act of Congress, and the year after I started high school, my school added the phrase "under God" to the Pledge of Allegiance, just before "with liberty and justice for all." That seemed to me, in my religious youth, blasphemy—taking God's name in a lie—for there was clearly little if any justice for Blacks or Indians. So I refused to say the pledge, or even to stand while it was being said. This may sound to some extreme, but there either is justice or there is not—there is no such thing as "partial" justice, or justice for some at the expense of others. I paid a fairly high price for this refusal, but it was and remains instructive, particularly about the contradictions of nationalism, which has its benefits as part of its costs.

Nation, as a concept that is supposed to mobilize a sense of belonging—a sense of we Americans or we Brits—can only fool so many, and it can only do so much with those it does fool. People know. That knowledge led soldiers in Vietnam—soldiers who had often volunteered, enlisted in the army "to save our nation," "to defend our way of life against communism and communists"—to shoot their own officers for trying to lead them into murderous, useless, and high-mortality battles, a truly ugly response to their situation, but one whose contradictions call out for understanding.

Against that knowledge, which can produce, simultaneously, a strong commitment to the idea of nation, my nation, our nation, while also realizing, somewhere below the surface of our commitments, the lie of nation, the lie of "we," is where culture comes in. Culture, in this perspective, heals the wounds the concept of nation carries within it, just as the concept of nation papered over the fault lines of race as a mode of unity of some people separate from, and often against, other sorts of people.

The sense of culture as a peoples' shared ways of life, their values, their beliefs, was introduced into anthropology, particularly in England and the United States, by Edward Tylor, in 1871. At just about the same time, Matthew Arnold developed and popularized an elitist concept of culture, connected to art, literature, and so forth. Both concepts spread widely into popular discourse over the next several decades. What is not noticed, and never a subject for consideration, are two major points about the concept of culture. First, these concepts were moving into the popular imagination in the context of a brutal economic depression lasting, with some ups and downs, from the mid-1870s to the mid-1890s—with slightly different starting and ending dates in different places. And this economic depression, as all do, both seriously intensified existing inequalities and helped develop new ones. Economic depressions intensify inequalities substantially, and what we call "culture," in both senses of that term, emerged in this, and a broader, context.

"Culture," in this context, whatever else it does in other more narrow contexts, is little more than a mystical and unspecific—even unspecifiable, and thus more flexible—version of race and nation. It is a "we and them" that is particularly flexible and particularly fluid, and this matters in part in explaining inequality to the unequal as if their situations were also fluid and flexible: you don't like being poor, working at shit jobs (if any) for low pay, living in a tenement, just learn to talk like us, to behave well in school and life, to share our culture and the manners behind which we hide, and you will live like us, with all our benefits and advantages over people like you used to be.

Right (in both the mocking and the political senses of that word). There should be a Broadway play about that, another version of My Fair Lady, called My Fair Grandmother. My grandmother could only very barely read and write, and she talked with a noticeable Yiddish accent. Some nice elite man should have taught her to read and write and talk proper, and while he was doing that, they could have sex or, after she was well trained in his ways, marriage, or if she was too young she could be adopted, and after she was trained in elite culture (which unlike race and birthright is learnable), she would have had such a nice life, with some other poor soul, with less culture, getting the opportunity, in this land of opportunity, to clean her floors. Bertrand Russell, in a wonderful critique of G. B. Shaw's play *Pygmalion* (on which the Broadway play *My Fair Lady* was based), noted that what might work for any one individual, teaching that person a more elite culture to give her or him a "better" life, would not work at all for a whole class or race of people. That is not what class and race are about.

The second major point about the concept of culture that is rarely if ever directly addressed—in addition to its emergence in the context of a major economic depression that intensified differentiation in populations, very much in association with state-sponsored assaults on working people— is that the concept is essentially undefinable.

There is an enormous literature in anthropology and related fields that seeks to define the concept of culture one way or another—mostly all absolute nonsense in terms of how people live their lives—with no one addressing the issue that the term "culture" may take on its force and its power by being undefinable. Unlike race and nation, which seem—falsely, of course, very falsely—to be definable, culture is not at all definable, so it has a fluidity that is crucial to what it does. And what it does is make inequality just as much and just as viciously as does class.

One of the crucial turning points in my understanding of what anthropology and its concept of culture were all about came on a demonstration down south in the 1960s. It was one of those demonstrations that went seriously wrong from the outset. There were more cops than demonstrators, and I was the only White. At some point soon after the very brief demonstration started, a very large and overweight sheriff focused on me and, pointing his fat finger at me, said, "Come here, nigger lover, I want to talk to you."

The African American man who taught me some very important lessons about civil rights struggles told me that if I ever got in serious trouble I should let my mind go blank, because I would get less hurt. So walking toward that sheriff as slowly as I could, I decided to think about anthropology. All of a sudden, I thought that if I ever could get my hands on my professors who taught me that culture is learned and shared and socially transmitted—the major concept of culture in the mid-twentieth century—I would do to them what that cop was going to do to me. For I realized in that deeply stressful moment that that cop was going to try to teach me to act as if I shared his values, and that the notion of shared values—including who does and does not share what, how, and why—names one of the most violent of the social struggles that make and contextualize inequality. So much for culture.

And in fact I did not get hit, for when I got to the cop I said to him, "You want to hit me, don't you?" Naming what seems to be on mentally unbalanced people's minds often quiets them down. He just told me to fuck off, and in gratitude for what I learned from that incident, I would subsequently just smile and say hello to my former professors when I met them at anthropology conferences, and not even pass on the get-lost greeting I got from that cop. They would have to learn their own way, if they still could.

I am actually glad for what I learned from that incident. Often when I am scared, or feeling overwhelmed and trapped, I retreat into joking or intellectual games to hide not from my fear but within it. So in that incident, which I mentioned in the introduction, when a town cop pointed a sawed-off shotgun in my face and said, "Don't make no sudden moves," my reply was, "I think that will be my motto for the rest of my life." That was a very stupid and provocative thing for me to say, for it held the possibility of increasing my risks, and worse. If he realized I was teasing him about how long the rest of my life would last, I might have gotten put to rest on the spot. Not all our protests are productive, not at all, and I learned little or nothing from what I did.

But being called an outrageous name by someone who had the power to teach me what that meant to him was fortunately more productive. It taught that the concept of culture is not, or not just, what it claims to be. To repeat a point I have made before, but one well worth repeating: culture may be, as Clifford Geertz (1973) has claimed, "webs of significance" (also called "webs of meaning"), but webs are spun by spiders to catch, and devour flies, and that seems to me a more realistic perspective on at least one aspect of what culture—and its concepts of significance and meaning—actually does.

If the concept of culture names part of how the active production of inequality is concealed, intensified, and also contested, it points to a process that has a far longer history than does the concept of culture itself. To take an example from the shaping of the modern world (although the process originates with recorded history, and probably well before), we can use a stunning illustration from the original and revised editions of Raymond Williams's *Keywords* (1976, 1985).

In *Keywords* (1976), Williams, a brilliant historian and critic of the formation of modern culture, took 120 socially significant words in the English language and traced their changes over time. One of the words he chose was "art." The revised edition of the book, put together by a group of scholars after Williams died, added several further words, including "genius." "Art," in English from the thirteenth century, referred to any person's skill, a meaning that survives in the word "artisan." Just about everyone had their art—it was what they did well. Each person's special ability was their art.

"Genius," from the Arabic *djinn*, meaning "spirit," via Latin, originally meant every person's guardian spirit. Almost everyone had an art, and everyone had a genius. By the middle to late 1600s, this was increasingly changing: artisans were manual laborers, but artists, who produced what we now call art, were special people, often geniuses in the modern, very restricted sense of the word. The rest of us were just . . .

A change like that works both ways. It is very likely that this shift in meanings can be in large part explained by then-changing social relations and inequalities, especially including how inequalities were being made. It is also very probable that the changing meanings of those words helped to significantly shape new ways of differentiating people. The point here is simple: that what we now call culture did not at all depend on the invention of that vague and troublesome concept. It has a much longer history. But we still need to pay attention to the invention of the modern concept of culture, for the process of its creation seems very much a part of the process of producing the new kinds of violent inequalities that came in the late nineteenth century and the twentieth, particularly with colonialism, the post-slavery brutalization of Blacks, and the variety of ways that industrial and service labor was put and kept in harness. All of these phenomena name huge struggles, not at all simple facts, and the point here is that what we have learned to name "culture" became an open part of all these struggles. It gets worse—both more hopeful and more deceptive, together. Hope and deception in what comes next take their nourishment from each other.

Democracy is, I think, the most deceptive of this sequence of terms—race, nation, culture, democracy—producing both victims and quiescence, for it encourages the feeling that "we" are responsible for the government we have. When I, or any of the people I know, all together have enough money to buy a congressional representative or a senator, or even a local politician, or reshape an election, I might believe that. Until then I marvel at the effectiveness of the belief that we have a democracy, although in a few limited ways we do, somewhat more in elections, when many people think that what they do in an election counts (bad but useful pun), than in what happens after the votes are counted. We can, with this, leave the terrain of how domination masks itself, and get back to the production of race.

## SHARECROPPING THE LANDS OF RACE

Our job here is not to grasp the range of meanings of each of these terms—race, nation, culture, democracy—but to use them to get a better hand-hold on the production of race and of related and interwoven manifestations of inequality.

On the pathways of this task, do not for a single moment let yourself think that there is any *derivative* connection between *actual* Black and White people and the fiction of racial categories—that the people, with their presumed differences from each other, gave us the categories. Maybe by now that is a bit of what is happening, maybe a bit even at first, but much more significantly the names made and still make the reality, rather than vice versa. Not only do the names make the reality, but also so especially does the violence these names call into being. An illustration will show what is at stake.

To see the illustration, you will have to know a bit about a way of organizing southern agriculture called sharecropping—a way of organizing rural production that came into prominence after the Civil War and died out in the 1960s and 1970s. After the Civil War, when slaves were finally freed, most of the land was still owned by Whites—especially the useful farmland. Freedom from enslavement without the resources to make a living—land and seed and the cash to start a crop and keep going until the harvest was sold, to name only some of the basics—was only a very incomplete benefit. After slavery ended, your family could no longer be taken from you and sold away, and you could not be whipped to work, but you could be starved to work, and your family could and often did die from lack of the resources for care (Downs [2012] is stunningly revealing on this).

So a system came into being in which the landlord, now without adequate labor after the slaves were turned loose, brought in families to work what was still his or her land. These families were mostly ex-slaves but also a substantial number of poor Whites and people who, when there were slaves, were legally "free persons of color"—supposedly freed slaves, but a category that more often than realized included survivors of the Native American holocaust who had disappeared into the wilderness not of forest but of the mix of tan peoples with all kinds of histories living quietly here and there with themselves and each other. All these sorts of people sooner or later wound up working on "shares" on land they did not own, for mostly White former plantation owners who, after the war, often did not have the cash to hire labor before the crop was sold. And the people who worked this land found it impossible to work their own land without also having all the resources—tools, seed, fertilizer, money or credit for food and necessities until harvest—that it took to "make it." Another brief detour before we get back to sharecropping and making race.

What elite Whites and the people they teach in the schools they supervise call "civilization," or "our civilization" contains more of a wilderness than is usually made visible. Race is both formed *and evaded*, in part, in the many wildernesses within so-called civilization. Some people get tossed into this wilderness but then survive and grow within it and against it. We will come back to that later. For now the point is only that all sorts of people, by the dominant society's unclear and conflicting ideas about how to sort people, were pulled out of one wilderness—the huge range of people and situations, living here and there, in swamps, mountains, borderlands, socially and politically constructed frontiers, and not fully governed spaces across and within the land—and by the late nineteenth century confined to another "wild," on land both well within the reach of domination and simultaneously far beyond the basic moral and legal foundations of what is thought of as "society" or "civilization." Sharecroppers were in such a situation, from the late mid-nineteenth century to the mid-twentieth, many held there by a legal arrangement, particular to the rural South, now called "debt peonage." This was actual, not symbolic, peonage. Sharecropping, for most of its duration as a major form of agrarian organization in the U.S. South (from the period after the Civil War to the intense mechanization of farming and consolidation of farms in the mid-twentieth century), was an extremely difficult arrangement for a sharecropping family to work their way out from. In that way sharecropping was like race—it carved tomorrow into the core of today, or sought to do so.

Two stories will clarify what is at stake here in the concealment and production of race in the wilderness of "civilization." One summer, in the early 1980s, I was working in the Lumbee Indian town of Pembroke, North Carolina. I was working for Lumbee River Legal Services (LRLS), a federally financed "poverty" law center, offering "legal aid" to people who cannot afford their own lawyers. This program was also very active in and deeply committed to working for the Lumbee nation, trying to help win federal recognition for this state-recognized "tribe," as both the state and the feds called it. I was there researching Lumbee history as part of this endeavor.

One day several tan, middle-aged and elderly people showed up, the men dressed in overalls, the women mostly in calico dresses. They looked like any very rural country farmers. They said they were Waccamaw Indians, living alongside the swamps near Whiteville, North Carolina. This was a particularly difficult town in which to be non-White, as the town apparently tried to live up to its name. These people wanted help being legally recognized as Indians by the state of North Carolina. They said that no one around them knew that they were Indians (one of the usual requirements for official recognition), but that they had more than one hundred years of tribal council meeting minutes in boxes in the trunk of their car.

That's what I mean by living peacefully in the wilderness of so-called civilization—having the sense not to reveal who you are, for fear of what would happen to you and yours. One of the things that did happen routinely to people recognized as non-White was to lose land from one ruse or another and become sharecroppers: a more difficult-to-survive wilderness, as we shall see.

Sharecropping was organized in ways that enabled White landowners—and the very occasional Black and Indian landowners—to obtain labor that was almost as controllable as were slaves. This starts with housing: the house on the farmer's land that was used to bring in a sharecropping family.

The landlord "gave" the sharecropper family—that was both wanted and needed, due to the huge amount of labor required—a cabin of sorts to live in, some land to work (a family using a mule or two to plow and harvest could work only ten to fifteen acres, more after tractors came in), plus seed and fertilizer, and also allowed the family to raise some of its own food on a very small plot. When the commercial crop was sold, at the end of the harvest, the landlord "settled" with the tenant. The tenant usually got a third of what tenants I knew called the "stated" sale price of the harvest—stated because paper receipts were rarely shown—minus all the stated advances that were made for food, medicines, and so forth since the last harvest, minus in many places half the stated cost of the seed and the fertilizer. Very often at the end of the year, the tenant owed money to the landlord and had to stay the following year to work off the debt, or else be arrested and jailed for robbing the landlord by leaving with a balance due. (Daniel [(1972) 1990] provides a stunning review of this, throughout the South.)

By the mid-twentieth century, as tractors replaced mules and the small farms were getting some mechanization, the tenant's share rose from a third to a half of the stated sale of the crop, as the tenant was supposed to supply the tractor and keep it running. But the system scarcely became more favorable to the tenant. Indeed, as the small and fairly old-fashioned farms came under increasingly intense cost-returns pressure, being increasingly unable to compete with large, corporate, fully mechanized farms, it seemed both to me and to many working the land that the squeeze on the tenant got harder. Or more precisely: after the Great Depression of the 1930s, with the better markets during and after World War II, some tenants were able to work themselves up to landownership, but many faced what is best named a terminal—life or way-of-life ending—squeeze. And the squeeze was very far from abstract.

In June 1967, one tenant family in eastern Robeson County that I knew about suffered their nine-year-old son's drowning in the farmer's pond, while they were out working in his fields, leaving their son back to shield him from the heavy work. In October, when the crop was settled, the landlord deducted $200 from the family's share of the sale of the crop to cover the cost of the funeral. The funeral was so paltry that the family could not believe the bill. When they went to the funeral home to ask about it, the undertaker showed them the bill to the landlord, $175, and a note from the landlord saying—as was often the case in the rural South in those days before credit cards were widespread—that he would pay the funeral home after the crop was sold. The landlord had turned a $25 profit on the death of his tenant's child. That's what we call race, and it mattered—I think—that it happened in eastern Robeson County, which was the area with the most Whites and the fewest Blacks and Indians, so that non-Whites had fewer "of their own" to call on.

"That's what we call race" because race, in part, is made by what people can get away with. Race is always defined by impunity. The impunity that shapes race has widely different temporal durations, for it encounters widely different opportunities for resistance or transformation. In some places impunity lasts only a few decades, in others a few centuries, so race—to just introduce a point that will be engaged later—is always historically volatile, because impunity also is, despite the fact that race is supposed to be grounded in enduring biological features. "What people can get away with" cuts both ways, from "above" and from "below," as it were: impunity is always a struggle, not simply a gift to some from the dominant. No one called the cops on my Indian mentor for shooting the trunk of that car. Victims and potential victims often engage a struggle against the impunity of the dominant and their allies, engage with their own strengths and their own resources, and yet they often also lose.

Back to sharecropping, and to the story that illustrates the larger and more general point that the categories make the people, rather than the people giving us the categories.

In 1967–68 I worked, two or three days each week, for a program primarily staffed and directed by African Americans, the North Carolina Mobility Project, which was funded by the U.S. Department of Labor and the Ford Foundation. This was the tag end of the years of the so-called riots in northern and western urban ghettos. It was years later that research revealed that most of the so-called rioters—the active protesters—were third-generation residents of the ghettos. At first, when the protests were happening, it was thought that the new migrants from the Black South were the source of "the trouble" (U.S. Riot Commission 1968).

So the U.S. government and the Ford Foundation, in their infinite wisdom, decided they wanted to alter the flow of migrants from the South to northern urban ghettos. Moreover, the old northern industrial cities were already starting to die an economic death—or, to put their problems more realistically, to be killed by government policies and practices, as will be discussed in chapter 8.

The North Carolina Mobility Project was designed to comb through the poorer rural areas of the state, talking with small, mostly Black and some Indian and White tenant farmers, to see who was being driven out of the bottom end of southern agriculture, where they were thinking of going, and whether some substantial relocation assistance, including help with finding housing and a job, and some tutoring in urban ways, such as figuring out bus routes from home to job, would get people to move to what was called "southern regional growth centers"—in North Carolina places such as Charlotte, Durham, High Point, and Greensboro. This was called "diverting the flow" of migrants, a polite way of quietly admitting that the point was to keep Black people from going to the large northern and western cities where they usually went, where relatives and former neighbors who had migrated earlier would help them find housing and jobs and show them how to get around. In these small southern cities they would supposedly have more of a future, and more: would be easier to control.

Almost all the people who worked for the Mobility Project were African American or Native American, and the director, Charles Davis, was African American, with very strong commitments to civil rights and social justice. This gave the people who worked in the program quite a bit of latitude to actually try to help the mostly impoverished farmers we encountered.

The following incident happened in the early summer of 1968. In eastern Robeson County (the same small area where a different farmer turned a profit on the death of his tenant's child), one rather small farm formerly worked by a single sharecropping family had recently been divided into two administrative units, and a second sharecropping family had been brought in to work the land. Let us use some artificial and rounded figures to explain what was happening in ways that can be quickly and clearly grasped. The figures may be artificial, but the situation they describe was unfortunately all too real.

Suppose the farm had one hundred acres of farmable land, and with one family working it, the farm produced 3,000 bushels of crops x and y, which sold for $6,000. The landlord took, supposedly but with no figures shown, half of the sale, $3,000, and the tenant got $3,000, minus costs, deducted before the income from the sale of the crop was split.

When a second sharecropping family is brought in, and given fifty of the one hundred acres to farm, then with more focus and more work and more attention to the smaller plots of land, the total output of the farm goes up, say to 3,500 bushels of crops x and y, which sell for $7,000. The landlord's half goes up to $3,500, and the two tenant families split the other half, the other $3,500, which gives each farm family an annual income of $1,750, minus the costs for half the seed, the fertilizer, and all the "advances" for food, medicine, and perhaps some clothes. In the 1960 census the *median rural family* income for non-Whites in Robeson County was actually $1,262, so this illustrative figure is in fact high (Blu 1980, chap. 1). "Median" means half got less than this, less than $100 per month. I don't know the actual figures in this specific case, but you get the point of how the system, and the division of the farm, worked.

When one of our fieldworkers who sought out families that might want or need to move encountered the two families on this now divided farm, in the early summer of 1968, the families were in desperate shape. One family had nothing much in the house to eat but green pecans, and the kids had lost all control over their bowels. The other family, whose home I was soon in, had nothing in their kitchen but a half-finished loaf of bread, some jam, and some tea bags. We pooled some money and bought these folks some groceries, as did a local church, but more needed to be done, for no one was in a position to support these two families over the long haul.

In the 1960s in North Carolina there were no food stamps, but people in desperate need got "surplus commodities"—blocks of cheese, powdered milk, and whatever else the U.S. Department of Agriculture had in surplus storage from its farm price-support programs. To get these commodities you had to prove an income below a certain level. In this case that meant the landlord had to sign a form provided by the welfare department saying that the family earned less than whatever the figure then was.

So the fieldworker, a young Black woman, went and got the form from "the welfare department" and took it to the landlord, asking him to sign. He chased her off the property with a gun. She then brought the form to me, saying he was much less likely to shoot a White guy, and urged me to go try to get him to sign.

Not wanting to volunteer to risk getting shot, or attacked by dogs or landlords unless the risk was unavoidable, I first went to see a local medical doctor, an Indian who had been born in Detroit, whose birth certificate said "White," and who, on that basis and before he returned "home" from Michigan to work in the county, and the hospital could "see what he looked like," had gotten what were called "admission privileges" at the local, then racist-managed hospital. To do so he sent in his birth certificate, which showed he was classified "White." I asked this doctor to sign a letter saying that the families were starving. I planned to take this letter to the welfare department and see if it would approve commodities on that basis. But the doctor very regretfully told me he could not do that, for fear he would lose his hospital admission privileges for his mostly Indian and Black patients.

So I went to the farm, visited the families, and then drove to the farm-house, being careful to position the car so that when I got out, it was between me and the house—a protection against the dogs, a bit of safety, and a bit of southern-style caution in case a woman was alone in the house and came out on the porch. In such cases you never wanted to be seen between the house and the car, and the landlord's house was visible from the road.

The landlord came out of the house and called back his dogs a bit. I asked him to sign not by appealing to his compassion but by saying that people who eat can work harder. I thought that explanation might convince him. But he just looked at me, when I was done talking, and then said what I can still clearly hear almost fifty years later: "If you give those niggers free food they won't work." And he turned and went back in the house, leaving the yard to me and his dogs.

One of the sharecropping families was White, the other was Indian.

Don't ever think that the people provide the categories—that the categories are named by what the people are. The current of power runs in the opposite direction. "If you give those niggers free food they won't work": that's how different kinds of people are made, by the imposition of categories, and the same violence that made them Black made the landlord and me—whether I wanted it or not—White. Whether I wanted this or not, whether the sharecropping families wanted this or not.

There is an old English phrase for situations like this—situations that put both the tenant farmers and me where we would try not to be: these are situations that happen to us "willy-nilly." The phrase is taken to mean that it happens chaotically, which it very much does, but the phrase actually means something that is imposed on, or happens to, someone "will he nill he"—whether he or she wants it or not. Both meanings call to mind the chaos-producing consequences of domination imposed upon our lives. This will turn out, at least at times, to be the basis for both our loss and our freedom: what the violence of such situations makes us into, or tries to make us into, can have only partial and temporary success, because while trying to create a social order, it simultaneously creates ungovernable social chaos. One tenant family split up, the mother running away, and the other left; the farm eventually failed.

Race is the name for this process of making order and chaos simultaneously.

Race is one of many names for this process of making order and chaos simultaneously.


The words we need to soon consider go beyond race, nation, culture, and democracy, are words that more intensely and directly both create and express the peculiar mixture of chaos and order that always comes with making severe inequalities. The words that most directly express, and in so doing reveal, this almost inextricable combination of chaos and order are "fuck" and "nigger." They bring into the arena the production of gender and noncitizens, but much more. It is this "more" that will enable us to talk usefully about the changing histories they create, and the changing histories that create them.

First we need to say a few words about the state, within and against which much but far from all of this happens.

——

# FIVE

# State Making

## HIGHWAYS TO LOSS

As usual we can most usefully start with the surprises: the way that the politics of progress and modernity, after World War II, and especially those begun under President Dwight Eisenhower (1953–61), became deeply interwoven with the production of race in the last half of the twentieth century.

Dwight D. Eisenhower was the "Supreme Allied Commander"—a title that sounds like it comes from a science fiction novel—of the military forces in Europe, from the winter of 1943 to the end of the war. He actively pursued a policy of bombing railroad hub stations and highway intersections in German cities, which had an exceptionally powerful effect because the transportation networks in Germany, as everywhere in what were then "modern" transportation systems, ran into the center of cities and back out again to multiple different places. The word "hub" is a precise metaphor: the transport systems were organized like wagon wheels, with cities and towns being the hubs where the transport-route spokes met.

When Eisenhower became president of the United States, in January 1953, in the context of both the "Cold War" with the Soviet Union and a wide range of American military-CIA expansionist and provocative interventions in the Middle East and Latin America, he was concerned to transform the vulnerability of the United States to the same sort of bombing attacks that he had used so effectively to undermine German production and the state—only these attacks might be nuclear and even more effective.

So he helped to push through Congress what was called the National Interstate and Defense Highway Act, which changed both transportation and race relations in the United States.

This highway act added a federal tax of about a dime a gallon on gasoline and diesel fuel and used it to finance the interstate highway system, which had two components: limited-access highways between cities, and ring roads around cities—sometimes two layers of ring roads, inner and outer. The act, passed in 1956, joined and massively expanded a slightly earlier system of limited-access highways, financed by tolls, that states had started constructing—the turnpikes and thruways. The so-called GI Bill constructed race along these new roads.

When U.S. soldiers in World War II were outfitted, their equipment was coded "Government Issue." As the soldiers were given similar haircuts when they entered the service, and similar uniforms, they themselves became government issue—GIs. In mid-1944, when the United States began preparing for the end of the war the Allies were already clearly winning, Congress passed the Servicemen's Readjustment Act, which entered into popular language as the GI Bill of Rights. The issue the act addressed was what to do with all the soldiers who would be "demobilized"—turned out of the armed forces at the end of the war. The memory of the Great Depression, which substantially was ended by wartime production and a massive mobilization of soldiers that "solved" the problem of mass unemployment, was still fresh, and there was substantial concern that tens of thousands of unemployed soldiers, and no additional major military production, would put the United States back into another economic depression.

The invention of the Cold War—anticommunist fantasy made into reality—solved the problem of the decline in military production, as did massive highway construction, along with the beginning of an era, still continuing and still intensifying, of almost constant armed "interventions" somewhere or another in the world. The United States currently has the world's largest defense budget, with soldiers stationed in 150 of the world's 190 countries, including more than fifty thousand still in Germany, left over from the Cold War (https://en.wikipedia.org/wiki/United_States _Armed_Forces).

The GI Bill solved the problem of what to do with the ex-soldiers. Two components of the bill are particularly relevant to the "modern" construction, or reconstruction, of race. First, it financed both higher education and vocational training for soldiers, including both tuition and living expenses. About half of all World War II veterans took these benefits, but for multiple reasons a higher percentage of White than Black veterans got this educational benefit, both receiving training for decently paying jobs in an expanding economy and being kept out of the job market while pursuing their education. Second, and crucially, the GI Bill provided guarantees for mortgages at subsidized interest rates and with no or minimal down payment. What made this provision crucial to the modern production of race is that this benefit was available only in "stable" neighborhoods, and an integrated neighborhood was considered unstable.

So the stables, called "suburbia," filled up with Whites and their families, while the Blacks and Hispanics and Asians were bottled up in the cities, with almost none of the National Defense Highway Act monies going to subsidize urban transportation. The so-called urban renewal that in many places came with urban transportation improvements was widely and correctly dismissed with the slogan "Urban renewal is Negro removal." It still is, although now in some places, such as Harlem, an African American elite, among others, is driving the former residents and their becoming-adult children out, with major increases in housing costs.

Compounding the problems of housing and employment were technological developments in manufacturing, which can be summed up in the industrial-jargon phrase "the increasing transition from batch processing to continuous flow." Batch processing means essentially that you take a quantity of materials, work on them, and then move them to the next site, where further work is done. Continuous flow means the materials enter on the conveyor belt or in the pipeline and keep moving. With batch processing you can have a great deal of production in urban areas, in tall buildings where goods are moved from floor to floor, if moved at all. Continuous-flow processing requires production to be on one floor—a horizontal, as opposed to a vertical, factory layout. This required manufacturing to move out of the cities to suburbia, to the ring roads at least, where the limited-access roads facilitated both the transport of goods and the transport of automobile-owning suburbanites to work on these goods, and where relatively inexpensive land was available for continuous-flow, horizontal-factory production facilities. There was little or no public transport to let the Blacks and Hispanics follow the work out of the city. If you did not or could not get a desk job, you were stuck in something, such as retail or service, that paid miserable wages so you could live what the state orchestrated, on purpose if silently: an often very stressed life, in decayed housing and with your children at decayed schools, because property taxes substantially finance schools, because an underground economy became crucial for many to get a living wage, which came to finance a prison complex increasingly profitable for White-owned and White-managed corporations. The realization that local property taxes provide a substantial portion of school funding mocks the fantasy of equality and democracy so intensely that it takes one's breath away, or should, were that inequality not the point and the purpose. Putting aside the racism and classism in the structure of private schools and most charter schools, the very ordinary notion that each state in the U.S. has "a" public school system is the lie that conceals the continuing making of race. And as Whites moved into suburbia, many office buildings moved out to the ring roads, for easier access by their workers. Urban ghettos quickly became the refuse dumps of this state-structured new capitalism, full to the brim with increasingly disposable people, not yet gentrified out of sight, and even before, but continuing with, the offshoring of U.S. manufacturing and back-office tasks.

The sale of an increasingly valuable suburban house, at least until the crash of the real estate market in 2008, provided a massive infusion into the inheritance packages—the estates—of the middle class, and thus the well-being of White middle-class children and grandchildren. The racism of the suburbia-intensifying reorganization of transport, coupled with the firmly enforced racism of the GI Bill's mortgage subsidies—real estate agents would lose their licenses if they sold a subsidizable-mortgage house to a Black in a "stable" White neighborhood—together excluded most Blacks from the wealth production of home ownership when home prices were rising. This rise has made a substantial portion—but far from all—of White retirement very much more comfortable, and the children of much of the White middle class also significantly better-off when their parents died, or even before death, when White parents could more readily afford the increasingly necessary subsidy of their children's down payment on that generation's home ownership and increasingly, also, their college education.

The implications of differential home ownership as a consequence of the GI Bill and the subsidized suburbanization of White folks have both endured and intensified, as illustrated by a study conducted by Tom Shapiro, director of the Institute on Assets and Social Policy at Brandeis University. An interview with Shapiro on National Public Radio about this study, which was titled "The Roots of the Widening Racial Wealth Gap: Explaining the Black-White Economic Divide," reveals the issue in all its force. As the interviewer explained: "In 1984, the total wealth gap between blacks and whites was $85,000. In 2009, that gap had tripled to $236,500. And the largest single factor that's led to the gap? Home ownership" (Ryssdal 2013).

## THE AVENGER'S MOMENT

There is a popular, but I think simplistic, semifantasy about the development of democracy in the "advanced industrial nations"—particularly in the leading case, the United States. This semifantasy is called "Fordism," taking its name from the work of the Italian theorist Antonio Gramsci.

Here is another place where I am likely to be misunderstood unless I take a moment or two to clarify what is and is not at stake. I am, in general, enormously impressed by the work of Gramsci, having learned from him a great deal that helps me understand, in very useful ways, how inequalities are made and continually transformed. But one of his concepts for understanding, the one he called Fordism, is much more complex than he realized. He is not wrong, which is why he is still very useful, only inadequate in important ways. And because Gramsci did most of his writings about industrialization and government in the 1920s and 1930s, we should be expected to engage the issues on an expanded terrain. Fordism, as a social-analytical concept, is rooted in the industrial organization that was put together by Henry Ford in the early twentieth century.

We will discuss the social arrangement Gramsci called Fordism in some further detail later. Here the introductory point to that discussion, and to all we should discuss on the way there, is that Gramsci saw the high wages that Henry Ford and then others paid, and the subsequent consumerism, as buying political quiescence. Indeed they do. But what he missed addressing at equal length and intensity is that high wages are meaningful only if many others are not also getting them. Fordism is not just the political quiescence of the well paid but their seemingly necessary collusion with the squeeze on the people "below" them, on which all the purchasing power of their wage depends. Ford himself was a racist; Fordism was the same, but more indirectly and more broadly.

Henry Ford brought together several prior developments in production to create something very effective and very powerful. He took the standardized part, developed by Samuel Colt in the production of firearms, and the conveyor belt, developed by Charles Goodyear, added the standardized worker, who could be quickly and cheaply trained to do the same thing over and over again, all day long, and put together a moving assembly line that could produce a car very quickly and very inexpensively, so long as a lot of them were produced, one after the other, all the same. This was one of the beginnings of mass production in industrial manufacturing—textiles were another—but the issues that Ford raised were more intense because even though his cars were comparatively inexpensive, they were vastly more expensive to purchase than daily-use textiles.

For Ford, in manufacturing cars there could be no mass production without mass consumption. This problem with automobiles was much more intense than with textiles, whose unit costs could be quite low when mass-produced. So Ford paid his workers—he advertised for "White Christian Gentlemen"—the then comparatively very high wage of five dollars a day. He had to do this in part to cut down on turnover among his workers, who hated the reduction of skill and intelligence involved in doing the same small task over and over and over and over again all the long day, and he had to do this to introduce the amount of money in circulation in the economy so that many more people would be able to purchase his cars. The broad consumerism that high wages made possible, including houses with mortgages, and later car payments, helped to stabilize both the workers and the system.

The people who run industries know the connection between large credit bills and staying on a job, know this well and clearly. Soon after the Converse athletic shoe company opened a large manufacturing plant in Robeson County in the early 1970s, one that hired a lot of local Indians and Blacks, it helped—with technical advice and, it was rumored, loans or loan guarantees—two Indians to open an Indian-owned new car agency staffed, most unusually then, with Indian and Black salespeople. The managers of the plant, it can be assumed, thought that their workers would be more likely to buy a car from one of "their own," and a worker with a car payment book in his or her pocket or pocketbook is not likely to be casually absent, or to not do whatever he or she was told, even when the belt was turned up (the conveyor belt that governed the speed at which people had to work was turned to and past the point of endurance, particularly for the older workers, as several workers in the plant told me). The production of race occurs, crucially, not just in actions done to people of a race but in how events within racially constructed communities are encouraged and channeled.

This includes how the feelings of abuse and the anger against control and manipulation are sometimes managed. For the production and maintenance of race as also the production and maintenance of class, and of producing White as well as Black (and of course Latino and . . . ), consider the following examples, which both illustrate the issues and push them beyond complex.

Mitsubishi is an unusual automobile manufacturing company. It makes some cars that it markets under its own name, but it makes a lot more cars that are marketed by other companies, with the other companies' model names attached. In the early 1970s Mitsubishi made a small car with a ninety-horsepower engine, somewhat underpowered by American standards, that was marketed in the United States, primarily to young women buying their first car, as the Plymouth Cricket. Plymouth is a Chrysler company. The identical car, with some slightly different trim and louder paint, was made and marketed in England through the 1970s by the Chrysler-owned Hillman Company, especially to the young and middle-aged male working class, as the Avenger. Suppose we ask ourselves, "What does the Avenger avenge?" Why would someone—in a fairly specific social location at a fairly specific historical moment, when the unions were being destroyed by political conservatives—want a car with that name? And we could also ask why mostly working-class and middle-class young women were being encouraged to identify with a small, noisy, seemingly chipper bug? On the way to an answer consider the following.

The second instance is yammering, as it was then called by managers and some workers. During World War II, factory production in the United States was very significantly speeded up, particularly in the "heavy" industries making trucks and tanks and other kinds of large war-related equipment. At the same time, there was what the government called "wage and price control," which meant that wages were frozen and prices, particularly on the black market and the under-the-counter market, rose quite substantially. The stress on the workers increased to the point that absenteeism and breakage were going up significantly. General Motors decided to allow, rather than suppress, yammering on the production line.

Production lines in heavy industry factories tend to be very noisy—in places on the line, painfully noisy. One way that workers deal with this is to make noise themselves—singing loudly, shouting, whatever. Yammering was doing this while also insulting, in very graphic and specific terms, the foreman, the supervisor, the bosses—detailing what they did with each other, with their genitals and the neighborhood dogs, their mothers and grandmothers, how they could pretend to see so much with their head up their ass—you get the point. Yammering was, before the speedup during World War II, usually suppressed. When yammering was allowed by General Motors, and then by other corporations, to help manage the stresses of the speedup during wartime production, absenteeism declined, breakage lessened, and production quality increased.

Yammering turns out to be more or less the same thing as driving home in your Avenger, and it may well be the same thing as smashing cockroaches on your mother's dining room table, racing motorcycles on the garbage dump, whatever. And since when driving home in your Avenger there is little to do by way of asserting oneself other than to cut off another worker on the road, it may also resonate with some aspects of lynching Blacks, for we have to wonder how people could do or just watch things like that and go back to work the next day, unless that return to work with an enhanced sense of power was part of the point.

It may also be related to why many people call getting bent and broken by drugs and alcohol "getting high" when they know, in many cases, that they are also "getting stoned." Among working-class folks in the United States, becoming seriously drunk, especially after getting high, is called "getting shitfaced"—a term I have heard only from White males, never Blacks. The process of distancing oneself from a difficult and uncomfortable world, getting high above your problems and troubles and doubts and fears, or just above the literally deadly daily grind, is more complex than it may first seem, for getting high above it all, as the people themselves well know, often does not end well. Getting high often ends in getting shitfaced. In the not so long run you lose, as well you know. But on the road to that ending you get to drive your Avenger, to call your boss an asshole, almost within his hearing, or to hop into your Cricket and make, in a far less openly aggressive way, your own annoying, interesting, and attention-calling racket. After three or four or five years of monthly payments, if the Cricket still runs and is still desirable, the car will be yours.

Robeson County, the primary locale for this study, now has, according to the public health nurses working there, the highest syphilis rate in the nation. We are back on the terrain of pleasure and thoughtlessness, of assertion and gendered assault (assault by lack of caring), of claim for something new, something different, and actual continuity or worse of the problems, of momentary joys and simultaneously communal self-destruction. The crucial point here is that making race, just like making class, happens not just between the differences being produced but also very much within each. Between and within are indeed as inseparable as the joys, the self-expressiveness, the caring or using, and the consequences of sex. We will return to this issue when we come to address all the meanings of the very popular and deeply contradictory sayings that are about people "getting fucked," and also about a deeply contradictory, as well as hatefully racist, language. Here the point—and it is a somewhat uncomfortable point, I know—is just to open issues that will be dealt with starting in the next chapter.

## STATES ROCK

Let us put aside all the discussions about what the state *is*—completely irrelevant to the situations at issue here—and focus on what states *do*. This will be the same as our treatment of race: it is not what race is but what it does that is at issue here. In this perspective on what it does, rather than what it is, and in the specific context of making race, states all seek to do two profoundly incompatible and contradictory tasks: produce and reproduce the changing inequalities that they or their sponsors consider necessary, useful, or important, with often a few more thrown into the hopper, just for kicks, to make a bad pun; and simultaneously manage, control, or "govern" these changing inequalities. This includes also trying to manage those who are no longer wanted or needed in the economy or, like so-called welfare mothers, people who need to be kicked just to remind them about their place in society. But sometimes this has been done so systematically, for so long, that it no longer politically shores up the pretenses of state to keep actively putting such people down, and the state can turn to what it once called "benign neglect" and start in on other kinds of people with other issues: the turn, for example, from a focus on "welfare mothers" to a focus on "drug addicts." African Americans were still the main victims of this shift in the focus of state, but the state continued its assertions of, or illusory claims to, power and control by changing its ongoing "response" to what it defined, or encouraged to be popularly defined, as a social problem. The foundation of state rests on the always defective cement made by mixing power and inequality, both making inequality and seeking and continually failing to control the unequals—so the state must continually expand and try to consolidate its reach.

Sustaining the state and its orgy of advisers, supporters, and opponents for this impossible dual task of simultaneously making and governing the unequal are a pack of intellectuals and engaged citizenries constantly producing one fantasy after another that this dual task could be, or was once, accomplished, if only we did this, or returned to that. For it is certainly not being accomplished today, whatever today you pick, for inequalities are, of course, unmanageable, ungovernable. They are usually too fluid and too tidal to be contained.

Race, like class, is a creation of state, and of course of more than state—but the engagement of state in this process is at issue here. We can imagine the state and the economy perpetually in the throes of their intercourse, making race and class—and gender and age, all of which in some of their manifestations can be summed up as differential citizenship. As soon as we make the simple and obvious but unsettling realization that the term "illegal alien" primarily—primarily—names what can be done to some people with impunity, and that is why they are wanted and needed and abused and destroyed; as soon as we make this simple and crucial realization about differential citizenship, we can also realize that there are many other kinds of people, including native-born Blacks, women, the disabled, the gays, and so forth and so forth, who all are, in their own ways, illegal aliens: they can be "done."

"Done" is a wonderfully fluid word used in the Bronx of my youth, whose meanings include being very badly treated, and finished, as in finished off. People could be "done" in ways that were not quite legal, or blatantly illegal in some readings of the law and justice, but despite the illegality of it all, or just the immorality, can be continually treated with almost total impunity. It was also a slang word for imposed, or differentially rewarding, sex—getting fucked, in all the meanings of that term, but here with the subtle extra meaning of fucked and discarded. You did not "do" a person you wanted to stay connected to in any positive way. To be an illegal—or a Black, or a worker in an industry that closes and moves away—is to be not just finished but done. And in the most intense use of the term, probably why the word got used that way, people who were "done" by those with power over them were finished. Not dead, but finished.

On the other end of this same stick are people like bankers, also differential citizens, for they can do almost as they wish to us and be very well rewarded for so doing. All inequalities are founded upon the rock of state, even while the rock continually crumbles, continually needs to be rebuilt. And, of course, the state is continually rebuilt upon the continually crumbling rock of inequality. Chase Bank was fined $13 billion in October 2013—$4 billion for cheating very many thousands of homeowners out of their homes, and $9 billion for harming other investors—just in case people did not understand what the state considered the more important transgression. And the news then reported an investor saying that now, just after that fine, is a good time to buy Chase stock.

The operative underlying metaphor for the rock of state is not Jesus changing Simon's name to Peter, a name that had a meaning something like stone or rock, and saying "on this rock I build my church." The rock of inequality is different. The underlying symbolism is not Peter but Prometheus, whose name in Greek means "forethought," chained to a rock for trying to liberate humanity by bringing to them fire, and the useful arts that fire makes possible. Prometheus was chained to a rock and perpetually tortured by birds that tore at his entrails but that could not kill him because he was immortal.

There is a tiny, *always* ignored point in the myth of Prometheus that turns out to have surprisingly significant implications when the myth is expanded, or shall we say exploded. Not only was Prometheus chained to the rock, but the rock was chained to him.

We will soon deal with the predictable wonder about how this could possibly matter to the rock. It matters to all of us who keep the fire in our bellies. The rock of state turns out to be chained to the people it abuses. The most obvious examples of this are the current relations between the U.S. state and the various increasingly uncontrollable countries of the Middle East. Our armies, our drones, our ambassadors, our huge financial commitment to governments that are utterly incapable of governing chain us to them even more than they are chained to us. Similarly, our state has made the unavoidable mistake of chaining itself to us—to the people it seeks to both diminish, if not injure, and simultaneously govern.

The state is no more free from what we can do to it than are we free from its chains. And the realization that rocks get rolled over all the time—the job of rivers and mountains—can be a cheerful thought. But we must also keep in mind that rolling that rock over has often been done very badly, very destructively, with a lot of innocent people getting hurt.


We are working to develop the perspective in which race and class and gender and all other so far immortal inequalities are chained to the rock of state, and thus, crucially, the rock of state is also chained to them—you cannot do one without doing the other. To understand the potential of inequalities founded upon chaining to the rock of state, we must start from the point that victims always struggle to liberate themselves not just from their chains but much more: from what put them there and what keeps them there. So we need to see what we can do with and against the state that is also chained to us.

It may be a simpler problem than usually realized—how to use our chains to pull the state off balance, so other work can be accomplished. Not easier, but simpler. To see this issue in new ways, we have to put aside, decisively, some of the central fantasies of twentieth-century social science, fantasies that have been so attractive to the bourgeoisie that they become the logical equivalent of wet dreams—fantasized desires that get transformed into fortunately unproductive realities.

Two of these central fantasies have been produced by Max Weber and his spiritual heir, Michel Foucault. Weber, as he got more and more mentally ill, descended from droll excursions into his own construction of reality—The Protestant Ethic and the Spirit of Capitalism ([1905] 2001) is the most flamboyant example of a droll excursion—to actually harmful, half-blind analyses.

In the Protestant Ethic book of essays Weber argued that capitalism was essentially dependent upon thrift and hard work, and that Protestants were particularly good at both. This was so very attractive both to capitalists and to those who have spent a good part of their academic careers licking the boots and the Gucci loafers of the capitalists, trying to explain, for example, why the Japanese were almost as good as the Protestants and certainly better than the Catholics. In fact—in simple fact—capitalism is actually founded on forced taking, on mistreatment, on enslavement, on child labor and brutal working conditions, and so forth, and if Weber had wanted to argue that the Protestants were particularly good at this, he would have been much less welcome to do so. Were his fantasy about what made capitalism not taken so seriously by so many, the book would be rather comic reading.

Far more dangerously misleading are his writings on politics, where he assumes—again with no basis whatsoever in reality—that power is based on order. He proposed several kinds of politically constructed order, based on the rulers' claims to their legitimacy—be they rational-legal, charismatic, or traditional (Weber [1919] 1958). In either way, power was about order, and compounding the problem—making his political theory into a form of violence-imbued political pornography to anyone who has ever been hit by a cop or by an unpunished domestic partner, or anyone who has had a loved one or a neighbor lynched—is his very widely quoted and accepted assertion that "the state has a monopoly on the legitimate use of violence." Wow. And this was written in the early twentieth century, when Blacks were being lynched repeatedly, not just murdered but burned alive, skinned alive, mutilated, with large crowds coming out to watch and to picnic, with souvenir postcards and pictures sold to the crowd, with none of the perpetrators, who had committed the felonious and capital crimes of kidnapping, torture in the extreme, and murder ever once punished, and in fact with none of the perpetrators, or the dignitaries who often gave speeches at the larger lynchings, ever bothering to mask, to conceal their identities (Tolnay and Beck 1995; Litwack 1999).

The absence of their masks was, of course, the masked presence of the state, granting impunity to the felonious perpetrators of these imposed horrors. And Weber could claim, in his naïveté and his fawning ignorance, that the state had a monopoly on the legitimate use of violence? The whole way the state works requires it to always engage in, encourage, or just permit acts that by its own rules are illegitimate. Not necessarily as violent as lynching, but still profoundly illegal. Impunity is a necessary tool of government, always: hello, President Obama, who was supposed to be different. His difference includes, in addition to whatever good he has tried to accomplish against Republican opposition, both bombing and deporting more people than the Bushes together ever did, plus snooping on the world, all against the "rules" of war and the laws of states. Impunity turns out to be one of the major ways that the contradictions of domination—of government—are both managed and perpetuated. Contrary to Max Weber, states do not work, cannot maintain themselves and their power, unless they act in ways that are both legitimate and not legitimate—by their own standards. Hello, fracking. Hello, waterboarding. Hello, funding schools by local property taxes, which seems an extremely clear violation of the Fourteenth Amendment's guarantee of equality.

And even more widespread in its consequences is the Weberian illusion that power produces order. To the very intense contrary, power always—always—*also* produces chaos in the lives of the governed, particularly among those sectors of the population that are being created and re-created as the vastly unequal.

Foucault reproduces, in either modern dress or Halloween costume, the same nonsense, the same notion that domination can create and manage the subjects of its domination. Even when they resist, the power over them supposedly defines and shapes how they and their resistance are constituted. In simple terms this makes some slight sense—one could argue that the conk rag, in small part, was designed by Foucault. But consider again the sheriff's deputies, who in Robeson County in the 1960s wore two pairs of steel handcuffs on their belt, and some people got handcuffed with one pair and whipped with the other. "Governmentality," as we painfully learned, *was beaten into you and often simultaneously out of you*—and the people who cared about you and for you as well—at the very same time, with the very same violence, by the very same "government" that dreamed in vain for a day it could govern us.

Those who suffered such beatings were scarcely people *within* whom domination created what Foucault called "governmentality." Foucault, like Weber, tries to make the process of domination, the process of state, look like it was rooted in a rational control. Not rational by any abstract standard, of course, but rational in terms of logically or coherently derived from the policies and plans of domination. Even in that more restricted sense, we are dealing with fantasy rationality. That's what makes Foucault's theory look like it was decked out for All Hallows' E'en—for the night of the dead turned into child's play—because actual life does not work like that at all, and his notion of "governmentality" is playing with a far more serious and often deadly process.

Domination actually is manifest in our lives in irrational, conflicting demands, incoherent claims, impossible tasks—for one example, all that comes with a factory that provided most of the jobs in a small town being allowed by state and national governments in the United States to just close and move away, and to even deduct the costs of so doing from the income on which it pays taxes. The mess and the chaos this leaves behind are crucial to the terrors, some of which cannot be named, that let factories that have not yet moved but threaten to do so, do much of what the owners and managers want to do to their workers and to their community. From the perspectives of the capitalists—the people who own the factory—this may be a rational strategy in the short run, increasing profits, but when the credit bubble bursts, they will find out that the consumption that made production possible, the consumption that sustained their driving wages and working conditions down, until the factory moved away, was sustained by the fiction of repayable credit, consumer and increasingly local government debt that has in reality become increasingly unpayable. The federal government can print money; local governments cannot.

One basis for the whole notion of governmentality is that the state, starting with its design of prisons and expanding now into its electronic snooping, can see just about everything. I went once to see the prison that Foucault described, and made a key metaphor in his book *Discipline and Punish* (1977). In that description he invoked a prison with a central observation and control hub, and spokes of corridors with the prisoners' cells radiating out from this hub. The point was that power could see and control it all, and do so simply and easily. It sounds good, eh?

The corridors actually rose and fell as they radiated outward, bent a bit, and the cells were all built on the sides of the corridors. It was not possible to see very far down several of the corridors, and not at all into the cells, not from the central hub. That is the crucial importance of not just reading books but going to look for yourself. Foucault worked from the drawing, the plan for constructing the prison, or more fundamentally the fantasy of how power would construct its control. Indeed, one prisoner escaped, I think twice. The diagram of how to build a prison that could see everything from a central, controlling hub had very little to do with reality, except in one crucial way: the fantasies of control by domination do have consequences. They name, or try to name and shape, the struggles they provoke, while the consequences of these struggles often spin out of control.

Bombing Muslims with drones, including very many ordinary civilians, points toward only the most flamboyant examples of the consequences of state fantasies of control spinning very much out of control in their uncontrollable consequences. And the bombs of the "terrorists" (as we call them, ignoring the terrorism of our drone bombing, of our "shock and awe") make it all too clear that all the electronic snooping that money can buy still misses a very great deal. This does not seem to stop the state, whose motto clearly is not "live and learn." Beyond all this failed foreign policy and practice is the fact that the soldiers sent to do this, when they come back more or less permanently hurt, damaged by what the state put them into and through, are mostly treated as if they too were now disposable. As disposable as the one child in five in America who at some point in the year goes to bed hungry.

It is not possible to have a "democracy" that is built on hurting so many of its own. That is why the United States can increasingly no longer allow non-Whites to vote, and must pour so much money into buying both elections and the elected. That is probably also, if not why, then at least a useful side effect of reworking the school systems so they teach "to the test" rather than toward thinking. So we have a situation, by 2014, as shown by the Pew Research Center, in which 43 percent of Republicans in the United States "believe" in the evolution of human beings. Just four years earlier, 54 percent did "believe in evolution" (Boerma 2013). The most scary aspect of this is that it is widely thought that evolution is a matter of belief—along with the causes of homelessness, poverty, health, inequality, and so forth into the night. There are real-world causes for all these problems that have nothing to do with the primacy of "belief," although fantasy erroneous beliefs can be part of the causes.

Over and over again I have invoked "the state" as if the state were unitary, as if it were a "thing," all of one piece. There are multiple possible serious objections to this, starting with the fact that whatever "the state" is, or is supposed to be, it has very fuzzy boundaries: for example, the public schools, which are both part of the state and part of civil society. Here a different objection to treating the state as a unitary entity is more relevant.

To the contrary of any attempt to treat the state as a coherent entity, states are always internally fragmented, at least in part, with the fragments in shifting antagonistic/collusive relations to one another. Indeed, the composition of the fragments, the chasms between them, and their cooperative merging often rapidly and decisively shift. How, then, can it be possible to speak of "the state"?

An answer, unpacking the supposed unity of "the state," can be developed specifically, by looking at the internal differentiation of a particular state at any one time and place, and then by looking at how this internal differentiation changes from one specific time to another. An answer to the question of how to speak realistically about "the state" can also be developed by looking abstractly, at the level of general processes. I think this latter approach is much more useful for grasping our situation, the situation of those vulnerable peoples who are the subjects of attempts to control and to administer, often against their best interests. Indeed, the approach to going beyond my initially assumed unity of the state—which got us started, but now must be unpacked—starts with looking again and a bit more closely at the attempt and the failure to govern a badly treated population. We start with the state-defined "minimum wage."

Keep in mind, to appreciate the range and the depth of attempts to "control and administer," that the unlivable minimum wage is not just a wage; it is part of policies that shape the lives of the working poor, as also more obviously is the school-to-prison pipeline for so many of the youth of the made poor. Such policies of course also make substantial segments of the working poor uncontrollable, placing significant parts of their lives, for good or for ill, beyond the reach of attempted administration, as they necessarily turn to the "underground" economy to support and sustain themselves and their families. So we can use this to look briefly at some general processes that make the notion of "the state" both more and less complex. This in particular will be processes that I will call "floating democracy."

Stuart Hall, in his famous lecture that he titled "Race, the Floating Signifier" (1997), argued that race was a "floating signifier" because it was so fluid in its formation and its entailments. That has been a useful perspective, against what is widely regarded as the enduring—because it was claimed to be both biological and theological—constitution of race. However, the notion of race as a floating signifier looks at it from what we might call the bottom up—from the perspective of the lives of its victims, witnesses, and low-level perpetrators, and also, simultaneously, from the lives of those who assertively and proudly claim what they consider "their" identity.

From the top side of the process, or processes, making race—which of course have multiple locations, in the state, in the economy, in civil society and more—we can also find a fluidity of formation and entailments. I want to look at just one location, emerging from what I have been calling "the state." My perspective here is based on the realization that democracy floats, and that its constructed ability to float gives it special powers for making and transforming race.

Almost everyone in the United States who has had any substantial connection to, or just an open and easy contact with, the working class and the unemployed, and has talked with them about bosses, landlords, merchants, and politicians, knows, or at least has heard, the phrase used to characterize segments of the dominant: "shit floats." Much as I get a certain droll pleasure from the potential analogy with what democracy has (once again?) become, when I now say that "democracy floats," a very serious transformation is in process. While the whole civil rights movement was based on caring deeply about what the state could be, and that sense of the possible has diminished greatly, that is not at all what I am implying. The appalling amount of money now used to buy elections, to turn democracy into a commodity, places what was once the sustenance of our collective society very firmly in the intestines of the elite, but that is not our main problem with the state.

Much more specific issues are at stake in our floating democracies. Two are particularly salient. Democracy floats in the sense that it is now exceedingly superficial—thin, light, and hollow—as NAFTA and the impending Trans-Pacific Partnership unavoidably demonstrate, along with oil pipelines and fracking and corporations continually permitted to move to places where labor has not only lower wages but also seriously fewer rights. These are crucial determinants of our lives where popular desires and sentiments have no purchase whatsoever, in both senses of the term "purchase." Democracy floats like oil on water, while we wade through the promises to vote for one or another supposed representative of and for our needs. Like oil, democracy very effectively lubricates the skids beneath us.

Democracy also, and crucially, floats in the sense that it can easily be moved from one segment of the populace to another: in the 1960s and 1970s in the United States it was decided that it would be OK—just OK—to let African Americans vote; by 2010 it was becoming increasingly no longer OK. And this is just a simple move: consider that in the first three-quarters or so of the twentieth century, when the U.S. South was solidly in the hold of the Democratic Party, it was legally decided, for example, in Mississippi, that the Democratic Party was a private club, and so it was free to forbid Blacks from voting in the crucial primaries, which chose the candidates who were assured of victory in the general election. More: Senator Theodore Bilbo from Mississippi, in the early mid-twentieth century, famously said that the night before elections, they knew what to do to keep the Blacks at home the next day. Democracy floats, like a toy boat in a bathtub or a cesspool, pushed back and forth from wall to wall.

Senator Bilbo was finally removed from the Senate for a too incendiary, or too openly descriptive, remark in his successful 1946 election campaign: "I call on every red-blooded white man to use any means to keep the niggers away from the polls[;] if you don't understand what that means you are just plain dumb" (Fleegler 2006).

Note that the infamous poll tax, used in the United States to keep the majority of African Americans from voting, also kept very large numbers of poor Whites from voting, and so doubly ensured that control both of southern states and also of the U.S. Senate, where seniority was crucial, stayed in the hands of a conservative elite. For a few decades after the

Civil War, Blacks were allowed to vote in substantial numbers. And the same for a couple of decades after the civil rights struggles from the 1950s through the 1980s. But our chief justice of the Supreme Court, who I think of as John "Bilbo" Roberts, along with his conservative allies, have figured out that they can more effectively float democracy back over to those they think deserve it if they speak the language of educated constitutionalism, with regard to redistricting, voter ID laws, and the free speech of large sums of money.

What we call the state, in its alliance-merger with finance capital, is now the primary mechanism making sure that democracy floats, and continues to float. In the United States this is done by letting corporate wealth largely, but not entirely, control elections; in Europe this is done by letting central banks, and the wealth of northern Europeans, dictate suffering to southern Europe; in Egypt this is done by having the general-president win more than 96 percent of the vote.

Once democracy floats, that becomes determinative of much or most policy and practice of government, no matter who is elected. The superficiality of voting and what voting does for most people, and the ability to shift whose votes actually matter—in some places, as we have seen, whose votes count, or get counted—mean that inequalities quite effectively are both reproduced and intensified—and in far more ways than the now well-known increasing spread between "the one percent" and the rest of us. Thus the vulnerable of yesterday are increasingly becoming the disposable of today and tomorrow. In all this the specific internal differentiation of the state—who is doing what to whom—has ceased to matter as much as it did even a few decades ago. Democracy floats, as those oppressed by the state would say, exactly as shit floats.

Decades ago, in a brilliant but flawed book, *Social Origins of Dictatorship and Democracy* (1966), Barrington Moore Jr. argued insightfully that revolutions, in order to succeed, depend upon a divided elite. While he had a limited grasp of the differences between what he called dictatorships and democracies—Zygmunt Bauman, in *Modernity and the Holocaust* (1989) and *Liquid Times* (2007), is more perceptive—that point about a divided elite was indeed insightful. Now, with neoliberalism more in control, I think elite divisions are about as transformative as the quarrels of couples who have lived together for decades, and our task has become not playing one segment of the elite or the state against others but more directly challenging the float in democracy. Audre Lorde prepared us for this when she told us that "the master's tools will never dismantle the master's house" (1984). As an autonomous Black lesbian feminist raised in the clutches of the twentieth century, she knew.

In part III, I will address the fundamental contradiction between citizenship, with its claims to equality, including equal treatment before the law and equal access to state services and benefits, and the production and management of those inequalities that are regarded as necessary or useful in the organization of production, consumption (including such basics as housing, schooling, and health care), and the social and political "order" of the country. Keep in mind that while the state is literally hell-bent on making and maintaining inequalities among us, the state's futile attempt to manage and control and justify both us and our imposed inequalities reinforces and expands the state. And all the while each "side" in this struggle—which of course has something much more complex than simply "sides"—has its own dynamics, its own issues and formations. If we stick to the contradictions, in the whole it seems to become clear enough for us to potentially get our hands on what is happening.

In addition to the contradictions between the rights of citizens and the need for inequalities, there is the problem of producing the consent of the governed to a state that is manifestly unfair, even more to some than to others, and when this cannot be done, controlling and channeling discontent. That will bring us back to the illusions of democracy. First we need to further discuss the three basic tools for constructing consent to what people with clear vision and good hearing would scarcely consent. These tools are called race, nation, and culture. We deal first with the workbench on which these tools both rest and work.

—

# SIX

**F&N**   Intimacy, Distance, Anger

**You can't fucking fuck me and then treat me like that.**

—A WOMAN IN HER MIDTWENTIES, TALKING VERY LOUDLY AND FIRMLY INTO
HER CELL PHONE, JULY 2013, 10:00 AM, ON THE CORNER OF THIRTY-EIGHTH
STREET AND EIGHTH AVENUE IN MANHATTAN

### GETTING MADE

The complexities of the outrage in the epigraph to this chapter are stunning. The woman's assertion simultaneously seems to say that she wants him or her back, but on other terms—or why not just say to disappear, or say nothing at all—or, alternatively, she wants the person gone if he or she can't change. In this complex utterance, "fucking" is used primarily as a word of emphasis, and simultaneously to convey anger. The "fuck me" here references a prior intimacy that was, in her terms, betrayed: an intimacy permeated with anger and distance at the outset, for that is how she named it, but an intimacy that was expected to diminish the anger and distance, and at least partially replace it with a warmer and more caring intimacy.

It is a well-known psychodynamic that angry sex is often very exciting, in some ways, or its own ways, pleasurable—but angry sex has to have consequences that for many are less desirable. "Fuck me" in the woman's complaint has, and simultaneously does not have, the same freight of meaning as "fuck you"—here said, in action and words, first about what was done to her and then thrown back by her. Intimacy, distance, and anger all together, all three emphasized as much as possible in the phrase "you can't fucking fuck me"—with an emphasis produced by the word "fucking" that has its own contradictory meanings.

It will help us to understand race in America if we can unravel at least some of the tangles of intimacy, distance, and anger—or shall we call it intimacy, domination, and anger—that shape the contortions within this poignant claim. For here we are not in the realm of what some call, in gentler moments, "making love," but neither she nor we have fully abandoned the claim to a giving closeness that still is attached to the outskirts of the word "fuck." This giving closeness is, in the long term, unequal. For good or ill, or both, she gets the pregnancy or just the concern about that, and usually also the bulk of the work of raising the child. Nonetheless, exactly none the less and often little the more, both the intimacy and the anger, simultaneously or sequentially, are still there.

Years before, standing under a movie marquee near Times Square, waiting for a cloudburst to subside, I was joined by two African American youths—young male teenagers, maybe fourteen or fifteen, freshly wrapped up in a not-yet-convincing macho assertiveness. One said to the other, while they stayed where I could hear them, "And then she asked me to take her nigger hand." Intimacy, distance, anger: the terminology of emphasized difference in the midst of shared and unshared identity. Such angry or incredulous distancing may well also be the framework for a special intimacy, as both the word and the African American people who use it to or about each other rise above and beyond its racist and hate-filled use. When one Black man says to another, "Come here, nigger, I want to give you a hug," it is a particularly powerful expression of love and intimacy, made all the more powerful by its transcendence of a pervasive and brutal racism that the word both carries with it and simultaneously denies.

I am fascinated when White folks use the phrase "the N-word." Can you imagine two Black men, happy in their friendship and their closeness, with one saying to the other, "Come here, N-word, I want to give you a hug"?

Because everybody knows exactly what is meant by the phrase "the N-word," what is supposed to be gained by this extra bit of distance from the word itself? Unfortunately, it is all too clear what is supposed to be gained—we are better now, we have progressed, we have changed. And that half fantasy enables the Supreme Court, with its current moral cesspool majority, to gut the Voting Rights Act that made it possible, for a brief while, for African Americans to vote in substantial numbers. Think how impossible it now would have been had the Roberts court said out loud what it actually did: "We are restricting the right of niggers to vote." What the court did, along with the "lower" courts not charging police for murdering African Americans, once again started the United States back down the road of making niggers, just as much as did sharecropping. The pretense of clean hands is vicious, dangerous, brutal—and absolutely crucial to how race is now made. Thus I find the claimed innocence of "the N-word" more dangerous than the word itself, even though it simultaneously is an attempt to cleanse our horrid and brutal history.

More than may be realized, the word "nigger" was itself about constructing a pretense of clean hands. America could do what it did to African Americans because they were, as the dominant called it, as the dominant called the shots, in their phrases, "niggers"—only very rarely worthy of respect or concern. So what "we" did to "them" became OK: not our problem but their fault. Our hands are clean. All that has supposedly changed now, with the use of the phrase "the N-word," is what happens "within the veil."

Du Bois named it so, in the title of one of his most important books, *Darkwater: Voices from Within the Veil* ([1920] 2007). Not behind the veil, but within it: that special kind of concealment is, I suggest, the power of the language of polite racism that makes the veil. This more polite racism is both a veil covering what is happening now and simultaneously a welcome distancing from the more brutal racism so deeply a central part of American, and Western European, history: the French have recently stopped calling the people they still quite intensely abuse "Gypsies" and starting calling them "Rom." It's so much nicer a word to use to name the people you are about to deport.

Du Bois, with his stunning brilliance, framed a crucial part of the dynamics of racism. When people are constructed as the deserving victims—for a current example, "welfare mothers"—their very existence on this earth, in our midst, constructs the veil concealing the full horror and the full tragedy of what the dominant society chooses to do to them, and by so doing to all of us.

The most difficult aspect of all this carnage for us to see is the intimacy that lies within the use of the word "nigger." This intimacy is not at all just when one Black uses it as a term of endearment to another; it also hides, very deeply, within the White racist use of the term, peeking out when it becomes part of the postemancipation continuity of slave-like relations in the term "our niggers." "Fuck" and "nigger" turn out to be the same kind of word; for both, the implied intimacy is very ephemeral, disappearing, like justice, in an instant.

We are not only dealing with fixed categories or stable forms of domination, despite the long-term persistence of racism, but also with a fluid intimacy deeply woven into an aggressive and brutal racism. In the early 1970s, when the high schools in Robeson County had been partially integrated—by taking the key athletes of the African American basketball and football teams "up" (as the locals put it) to the White high schools—there was a high school basketball game in which one Black player was guarding a Black player from the other team very closely and assertively. A White male adult spectator in the stands called out, very loudly and with clear anger and upset: "Get your nigger off our colored boy!" That's what passes for intimacy in this strange and dangerous world.

It is the inescapable fluidity of the words "colored boy," "fuck," and "nigger" that provides the center of our work unraveling the changing production of race in America, for this fluidity is the center of what is happening, and thus must also be the core of our opposition to the continuity of racism.

Sometimes I wonder and worry if the fluidity of these words—their ability to convey so many conjoined and different meanings sometimes simultaneously, more often one right after the other, or one within the other—is like the fluid of an automatic automobile transmission. These transmissions work by the way the dense fluid within them makes possible quickly and smoothly changing how the power input gets conveyed and converted to output, so that the car adjusts to pulling loads, accelerating, coasting, whatever is called for. Race and gender are also about getting whatever is called for, smoothly and efficiently.

If ever there was a metaphor, or more, a template, for the production of disposable people, or for the dance of getting fucked, in any meaning of that term, this is it. Our struggles are not against something fixed but something fluid, something constantly trying to change the relation of input to output. When we organize to struggle, when we organize our struggles themselves, we must keep this very firmly in mind. While all the brutality against us makes us think that our situation is more or less, but mostly more, fixed, in fact our task is to pay attention to, and use, the fluidity within this brutality for, as we shall see, the weaknesses and the contradictions of domination are sometimes very clearly exposed in their shifts—in how they shift, or try to make us shift.

## GRASPING INEQUALITY

> Struck by Will Self's description of Battersea Power Station as "absolutely fucking huge" (LRB, 18 July), I wondered if he would use "fucking" in other inoffensive contexts, say after Matins—"Absolutely fucking challenging sermon, Vicar"—or on his birthday: "The socks were just what I absolutely fucking wanted."

JOHN BAILEY, LETTER TO THE LONDON REVIEW OF BOOKS, AUGUST 8, 2013

I love the use of "Matins"—it so quickly situates this complaint within the smart sniffery of the British elite. But the complaint, beyond its simple cleverness, raises complex and crucial issues for us. For what John Bailey has done in his letter, to begin, is point toward class—you don't speak to a vicar that way, provided you know what a vicar is, for there were none on my block when I was growing up, although I bet the costume they wear would announce my need to be careful. But he is also pointing to something that goes far beyond class, something both related to intimacy and yet opposed to it, for Bailey notes that you would not thank a relative for a birthday token in that way ayther. Not even if you pronounced it "eether."

At issue here is far more than the theater of delicacy and its transformation. At issue is what both emerges from and goes beyond class to create a language that simultaneously speaks of equality and inequality, in the languages that address, from within or against, gender, race, class, and locality.

We are standing at the doorway of a world that lets you and me grasp the multiple meanings of Will Self calling the Battersea Power station "absolutely fucking huge"—for such monstrosities are built in our neighborhoods, polluting them with smoke and noise and by-products and making some very steady jobs on the way—a subtlety conveyed by that one word, telling us who grasps what and who does not. We can imagine this happens with a very different content in the training you get attending what your congregation calls Matins. This is not, however, about the dialects that make and express class, not at all. At issue here is what goes beyond class.

And that, I want to suggest, is the way intimacy and distance and domination are continually combined into one social dynamic, combined in very different and continually changing ways, to make and break apart transient collectivities—momentary alliances marked also by the distances and tensions that keep them momentary while announcing and harnessing them as alliances.

This is the fluid language people who do not know each other use to speak to each other at protest marches, left and right, racist and antiracist. This is the way workers in a factory or a bar talk to each other, people who are glad to be together but cautious about being too together within and across lines of class, gender, race, and obvious citizenship.

And this is what makes class, gender, race, and citizenship never reducible to just those parameters, however open the violence and the alliances formed to perpetrate and evade and confront that violence, however open or concealed the hand of the state in the production and reproduction of these categories. For the mixture of intimacy and distance, anger and closeness expressed in the phrase the "fucking huge" power station in the midst of our neighborhood, and again in the languages of race and gender, all this simultaneous intimacy and distance and acknowledgment of the domination over our lives, that we can still name and curse, both unites and divides. For some of our cousins and neighbors work in that absolutely fucking huge power plant stuck alongside our homes and our children's schools.

This is why, to grasp the continuing production of race in useful ways, we must never stop at the boundaries of any of the categories, nor of all the categories put together. Race is not just race, class is not just class, gender is not just gender. The dynamics of intimacy and distance both shape and cross all these divides. It is this unstable mixture of our intimacy and distance from each other, and from those who continually seek to and in some ways do dominate us, that is so crucial to our confrontational engagement with domination and the inequalities it makes in our lives.

The point here is to use the fluidity of intimacy, distance, domination, and anger to reveal otherwise hidden complexities in our relations both to each other and to domination. This may help us be more effectively prepared to confront what we cannot avoid confronting. Power might be like electricity: it flows through lines of differential resistance. Some of our resistance to domination may strengthen it as much as does collusion. In fact, some of our voluntary collusion can undermine the control over us. We have entered the contradictions of maintaining and opposing inequality.

# PART III

---

## BEYOND

# SEVEN

# Living in the Beyond

I am glad to travel in my memory to that other world, hedged in by custom and sorrow, cut off from History and the State, eternally patient, to that land without comfort or solace, where the peasant lives out his motionless civilization on barren ground in remote poverty, and in the presence of death.

—CARLO LEVI, *CHRIST STOPPED AT EBOLI*

Carlo Levi, for those not familiar with this signature but now distant work of the twentieth century—a defining part of how the twentieth century claimed and, for a moment, sought to transcend its brutal and brutalizing identity—was an antifascist Italian doctor exiled, in 1935, to a mountain village in remote southern Italy, a village in the mountains above and beyond the valley town of Eboli. This was the world, before the obscene wealth-constructed inventions of contemporary politics and our mostly historically illiterate "representatives," when those who opposed the state and its more flamboyant outrages were "only" exiled to the local equivalent of southern New Jersey, or rural Texas, or more specifically West Virginia and inland South Carolina, and trusted to do what they were told while living there. Edward Snowden, Chelsea Manning, and Julian Assange should be so lucky as to have lived in and struggled against a state such as Italy in the 1930s, as opposed to one with far more dangerous and illusory "democratic" pretenses. And although Italy so very soon became much worse, we can only hope and struggle against what is now increasingly happening here with the realization that opposition to the state did not always end as brutally as it now does.

The issue in Italy in the mid-1930s was not yet World War II, nor even the Italians' support of fascists in Spain, but the Fascist government's brutally destructive military assault on almost utterly defenseless Ethiopia—the equivalent, in some respects, of our drone-airplane mass murders of Pakistani and Yemeni villagers, as part of protecting and expanding our "legitimate" interests. A dozen or so people at a wedding or having a meal in a home who are bombed in a surprise attack, with no chance to run or hide, much less to explain their innocence, is not "mass murder"? Think what would happen if an armed psychopath came into a dinner or a wedding in the United States and killed a dozen or so White people. How the media would dance the details before us. But Pakistanis and Yemenis are Muslims, like Ethiopians were, for the Italians, Negroes, Africans.

Put my feelings and political sympathies aside, if that makes you feel more at peace with yourself, even though they are relevant to the issue at hand. We can deal with them another day. The issue before us here is the fundamental and very relevant contradictions embedded in Levi's poignant description of the peasants that he loved, separated himself from, and clearly cared about greatly.

We start where he started: that the peasants were "cut off from History and the State"—with those wonderful and brilliant capitalizations—his, not the translator's—indicating that they are not cut off from their own history and their own government, but from the History and Government of domination—of the dominant state and its "cultural" constructions. These capitalizations point to "real" History and "real" Government, not to the continuing and supposedly unchanging and not very significant dance of folk.

This perspective is a natural and logical extension from the title that introduces and frames his work: Christ Stopped at Eboli. Eboli is a town in the valley, a bit south of the industrial and politically central city of Turin. Eboli is where the railroad then stopped: seemingly—only seemingly—the end of the line of capitalism and the expanding state. The villages where Levi was exiled, for a year, were in the mountains beyond Eboli, south and inland. To say that Christ stopped at Eboli, in his journeys that brought

Christianity, and what is called Civilization and History, is to say that civilization in motion, in continual and progressive development, stopped at Eboli, as opposed to the "motionless civilization" of the peasants in the hills beyond. History in motion, in this perspective, is for those who live in the valley cities and towns with Christ, people who have lives that end with the possibility of heaven or hell.

If Christ stopped at Eboli, a town in the valley, the people in Eboli have a history that both produces and recognizes the essential humanity of its subjects, its Christian subjects, for only humans (in the narrow Catholic sense then of the dominant Italian state) can qualify for either heaven or hell. Animals just die. To say that Christ stopped his journeys at Eboli is to say that we who live in the hills beyond are ourselves the beyond—even though the people in these hills had been providing industrial Turin with a substantial portion of its labor force and its food.

But of course the people who lived in these hill villages were also Christians, and they themselves may well have originated the claim that Christ stopped at Eboli, in part to explain their marginalization from the rewards of state, or they may have adopted what they knew was said about them, to make it their own, and given it back to Carlo Levi.

Similarly, the African Americans living in the villages beyond the interstate highway economies, living beyond the need for their labor, living seemingly beyond History and the State, are also of course very much living within and against the state and its historical violence, constantly creating and expelling the peoples beyond. So the initial contradiction is between the processes that create, within History and the State, the peoples who only seem to live in the beyond, who are actually very much part of the state and the national economy, but at the same time are treated as if they exist beyond History and the State, which makes them disposable, or if disposable is too harsh, at least inconsequential to History and the State. This even by people like Carlo Levi, who clearly loved and cared both for and about them.

And all this despite the fact that so much wealth and power is extracted from those who do not belong, who do not really matter—slaves, free Blacks, peasants, undocumented workers—that they seem to be, in one perspective, the goose that laid the golden egg, thoughtlessly torn apart by greed to try to get more from them, and at the same time continually produced and reproduced by domination as useful but not fully human people. That is a crucial contradiction, between people who don't count yet who produce so much of what gets counted.

A further contradiction hidden within Levi's sympathetic formulations is to call the people he so much cares about "eternally patient." Indeed, on the one hand they have had most possibilities for a better tomorrow robbed from them, so it seems as if all they can do is be patient with and within a continuing and supposedly unchanging today. On the other hand even a small familiarity with the situation of African Americans in their long struggle for rights and justice, especially in the mid-twentieth century, will recognize that power—in the form of President Franklin D. Roosevelt and his Congress, plus all sorts of local "liberal" and "sympathetic" collusionists— kept counseling African Americans to be patient, to not struggle so openly, to not struggle for change in ways that constantly at least embarrassed and always needled domination. Be patient, be eternally patient: domination's mantra when challenged. For Levi to call the people he so cares about "eternally patient" is, against and underneath his own sympathies, to side with continuing domination, to side with the forces that continually made and remade the suffering that called forth his deep concern.

Patience is quietude, scarcely what was wanted by the communists and others, who struggled so well and in the very long run so futilely against fascist domination and now World Bank and International Monetary Fund and German economic impositions. It has been a struggle against a domination whose name is now no longer occupation but austerity. Name the underlying differences, in Greece, for example, if you think you can do so with a straight face.

The point again is not my politics, nor my anger, nor my realization that it increasingly now seems as if Germany has won World War II, at least in Europe, Israel, and the Middle East, but the contradictions embedded in the claim that the natives are and should be patient, now extended to the Greeks and Italians and Palestinians and Iranians and Kazaks and Tibetans and more ands—they should all just quietly and patiently accept austerity and poverty. To the extent that they have once been patient, and their governments still mostly are, they are also now becoming the flamboyantly allergic patients of austerities' imposed medicines.

There are two further contradictions pointed toward in Carlos Levi's wonderfully sympathetic approach to understanding the plight of the impoverished and seemingly abandoned Italian mountain peasantry: the contradictions raised by his use of remote and by his invocation of peasants that live with—and we imagine against—the familiar and intimate presence of death.

We have invoked both in our discussion of Maxton: that Maxton is remote from the economic dynamism along Interstate 95, the major north–south interstate highway in the eastern United States, and that it is the locale for a very high infant and child mortality rate—as well as having a comparatively high adult death rate. But these can never be reduced to simple facts, as brutally factual as they are.

On the other side of both remote and imposed death, the other side that makes the contradiction, and more precisely the opposition to remoteness and imposed death, very surprisingly is the conk rag. This is the part of my perspective that is most likely to be misunderstood, to be assaulted as a fundamental betrayal of the issues at stake. To the contrary.

What I am pointing toward is not at all the conk rag as a desire to be White, to "play ball" with the Whites, to be like the Whites. Very far from this, in many ways. I knew the candidate whose nomination and election struggles I discussed earlier. He was a very special person, imbued with his own dignity, deeply and assertively concerned with the education of African American and Native American children. He thought that if he straightened his hair he might have a better chance of winning the election, for some Whites might also vote for him, countering the Black and Indian vote that could be pulled away from him, or wanted to turn away from him. But the world of his potential supporters had not changed that much. If the worldview of the local Whites had also changed, and some substantial number would vote for a "Negro," a "colored man," his strategy might have worked. But change always comes last to the dominant population, even though the elite of the dominant often shift first, from their needs, not their decency.

The conk rag of the candidate was, in sum, deeply embedded in the illusion that if the African Americans were changing, to become by their claims and assertions more an equal part of America, the Whites might also be changing, and in this area, then, vote for a Black man. This is the opposite of "remote." But there was only a fat chance that the Whites would have changed or, more precisely, a thin chance in a fat world—in a world getting fat by stuffing itself on its racism and its illusions of the "gift" of equality. In the generosity of his hopes that Whites might be changing was his dignity and his humanity, in the midst of a world that sought to make and keep him remote.

So ultimately the contradiction raised within the notion of remote, for people seemingly shunted aside from History and Government, people who literally pay for their marginalization with their own and their family's lives, is not the fact that they are in reality the continuing creation and re-creation of the policies and practices of History and Government. Their remoteness and their tragic intimacy with early and unnecessary deaths are both denied and contested by hope—by the claims that lie within the conk rag.

Hope does not have to be realistic to be crucial. If remote is itself an illusion, an illusion about people who remain significantly within the eagle claws of a broad-winged and fast-moving inequality, we can expect that many of the hopes that confront both this inequality and its consequences will also be illusory. And each is not less important, not less life shaping and life denying for being illusory. We can work toward less illusory hopes in the belief that they will be more effective, but we don't know and we should not presume to know. The point here is that the remoteness of the southern mountain villagers that Levi took for granted, and that in the 1930s, with poor roads and no railroad, had some basis in reality, was also an illusion. For these villagers were both a self-creation and also a continual creation of the state and its policies and practices. They were remote in the very same way that Maxton and the other predominantly African American towns of this region are now remote. Looked at from the point of view of the people who live in Maxton, it is both a remoteness that distances them from work at a living wage and some of the rewards and excitements of urban life, and a remoteness that shelters them from continual confrontations with the nastiness of the dominant society.

From this complex and contradictory perspective we can address the last contradiction Carlo Levi pointed toward in his introductory phrase "that other world, hedged in by custom and sorrow . . ."

"Custom" is a wonderfully useful term—I much prefer it to the far more vague and vacuous term that took over anthropology and popular discourse: "culture." Customs are both local practices and practices that both define and shape the local by regulating, or explicitly by not regulating, goods and services and people. We can get a sense of this meaning of custom as a local place with its own rules and ways when we "go through customs" at ports and airports.

So a world that is "hedged in by custom and sorrow"—including the customary ways of dealing with sorrow—is partly created by the locality itself, claiming, defining, and defending its boundaries. Does this isolate the local from progress? Perhaps in some very small way. Does it defend the community from even more destructive intrusions, including the intrusions that make it remote and sorrowful? Yes. Is remoteness still an illusion? Yes.

All this just introduces, here, the notion of contradiction, as the contradictions unfold in the production of race. We can now get back to the work at hand.

_____

# EIGHT

# "Out Here It's Dog Eat Dog and Vice Versa"

## SLAVEY WORK

Stephen Jay Gould (1977), a brilliant evolutionary biologist, popularized over the space of several books, backed up by his research articles, a theory of evolution he called "punctuated equilibrium." In his perspective, the evolution of plants and animals did not occur as simple linear changes over time but more usually in brief periods of relatively rapid and major transformations that punctuated, as it were, much longer periods of relative stability, or equilibrium, during which, in some cases, the pressures toward the spurts of rapid change either slowly developed or quickly emerged. To use this as a metaphor for social change, we have to be careful about invoking the long periods of relative stability—which seem to be rather rare—but there do seem to be comparatively brief periods where major transformations occur. At issue here is one such time.

The most massive transformation in the recent production of race in the United States began, in this region of the Carolinas, in the 1960s with the nearly simultaneous intensive mechanization of agriculture, making ultra-low-cost labor by people with few if any rights much less _necessary_ to control, year-round, and at almost the same time the rapid development of large-scale textile production and other kinds of manufacturing, including athletic shoes and carcinogenic auto safety glass. The transformation of race was then given a further burst of activity two decades later, with the sudden collapse of manufacturing, as all the cut and stitch factories moved first to Mexico and then to China, leaving behind thousands of unemployed, mostly women.

This double move—to Mexico and then to China—was doubly devastating for Mexico; first, because NAFTA allowed the duty-free importation of subsidized U.S. corn (maize) into Mexico, which as we have noted destroyed a great deal of small-scale Mexican agriculture, and second, when vast numbers of factories that had been making goods for U.S. markets moved on to employ even cheaper and more abusable Chinese and Bangladeshi labor. Estimates are that in this transition from Mexico to Asia about 175,000 people, mostly women who were major contributors to their family income, became unemployed. There was not enough of any kind of work in Mexico, no matter how low paid or degrading, neither domestic service nor prostitution, to provide income to all these displaced people, and it is no longer possible to live without income. They, or some in their families, had to come north. Had to. And in the north they found a market for people who had no effective rights whatsoever, because Blacks had largely fought their way out of that category, and because it has been relatively easy to keep people without documents in that situation.

The trigger for this life-breaking assault was NAFTA, which began in 1994. Over the next five years I became increasingly concerned with what was happening to all the workers—more than eight thousand in Robeson County alone—who lost their jobs when the cut and stitch factories closed. The majority of these workers were "women of color"—Blacks and Indians.

As I have already noted and discussed, it was surprisingly difficult to find out what happened to these women when they lost their mill jobs. But I kept trying, kept being disappointed. There were several ministers in the county pastoring Indian and Black churches who still knew me from 1967 and 1968, when I registered voters from their churches, or who knew me from the early 1980s, when I worked on Indian recognition and rights. We had long-established practices of talking quite directly to one another. When I asked several of them what happened to the people in their congregations who lost their jobs, or asked what those who lost their jobs were doing now, they did not know. Not one. The people and the problems and issues they carried with them, on them, into what for many was long-term unemployment or employment at very much lower wages, had disappeared. There was not even any more agricultural work they could fall back upon.

And the new industries that came into the region five or ten years after NAFTA—the chicken- and turkey-packing operations and, in somewhat different fashion, the hog deconstruction factories as well—had two special features with significant consequences. First, the textile factories mostly had ten-foot-high ceilings, sometimes twelve, sometimes less. The new poultry plants used overhead conveyor belt mechanisms and needed new buildings with ceilings that were at least fourteen and sometimes sixteen feet high. So they were brought into one county rather than another with significant start-up subsidies and write-offs for their construction costs, which meant both higher local taxes and, especially relevant here, local governments that, after their very costly subsidies to get these corporations, were not going to look too closely at what kinds of labor were employed in these new factories or how that labor was treated. The local governments had too much of their tax revenues tied up in subsidizing the start-up costs of these new plants.

Thus, because these were all high-injury occupations—jobs in chicken parts factories reputedly have some of the highest injury rates in the United States—it was not likely that people who now had "civil rights" would either get or perhaps even want such jobs, nor was it likely that governments that had invested so heavily in attracting these industries would look at all closely at whether the new workers in these factories had any rights whatsoever. So these new poultry and pork plants could use mostly undocumented workers quite openly.

And the former manufacturing plants, no longer wanted, just stand empty, decaying symbols of the lives corporations were so casually allowed, or encouraged, to discard by the U.S. government and its corporate tax-deduction policies. The federal and of course also state governments have a much greater role in the production of abused and abusable people than is usually realized, even now in the context of current struggles against an unlivable minimum wage. These struggles have highlighted such major abusers as Walmart and McDonald's and have only started to popularize the realization that the primary culprit is neither of these corporations but the federal government itself, for its contractors, not Walmart or McDonald's, are the largest payers of what we must understand as abuse wages.

But there is more to it than even this. During the whole process of imposing NAFTA and its consequences, the unemployment compensation regulations in the United States were changed, within a veil of silence. It "used to be" that if you were unemployed through no fault of your own— that is, laid off rather than fired—and offered a job at your former pay, and did not take it, your unemployment benefit payments stopped. If you were offered a job at less than your former pay, you were free to say no without consequences. The government knew what you were being offered while you were getting unemployment compensation checks, because to get your unemployment partial income replacement, you had to register at the state employment office each week, to see if they would "send you out" to any possible jobs. The rules were changed so that if you were offered a job at any legal wage, no matter how much lower than your former wage, you had to take it or lose your benefits on the spot. That is a crucial subsidy for abuse and exploitation, whose silence depends on how little it has been known.

And there is a further major feature of the state production of abusable people, hidden within the ways that state statistics are produced and disseminated. If you stopped going to the unemployment office because your benefits expired, because you did not need their help finding a job at McDonald's, because you were cut off from benefits, because you got discouraged, whatever the reason, you are no longer counted as unemployed. To put it more directly, in terms of how it is being suggested you live, you no longer count. And the government can advertise its fantasy unemployment figures of only 8 or 10 percent, and only double that in the ghettos, because you are now officially out of the labor force, just as the undocumented workers are out of the protection of the state and its laws. And the imposed task becomes to construct a life on these terms. Fortunately we do not only live the lives that government tries to impose upon us.

The fact that it is often not easy to create and shape our own lives, and that many pay a very high price for trying to do so, for example, in the underground economy, should not conceal from us the power and the prominence of what emerges from below. The following two stories illustrate profoundly different dimensions of people trying to shape and own their own lives.

The first happened about 2005, while I was still teaching undergraduates. The course was Urban Anthropology, and it was a night class, with mostly adult students. One of my students, a clearly hard-pressed middle-aged African American woman, had trouble at times staying awake during class. As soon as class was over, at ten o'clock, she went to a large chain drugstore, where she restacked shelves until she ran home in the early morning to get her fourteen-year-old son up, feed him breakfast, and send him off to the local high school. She was trying to complete a couple of years of college so she could get a job as a teacher's aide in the public schools. One evening she came up to me at the end of class and asked if she could talk to me in private. In my office she started crying and told me she had started finding twenty-dollar bills in her purse every week or so. In, not gone from, the purse she left on the kitchen counter. She asked me if I would talk to her son, her only child, because she could not, and there was no father in or near her house.

So I met her son, one day after his high school classes ended, and we spent a couple of hours walking around the college campus or sitting on a wall, talking. I offered no moralizing whatsoever, and as much practical advice as I could figure out how to communicate.

The underlying situation is stark, and again created by people living both within and against the state. Wholesalers dealing drugs, even simple stuff like marijuana, used children under sixteen to "run" it from one place to another. Children when caught got relatively brief sentences; those over sixteen got "put away." So the older people running drugs, as part of a plea bargain, were much more likely to snitch on where they got what, and where and to whom they were bringing it. It was a matter of safety and self-preservation for the dealers to use youngsters. Besides, they were much cheaper workers.

Essentially, I tried to tell this fourteen-year-old youth two things. First, plainclothes undercover cops no longer looked like they grew up in suburbia eating well. When I got fingered by an undercover cop at a demonstration, he was someone who stepped out of the demonstration when the uniformed cops arrived and pointed activists out to the uniformed heavies whose idea of proper policing was hitting, dragging, and insulting. This informer was a ninety-pound, flamboyantly gay young Puerto Rican man with dyed blond hair, whom we were all being nice to, to show how liberal we were. So this youth helping his mother—among other things—should never trust anyone based on looks or the identities that they presented. The second point I tried to make was that in the long run he could do more for his mom by doing well enough to get into college—I would help him with that if he wanted—and getting a decent job. He could get there by the time his mom was old enough to need that kind of real and sustained help, if he got himself on that track, which I tried hard to make sound as attractive and easy as possible, even for someone from the working class who did not have much background in such things.

He in turn bowled me over with his counterclaims, making him sound something like I imagine a midwestern White Republican would talk. He told me, this skinny fourteen-year-old kid, that he was a man, that he was not going to let his mom hurt, that he was going to take good care of her, because that's what men do.

A year later his mom came to see me, to tell me that he was in jail. It hurt to hear this, and it hurt to realize the extent to which the *perceived* values of the dominant society about men taking care of women, especially their mothers, work their ways as they are repackaged for the excluded. These of course are not the actual values of the dominant society, but what is fed to socially illiterate Republicans (and to only a slightly lesser extent self-satisfied elite Democrats) and to youngsters trying, against the odds, to take care of people they love, people whom the dominant society is squeezing against one wall after another. This young man paid a very high price for his genuine concern for how hard-pressed was the mother he loved.

The second story is a different, equally tragic, story of a person claiming her dignity in the midst of an even more oppressive world.

The low-end motel room in Robeson County, North Carolina, where I stayed in the summer of 1999 was cleaned by an African American woman, probably in her late forties. She was very thin and had a lot of missing teeth—markers of a hard life. She cleaned in the early morning, while I wrote, and we got into the habit of talking. I very much wanted to find out from her what happened to the women who lost their jobs when the textile mills closed and, because she came from a rural part of the county, especially and even more to find out from her what happened to the African American women who earlier had been displaced from farm labor—which I was still having immense difficulty tracking.

As I followed her about the room, talking, I saw that she took a washcloth from the towel rack and, with her bare hand, soaked it in the toilet and used it to wash the inside of the toilet bowl. I talked to her a bit about the serious diseases in circulation, particularly hepatitis, and the risks she was taking with her health, and offered to buy her rubber gloves, a brush, whatever. She completely refused to let me buy her gloves, or to give her the money to get them herself, although I had been giving her money every few days to thank her for the extra coffee she left and the work she did. She said she couldn't work as well with gloves.

The next day, again with her bare hand in the toilet, when I asked what happened to the women who used to work on farms, she looked up directly at me (which she rarely did) and said, "We're not doing that slavey work anymore."

It is to this heart-wrenchingly powerful assertion of memory and dignity that we now must turn.

## IMPUNITY AND THE STRUGGLE OVER THE INTERCHANGEABLE PART

Our whole discussion of these inequalities so far illuminates the fact that capital does not, and indeed cannot, itself produce all the inequalities that it uses. It is also clear that the state is deeply involved in producing the fresh and changing inequalities that capital, in its continual transformation, uses. The state also is deeply involved in producing all the inequalities the state itself needs or wants, plus managing all the consequences of currently useless former inequalities now cluttering the neighborhoods of dying cities, rural jails, local White job centers, Veterans Administration hospitals, and homeless shelters.

As the whole postemancipation history of African American struggles and claims makes clear—and in particular the long struggle for citizenship rights, and the subsequent marginalization of ordinary African Americans after achieving some of these rights—there is a fundamental contradiction between the rights and benefits of citizenship in a modern "liberal-democratic" state, and the production of those inequalities that capital and the state uses. More than simply uses: if we look, for only one example, to the mobilization of labor on the farms and food-processing plants of North Carolina, or all the women working in "service" industries, including retail sales, we can see the kinds of inequalities upon which capital claims it depends. And if we look at how "volunteer" military forces are staffed at the bottom end (enlistment among the bottom end of the working class was called signing up for "three squares and a warm," or three solid meals and a warm bed, plus a chance to show how tough you are, in a world that always takes advantage of your actual weaknesses); and if we also look at how dumb and vicious congressmen get elected, with very substantial financial support from industry and wealthy individuals who know how easy it is to turn these opportunists into ventriloquists' dummies; and if we look at how much money states save providing fifth-rate schools, little or no health care, and bottom-end basic services to poor folks in poor neighborhoods, we can see in all this how very much the state itself depends on, and benefits from, the inequalities it so generously produces and gifts to whoever still uses the current occupants of the state- and culture-manufactured hard-pressed category. These are people no longer so openly called racist and sexist names, but now called something slightly more polite than formerly, especially if they are watching your kids and cleaning your house while you are out doing one important thing or another. It is an immensely complex question: What else changes when the horrific names change? In the past the answer to the question of what went with changing names and changing situations was a great deal of continuity, wearing a different mask.

Pete Daniel ([1972] 1990) is extremely revealing on how legally enforced debt peonage kept African Americans in bondage long after slavery ended, and Jim Downs (2012) is equally revealing about how the end of slavery scarcely diminished government-orchestrated suffering among the newly freed. Much more than is usually named, the suffering of categories of people is not simply, or not at all, "local culture" but government policy and practice.

Impunity in any of its manifestations, from unpunished lynching to stop and frisk and fuck over, to the appalling differential rates at which Black students are expelled from schools or arrested for drugs when Whites in fact use more and deal more, turns out to be crucial in "resolving" these contradictions—not resolving them in the sense of making them better or easier to live with, but stabilizing their perpetuation, so that the state can either wash its hands of what is happening, or pretend not to see, or pretend it is helpless to remedy the abuse, and in all cases also claim that it is the victims' own fault. All that, even more than the acts it permits or encourages, is impunity.

Cheap labor, to emphasize a point already made, is ordinarily not just labor with low wage cost, not just laborers who can be pushed on the job far beyond reasonable boundaries, but labor that has very low social costs. Undocumented immigrants who were not educated with our tax revenues, who cannot claim the Social Security benefits whose costs are deducted from their paychecks, who have diminished access to hospitals, to garbage collection, to many of the social amenities and social services—all of this is what constitutes low-wage and low-tax-cost labor. Although their children often go to U.S. schools, they did not; as working-age adults, the costs of raising and educating them were donated to U.S. corporations by the increasingly impoverished villages and towns where they grew up. And much of what is not given to them, or what is given that should not be, occurs in defiance of the supposed equality of all people. In that sense impunity runs much deeper than the cops beating or shooting a Black, knowing that there will be no consequences. Impunity means the schools can be terrible, the hospitals third rate, the housing below code, and scarcely anyone except those constrained to be there cares in any way that matters.

Lynching, the most intense expression of the impunity that produced race, was primarily an agrarian, not an urban, phenomenon. The transition from "race" to "citizenship"—from "Blacks" to "Mexicans"—as the superficial matrix for producing and specifying the victims of impunity, represents also a shift from agrarian production as the context for Black labor to a context now so intensely capitalized, for example, in the production of tobacco, chickens, turkeys, and hogs, that the distinction between farm and factory, rural and urban, often becomes trivial. The production of Black labor at first and intensely entailed people tied to the land after post–Civil War emancipation, tied as far as possible to one locale by sharecropping arrangements, debt peonage, and the massive denial (for those who stayed in the South) both of alternatives and of access to the preconditions for alternatives, such as education and credit (Daniel [1972] 1990).

When Blacks moved north, or into cities, to manufacturing jobs and also to mining, they were used to diminish the power of unions, and to do work that corporations claimed could not readily be assigned to Whites. General Motors—shall we call it a key corporation in the United States?—was proud of the fact that more than Ford or Chrysler, up through the mid-twentieth century, it hired African Americans. What it did not brag about was that a high proportion of the workers in the grinding room, where metal welds were ground down smooth, and in the painting room—the two most toxic locations in automobile production—were African American. It is a bad but important pun to say that African Americans were being given lifetime jobs.

The production of illegal aliens at first was far more connected to labor that was made to be so mobile that workers disappeared almost the minute they were no longer being used, and reappeared again when wanted. Without Social Security cards it is not possible to open a bank account or even to rent a safe deposit box. When the harvest ends and the workers are paid off, everyone knows that the harvesters, those short brown people with funny accents, are walking about with several hundred dollars in their pockets. The safest thing for them to do is leave, that day. Although race was, in fact, differential citizenship, the shift from race as the surface manifestation of labor that could be treated with impunity to workers without citizenship documents was part of a transition from labor tied to the land, to the place, to labor that had to keep moving.

That period in the history of abusive domestic capitalism is over, for undocumented workers are now primarily rooted in relatively stable communities. They have put down roots in place, in many places, working continually in meat- and poultry-packing, in landscaping, in manual labor construction jobs, but within these places the work they do sometimes shifts constantly. With this change the task of impunity has changed.

At the absolute core of the material organization of modern industrial capitalism is the standardized, and thus interchangeable, part. The interchangeable worker, as the human result and the human cost of the interchangeable part, has also been central to industrial capitalism. The interchangeable part meant that every part made at a specific point in the production process was as nearly identical as possible to every other part made at that place on the production line for the same purpose. So the worker making these parts did the same thing over and over and over and over and over and over, hour after hour, day after day. As I have already noted, this was Colt's invention, along with the Colt revolver, and it changed production in the last half of the nineteenth century.

The process of producing standardized, interchangeable parts culminated in the assembly line, introduced in Ford's River Rouge plant, and it simultaneously became the process of producing the standardized, interchangeable worker on the assembly line, with the replaceability of workers being crucial to control over their labor. A worker doing the same dumb task over and over again—dumb in the double sense of mindless and unspeakable, because what can you say to your family or your friends about your work today, like yesterday and the day before and the day before that, tightening the same effing bolts over and over again? Such "standardized" workers doing standardized tasks can be easily replaced, as the training costs are low. But now the whole notion of how to create interchangeable workers, easily disciplined and pushed to their limit because they are easily replaced, has changed profoundly, and it has extended to areas of production, like construction, where workers do very different things all day long.

Impunity, which makes it possible to treat people however the bosses and managers want to treat them, in Amazon warehouses, in Walmart stores, whatever, in a context where there is now little work on assembly lines, does the same thing to workers as the repetitive, dumbed-down tasks on an assembly line did. It makes the workers interchangeable, easily replaceable. One person called a "Mexican" (wherever in fact they came from) is the same as almost any other "Mexican." If they get hurt, or arrested, or deported, or just disappear, there are lots more Mexicans waiting for that job, as once it was with African Americans in many occupations. All that mattered was what specific kind of person did it, not what specific person. *Their status was their skill.* That is impunity in production.

Impunity—or more diffusely but equally destructively, concepts of race or of shared culture—does the same thing the industrial assembly line did to its workers. It creates utter substitutability among similarly categorized people. Just as a person on an assembly line who spends the entire day tightening wheel bolts or cutting the heads from chickens can be almost instantly replaced, so also can be a person called—and treated as—Black or female or Mexican and put to doing work reserved for people in that category. The impunity of domination produces the completely interchangeable abusable worker in contexts far removed from the routinization of a specific spot on an assembly line. Or, more precisely, as we can learn from the woman cleaning the motel room: it tries to.

To more fully understand what that woman with her hand in the toilet was saying to me when she said, "We're not doing that slavey work anymore," you have to begin by understanding just how misleading are the analyses offered by James Scott, in *Weapons of the Weak* (1985), and by Foucault's *Discipline and Punish* (1977), which Scott's perspective supports. The individualism embedded in James Scott's perspective in his popular book—an aggregate individualism, multiplied many times over, but still an individual response of foot-dragging, feigned ignorance, petty destruction—is what we used to call, in the 1950s, when I worked washing dishes in a restaurant, pissing in the coffeepot, done to get even with the customers who abused the staff. This did and still does little or nothing to rattle domination. They never even knew, not if it was only a little bit of pee. More: no individualized response possibly could bring change. The only things that could possibly have a chance of forcing change are not the kinds of actions that are repeated by separate individuals but the kinds of actions that can be done by people using their relations to one another. (See Piven and Cloward [1977] for a similar perspective.)

Pissing in the coffee pot may well make an abused worker feel a bit better, feel like a bit of vengeance has been extracted, but it changes nothing else. So long as we follow Scott, Foucault is right: power inscribes itself within the victims it produces, creating the dominated people who know power as it comes within their lives, and in their individualized resistance actually help to perpetuate power.

A similar point, more fully developed, was brilliantly made in two ethnographies of race and class in Washington, DC (Hannerz 1969; Howell 1973). The examples used included workers in a chain drugstore who engaged in petty shoplifting of supplies from the shelves. It turns out the managers and owners knew—everything was caught on the hidden security cameras—but they ignored the shoplifting so long as it did not get too intense. They ignored it for three reasons: First, it let them continue to pay truly miserable wages, for the cost to them of what the workers took still did not rise to the level of a livable wage. Second, it gave them the possibility of firing any worker whenever they wanted, for whatever real reason. If workers are laid off during seasonal downturns, for example, they qualify for unemployment insurance, and somehow the place that hired them is given higher rates. If workers are fired, they do not qualify for unemployment insurance, and the company's rates do not increase, so from the manager's perspective it is, or then was, always better to fire someone than to lay them off. Third, this petty shoplifting made the workers feel good, so they could be squeezed even harder on the job.

All that is why pissing in the coffeepot and any of the other so-called weapons of the weak are very far from what they seem to be on the surface. In many instances they are more part of control over the weak than the weapons of the weak.

We are now back to the woman who cleaned the motel room, and how her claims upon the world, her claims against the impunity with which she and her ancestors and her family and her community have long been treated, were profoundly different, profoundly more of a claim for her dignity and her rights.

When the woman with her hand in the toilet, who was neither dragging her feet nor feigning ignorance, but doing her job well, and proud of it; when she looked at me—which she rarely did—and when she said to me, "We're not doing that slavey work anymore" (note the "we"; it is crucial); when she said this to me, she was claiming her dignity and her humanity in the midst of doing the dirty work of the "service sector." Her saying, "We're not doing that slavey work anymore"; that assertion of we, for the women I asked about, hints, only hints, for the "we" is also not sticking her personal neck out; that "we" hints at the world she together with others can potentially build in the midst of domination. Half toothless, emaciated from a life of too much work and not enough care, she still had the strength and she still could call forth the connections to others like herself not only to surprise me with what she said but to put me in my place. My—and perhaps our—inability to understand clearly what is or where is that place she put me in: my failure, that failure of ours, is her second victory, her freedom from the totalization of the Foucauldian worldview, and her freedom from the petty and ultimately trivial claims of the equally elitist *weapons of the weak* perspective.

She did not choose to stop doing slavey work; power largely, if not entirely, chose for her when mechanization and corporate takeovers of small farms changed the labor demands in agriculture. Nor did she choose to wash toilets for minimum wage or less; power defined the kinds of jobs that would be available to her, and also made the rules that, sick or well, she would have to do one or another of those jobs. She chose, however, to remind me that she, and other Black women in the region, had their own values.

*Impunity is designed to produce shared culture or, more forcefully and significantly, to produce an enclosing and excluding "us"—to produce among the excluded people who are supposed to share in the culture but not in the nation. Impunity defines differential situations, once among the dominant and differently among the dominated. In both cases impunity makes the illusion, first of race and more recently of citizenship and "illegal alien," both seem real and be real.* Fortunately, culture is not shared, despite what anthropologists and other apologists for "society" once said and still cannot quite transcend. All such apologists still think that "we" "have" "culture." I'll tell that to the vicar next time I go to Matins.

There is a wonderfully perceptive T-shirt from the perspective of the victims of such fantasies as the dominant concepts of "our culture" and "our nation." It shows an entire digestive tract, from the mouth, down the esophagus to the stomach, to a very, very long coil of intestines ending at the anus, and around this drawing on the front of the T-shirt are the words "Shit does not just happen." We know that, even if the folks who grant each other impunity do not, and even if they are taken in by our jest to each other, our momentary acceptance or dismissal of our situations and our circumstances: "shit happens."

Impunity is more than an aspect of the production of low-cost, interchangeable workers who can be quickly shuffled from cotton to tobacco to motel toilets, or people who can readily be shifted from chicken packing to construction to gardening to whatever. It is, beyond this, another instance of the production of ultimately ungovernable and uncontrollable people. For impunity does not fully work, not at all. We can see in the woman's we-invoking rejection, both of slavey work and of my "progressive" concerns for unemployment and poverty, not simply her freedom and her dignity but her threat to our power. It may as likely come from her Pentecostal religion as from open confrontation, but that too is her choice, not ours.

The issue now becomes the shift between a world shaped by impunity, and people trying to go beyond their impunity-shaped pasts by claiming a different future, their own future, no matter how grim. The life she now lives is both her freedom and simultaneously the harness that chains her to a life of stress, ill health, and probably hurt, but hurt in the midst of her pride, all the pride expressed in her assertion of "we."

That "we" now commands our attention, along with the realization that much of its historical dynamic is taking shape beyond our current capacity to know, to understand, and especially to grasp. That is why I have picked, as an introduction to the general and larger issue, a phrase about the social relations among oppressed and exploited people that seems to make no sense, that even seems to mock the project of making sense: "Out here it's dog eat dog and vice versa." When this phrase turns out to make a great deal of sense we will perhaps know something we did not know before.

### TOMORROW'S DOGS

To start I should remind a younger generation of the development of a metaphor that once had very deep meanings in popular consciousness, from the beginning of the Industrial Revolution to the early mid-twentieth century—the period before the predominance of "open-pit mining" when industry and rail transport and home heating were fueled, literally, by coal mostly mined in long tunnels into the seam with pick and shovel and pony-drawn or human-drawn carts. Coal mines can at times produce, and their shafts sometimes trap, a lot of carbon dioxide, carbon monoxide, or methane gas, or just run out of breathable oxygen with the twists and dips of tunnels, and the general lack of ventilation in the older mines. Two deadly possibilities emerge in this context: the miners run out of oxygen, or the shaft explodes. These disasters were both frequent and widely known. For centuries miners took caged canaries into the mines with them. A canary has a very delicate set of lungs, and as oxygen declines or toxic gases accumulate, the bird quickly dies. When the bird fell over, you ran, as fast as you could, because you were next. So people in many contexts would use the image of the miner's canary: the warning sign for what is likely to soon be next for them. (Émile Zola [(1885) 2004] has one of the most powerful depictions of this type of mining.)

One of the several reasons I have long been fascinated by Newfoundland is that the people there are the miner's canary for the United States. Behind the very well-developed politeness of ordinary Canadians, their government treats its vulnerable peoples with a mixture of stunning unconcern and active destructiveness. A bit of explanation of how recent events in rural Newfoundland have developed will introduce the usefulness here of the complaint from Newfoundland about dogs eating dogs and then being eaten by the dogs they just ate.

Rural Newfoundland, for most of the nineteenth and twentieth centuries, was a thousand mostly quite small villages strung out along a rocky and indented coastline in this far northeastern Canadian island, out in the North Atlantic. Most villagers earned their living from the small-boat, near-shore cod fishery, catching and dry-salting the fish along the beach—the northern equivalent of handpicking cotton or working in a U.S.-based textile manufacturing plant. It was hard and stressful work, very poorly remunerated, but the center of a whole way of life that had its own satisfactions (Sider 2003a). By the mid-twentieth century these fisher families were being driven to the wall by a large-boat, offshore, commercial fishery prosecuted by trawlers from several nations, dragging huge nets along the ocean bottom in ways that both scooped up everything swimming there and simultaneously destroyed, by tearing up, the codfish breeding grounds on the ocean floor. These larger boats brought their catch to central freezing plants, bypassing the local processing facilities that had provided the bulk of local employment.

For a while in the 1970s and 1980s, there was a lot of money to be made, at least by the corporations, from this utterly destructive practice, so the politicians either encouraged it or closed their eyes to its destructiveness, or did both. Then, in the late 1980s, the codfish stock collapsed, and the codfish were just about all gone. In 1992 Newfoundland closed the cod fishery and for a few years made support payments to fishers and fish processors, in the belief that the cod stock would rebound, but after seven years or so, when it was clear that this was not about to happen, the support payments dwindled and stopped. The people still left in the villages were mostly suffering greatly, except for a few who had the resources to get into the distant-water shrimp and crab fishery, where the same destructive overfishing is now being repeated (Sider 2003a, preface).

This was the context when, in early 2000, I was in Newfoundland, listening to a radio talk show that was very popular among fishers and former fishers, who called in to discuss their issues and problems. One evening an elderly fisherman, from a small community far out on a northern peninsula of Newfoundland, called in and, trying to explain how social and work relations were changing in his and other fishing villages, said, in the passion of his comments, "Out here it's dog eat dog and vice versa." A few days later I drove out to his village to talk to him; he meant exactly what he said.

In the midst of our droll amusement at the vice versa, which seems a peculiar, illogical, unnecessarily circular intensification, we are in for some very substantial surprises. Woven within the deeper complexities of what this fisherman said, calling to us from his heart, his anger, his upset, and his dismay, are some fundamental challenges to the ways we understand how histories are made.

For a moment let us put the vice versa aside and focus on dog eat dog. It would make more logical sense to say dog eat rabbit or dog eat cat, but all that we know about our world helps us to realize that dog eat rabbit could never be a widespread folk saying. One would never say, "Out here it's dog eat rabbit." Dog eat rabbit has no surprises, implies no deeply underlying moral claims; it simply and superficially describes the way the world works. Dog eat dog raises other issues, issues that emerge from the fundamental identity of the participants—all are dogs—and simultaneously the equally fundamental, life-taking inequalities between dogs. The phrase dog eat dog, or more specifically "Out here it's dog eat dog," thus both describes and very deeply critiques the way the world works. It is difficult to see the power of this critique until we try to think why the phrase dog eat rabbit has no compelling moral force whatsoever. Dog eat dog is about the strong devouring and destroying not just the weak but their own; dog eat rabbit is, at best, trivia.

The fundamental problem before us, as we come to take the quote more seriously, is: What then is the vice versa? Let us start with what it is not, perhaps unfortunately. The vice versa figures in two very widespread and intense discourses, one rooted in Judeo-Christianity (and several other major religions) and the other in left revolutions. Christianity insists that the meek shall inherit the earth, after suffering the predations of the dominant, very pervasively downplaying the point that the word "inherit" ordinarily refers to the death of those who currently hold the goods. The left has the same belief, albeit for different reasons: it is just a bit noisier about it, and it once tried a bit more actively to help reach the goal implicit in the notion of inherit.

But in the rather typical Newfoundland fishing village to which the caller referred, and in which he lived, the vice versa points to something very different and very much more complex than a reversal-elevation of the meek or the mistreated. Indeed, at stake in the vice versa will be an introduction to a new perspective on how history is being made down at the bottom.

At the core of what is implied in the phrase "Out here it's dog eat dog and vice versa" is the fundamental point that no one can win, ever, no matter what. It is also saying that in the realm of their current everyday life no one has a future. If one dog ate another, there would be a future at least for the victor. If it is also vice versa, then life continues, if and when it does, in the midst of utter and oppressive contingency, uncertainty. What people are harnessed to, most of all, is this inescapable contingency, this inescapable and increasing uncertainty, this increasing uncertainty about what academics, with their love of abstraction, call social reproduction or what we, more directly, call tomorrow.

More concretely and more specifically the vice versa calls to the foreground the likelihood that tomorrow cannot be more or less like today and yesterday. This phrase is not primarily about people attacking one another, although as the possibilities for livable income diminish greatly, the competition for those situations intensifies greatly. That is exactly what, for one example, the current brutal increases in college tuition measure: the cost of thinking you can be in, or get to, a position to have a regular income and a place of your own to live—the cost of having the illusion that this might well be possible without a debt that constrains you for a substantial part of your adult life. The vice versa, to the contrary, first and foremost expresses the fact that no one has much if any future, not in that place, not in their communities, not in how they live their current lives, not, to get to the heart of the matter, the hearts of the people in such situations, in their current lives with family, friends, and neighbors.

The continuities of place, of tomorrow after today after yesterday, were crucial to the anthropological concepts of culture and social organization, and beyond these old-fashioned claims, to the notion of everyday life. The whole idea of culture and social organization, central anthropological and social-historical concepts in academia, depends on tomorrow being more or less like today, here. Concepts like capitalism have a certain portability to them—if a factory closes here, it or another opens there, and capitalism itself continues, at least for the while. When the people move away from the village where the factory that closed was located, or when the people are more or less forcibly moved away from a place near where a new factory is to be built—to make a dam or a road—or when people have to migrate to survive, their social organization is broken, and the vice versa is imposed upon them.

The United Nations says that in 2013—the last year for which an approximate count was developed—forty-five million people were refugees or displaced people (DW 2013). Much as the metaphor of dog eat dog is compellingly, if gruesomely, attractive, it turns out that it is the vice versa that names what is happening in the world: no one in the places that have become disposable, as have the people within them, has any future beyond an absolute and inescapable contingency, defined by the very much intensified uncertainties people must live within and against. "Dog eat dog and vice versa" means there are, and there can be, no winners, no future either for one or for all.

The vice versa names what is happening in this useful way: The production of race is always fluid. A world that produced abusable Blacks one day on the next makes illegal aliens and then has little use for Blacks. The people who now become useless have thus also become disposable. This is a crucial characteristic of the modern world, extending far beyond race making to all the no longer needed rural producers in India and Southeast Asia, to the fourteen million AIDS orphans in Africa, to all the no-longer-needed peasants and in-the-way tribal peoples of Latin America, to all the former industrial workers in U.S. and Canadian and Greek and Italian and Spanish cities, to . . . *There are now far more disposable people in the world than domination can dispose.* We are living in the vice versa.

Moreover, few are willing to cooperate with being disposed. The central lesson this fisherman was trying to teach seems to be that there is something beyond people in this situation preying on one another. That lesson is that no one has much by way of a tomorrow, in the place they are now. And this seems to me to be the start of new kinds of collective actions, focusing, to begin with, on remaking, on completely new terms, both place and tomorrow.

I was asked: What does this mean in practice? It means that part of the route to a different and better tomorrow—only part, but an important part—lies in what the working class and the even poorer victims of the current situation have long known and tried to use as a strategy for starting to claim their own lives, their own future. This strategy is properly called fucking over the bosses, or the people seemingly responsible for our current situations. While I very much regret the sexism of this formulation, and while I worry intensely and mourn intensely about good people getting hurt in the process, I want to assure readers that when this is all we have left, it is at least a useful, and at times a productive, strategy, minus its sexism and incorporating its angers.

That, unfortunately, is precisely what the murderous fundamentalists are doing in the Middle East and elsewhere, not only to those in their governments who have colluded with neocolonialism but, as also with neocolonialism, to vast numbers of innocent victims. The current violent destructiveness of the struggles between Sunni and Shia Muslims is all too painfully reminiscent of the Thirty Years' War in Europe (1618–1648), when Protestants and Catholics devastated central Europe, destroying 18,000 towns and villages and killing many millions of people. No one has had a monopoly on murderous confrontations, but as the world changes we must find more mutually caring totalizing confrontations with those whose policies and practices actually do us harm, lest all we do is destroy each other.

The reach to confrontation has the advantage of making the dominant rather more willing to listen to the more polite sectors of their opposition, for fear of what we might do if they did not. That was the very special contribution of Malcolm X, the Black Panthers, and the Young Lords to the civil rights victories. May we learn from what they did for us, although they each paid a very high price for this contribution. If you don't like this way of posing our situation and our route to a more just future, figure out something else rather than just turning your back on the problems.

# PART IV

LIVING CONTRADICTIONS

———

# NINE

# Civil Society and Civil Rights on One Leg

## ONE-LEGGED CHALLENGES

Peter Newcomer, the same colleague who talked to me about the mechanical cotton picker as the prelude to and precondition for civil rights, also told me, when I went down south to join the struggles, that I was going to be like a one-legged man in an ass-kicking contest. I would have to get used to falling down, picking myself up, dusting myself off, and getting right back in the fray. Further, he said, I would have to learn to enjoy the struggle, because that pleasure would be one of the major rewards. We both thought that civil rights would be won, that "the movement," as it was called, was unstoppable, but the warning about standing on one leg was good and useful, as many of the stories have sought to show, for the struggles have been endless and, while we are on our way to tomorrow, frequently lost.

I now think that this is also crucial advice about how we must organize current struggles. We are going to lose, almost all of the time, but I think if we keep at it, in the long run we have to win at least a good part of what we seek because domination cannot stand the chaos we can introduce into the lives and practices of the dominant.

The general question before us now is how to organize, at the deepest level, the struggles that, for the most part and at least for now, only for now, we are often doomed to lose.

The answer to this starts with the basics of why we are doomed to lose. Here I want to put aside the obvious, the money and power and control—of media, of police, of courts, all and more—that can be mobilized against us. As painful as that may be when we get hit by one or more of these forces, that is not the main problem before us.

I think the main problem is hinted at by the name "civil rights." And when we see what that name reveals, we will also know a bit more about our broader struggles. Be a bit patient as we work through this; it will take several pages, but in the end we will have more standing, and more basic standing than in a court, and hopefully we will wind up standing on one or both legs.

In a court, "standing," which must be proved against potential or actual challenges, is the right to be there as an aggrieved party and to sue for redress. Many cases are dismissed because the clearly aggrieved parties are held by the court not to have this "standing." We do not want to ask anyone for standing; we want to set up our struggles so they belong to us, for we are the ones who more than *have* standing, *are* standing.

There are two useful ways to approach the task of strategizing struggle. The first, and I think surprisingly less useful, is to ask what they want from us—to ask why the dominant society, the superrich, and their bought politicians can't let go of the whole process of producing abusable, marginalized African Americans when there is no more need for them in the productive economy. There are a whole freight-load of possible answers to this question, many invoking the need of a declining or status-threatened "middle class" to have someone beneath them not just to feel better than— my grandfather's cockroach fantasy—but also to clean their houses, mind their kids, mow their lawns, and so forth. Probably most of the folks in these jobs, in many areas of the United States, are Latino/a, but in terms of the dominant perspectives that is not too much of a change—they are all the colored folks of the world, who have always been foreigners, not really citizens, for they did not and still do not come under the protection of the law.

This category—not quite citizens, not quite us—also includes a substantial portion of the 8 percent of U.S. households that live in "mobile homes" (17 to 18 percent of the households in the Carolinas) (StateMaster .com 2004). These folks are the so-called trailer trash who now hang on to their few paltry and mostly declining opportunities "by the skin of their teeth," as what has become an American saying fibs, for teeth of course have no skin. It also of course includes all the poor, of any color, for here color is scarcely relevant, who live in declining or dying cities, or who live in the not-yet-gentrified slums near the expanding neighborhoods of predatory refinance capitalism. What is Maxton is now also Detroit, as that city, under a manager appointed by a Republican governor, turns off the water of thousands of people who can no longer pay their water bill in full. And what this does is make the water supply system more attractive to a corporation, as the city and state seem to be considering, as usual with neoliberalism, privatizing for profit what should by now be a human right.

It is clear that the dominant still want to use at least some of the well-behaved people "below them," so it is not useless to ask what they are trying to do to us and with us, and how we can resist what they try to make us into for their purposes. This will be one of our hardest tasks, for as John Iliffe (1987), a Cambridge University economist of African origin, put it, there is only one thing in the world worse than being exploited by a multinational corporation, and that is not being exploited by a multinational corporation. (The originator of this phrase seems to be the British economist Joan Robinson [(1962) 2006], but although it was meant somewhat critically, it is now so widely used as an excuse for exploitation that it is hard to track it down.) They may scarcely need some of us, and the rest they will as quietly as possible throw to the dogs, but we still need them and their increasingly paltry and insecure offerings, so it is on this basis alone that we are in a profoundly unequal struggle.

But it seems much more useful to turn away from asking what the dominant want from us, and how to engage them on those terms and their terrain, and instead ask what we ourselves are doing wrong in our struggles for justice, because we can more easily change what we do than try to change "them," or engage them on their terrain. President Barack Obama and his only partly invisible conk rag, which also went on shortly after his nomination, however much sympathy we might feel for him, considering the enormous pressures put upon him, should have finally taught us the lesson that the dominant are hard to dislodge.

So two tactical issues emerge from this. First, when I am asked who specifically we should organize and struggle against, my answer is go after everyone responsible, for that will more likely put them on the run than if we were to focus. And there are now enough groups and grouplets, from those opposed to fracking to those fighting the increasing restrictions on voting rights, so that we can mount very broad challenges. There was an old left, too romantic slogan, "let a hundred flowers bloom," that once named a very illusory loosening of Communist Party discipline in China. But there is a better version: let a hundred intrusive plants be deadheaded; have their taking-over tops be removed, down to their roots.

Second, and a related question, when I say that our problems come from "them" or "they," I was asked by readers of the manuscript to specify to whom I am referring. That misses the point: we cannot tell who will oppose us until we demand justice—and remember that the opposite of poverty is not wealth but justice, as Bryan Stevenson, the founder of the Equal Justice Initiative put it. So it is always a mistake to name those against our search for justice in advance.

## CIVIL? RIGHTS

To see our situation more clearly we need to return to the point I raised at the opening of this work: the issue of civil rights. What we have been doing wrong, partly—for much of what we did was fine—was to struggle for civil rights. It was such a nightmare to not be able to vote for the people who ran our schools, our towns, counties, and states; it was such a nightmare to not be able to be protected by the courts, the police, or anything else; it was such a nightmare to suffer the constant humiliations, with spouses and children often watching helplessly; it was such a nightmare to have children, parents, and friends suffer and die from lack of care and caring; it was such a nightmare to live with and against all this that we can ask, in justifiable anger, what is the problem with struggling for civil rights?

For any and all of the above, and far more, the answer of course is absolutely nothing is wrong with that struggle, those struggles. The problem is that by struggling for civil rights we stopped there, so in the long run we had to lose as well as gain. We had to lose, just by the terms of the struggle we paid such a high price to engage.

To explain this we return to the notion of civil in civil rights, where the limitations we imposed on ourselves, or accepted as they were given to us in our struggles, become more clear.

In Western political philosophy there has developed a notion of civil society—the domain of society where civil rights are to be found, and where the struggles for such rights take place. The concept was formed by Aristotle and was given its modern force and utility by the German philosopher G. W. F. Hegel, in the early nineteenth century, in a way that it became a key part of a broader field of social thinking. Hegel saw civil society as the realm of the individual, particularly and revealingly the property-owning individual, the multiple individuals who had to coordinate their needs and desires with one another. In simplified terms it was the domain of a society that was not either the state or "business."

But as I have already noted, the term in German that Hegel used for what we have poorly but routinely translated as "civil society"—and this is crucial—was *bürgerliche Gesellschaft*, which can be more specifically translated as "bourgeois society," the society of, and for, and ruled by, the burghers, the special citizens and property owners of the city, the city as the core of civil society, civilization. The burghers—the people whose descendants became the bourgeoisie—were the people in the Middle Ages and the late Middle Ages who owned property in the cities, who were thus and almost exclusively the citizens of the city, the rulers of the city. Civil rights are rights in and within the world that these folks control, and they have scarcely ever meant us well.

To seek civil rights, however wonderful they may seem when we don't have any, is inescapably to seek to play by the bourgeoisie's rules, to play their game on their terrain, to seek admission to their society, their enclosures, to get their rights. It can never happen, because the rights they are willing to give us, to let us win without appalling bloodshed, are mostly the rights that can be harnessed to support their rule over us.

This is not to say that we are given rights just to have them taken away, although this is much of what is happening with the Supreme—or better: Supremacist—Court and Republican state governments very intensely now restricting the ability of African Americans to vote. More is at stake. Sometimes the rights that African Americans were given, such as their civil rights, are subsequently used to displace them, as when in high-injury jobs they were specifically replaced by undocumented workers with little if any such rights. And sometimes their rights are used to harness them to tasks against their well-being and long-term interests: the army, in Iraq and Afghanistan, became very much an equal opportunity employer, if not proportionately more so. We can have another conversation about people being "given" or "winning" civil rights when the proportion of African Americans in Congress, or state houses, is about the same as the proportion of African Americans in Afghanistan and the Middle East.

We talk, or did in an older generation that read with their eyes, not their thumbs, of people who live "beyond the pale"—outside, beyond the bounds, marginal in more ways than one. What many people then did and now still mostly do not realize is that the word "pale," in the phrase "those who live beyond the pale," has the same root word as "palisade"—the fortress defense of a boundary made by sharpened poles stuck, side by side, in the ground to make a fence, to mark a boundary, and more: to mark a boundary that can be defended against those "beyond the pale." We who still live most of our lives beyond the pale, except when we are called inside to clean up their messes, to police each other, to wash their toilets if we have the experience and the references, we who live beyond the pale can win, or will be "given," some of the rights that come with being inside the pale, being within bourgeois society, but we will never be a part of it—except for our elites, who then will all too often turn around and stick it to us, and enjoy the rewards bourgeois society gives them for both doing that and helping to control us in the process.

So we must simultaneously fight for our civil rights, our rights within bourgeois society, and at the same time fight against the bourgeoisie who so cheerfully and contemptuously exploit and abuse us. That is why I say our struggle is for rights and justice, not civil rights—and a justice that can no longer be expected to come from the courts of civil society. Until the Supremacist Court just took it away we had, for a brief while, the right to vote for corrupt and opportunistic congressional and state representatives and governors, many of whom were on the take from whoever could and would support their place at the public trough. A few not, very much not, but they are the minority both in Congress and in any state legislature. The supporters of what I call "the take and make politicians," or the agents of those supporters, have the deeply deceptive name "lobbyists," as if their bribery and their organization of corruption were restricted to the lobbies of the legislature.

The courts have always had a deeply ambivalent role in protecting or ensuring rights—both granting significant rights and taking significant ones away. They seem recently to be shifting more and more in the direction of denying rights, and it is unclear why. It could be the vastly increasing inequalities in America, destroying the last pretense of democracy; it could be the intensifying arrogant illegality of recent U.S. governments, both Republican and Democrat, from the unpunished police murders of African Americans, now almost matching lynchings in their frequency, to "extraordinary renditions" that have become ordinary, to murdering innocent civilians with bombs from unmanned drones, to not jailing bankers, to the sequester here and the enforced austerity there, to the

United States, under at least Presidents Obama and the previous Bush, helping the Colombian government find and murder its opponents—and apparently also, decades ago, using the CIA to help put Nelson Mandela in jail for twenty-seven years, to, to, to. Most of all I think rights are being increasingly denied because they have to be, in a vain (in both senses of that word: futile and self-aggrandizing) attempt to preserve a crumbling state.

But the main point is that it doesn't matter why the courts cannot be trusted. They are a central part of the civil society that is built to keep us out, to keep us down. In the long run they are profoundly inadequate for our task, our struggles for justice.


The answer to where and how our struggles might productively be focused will come as quite a surprise. The phrase "law and order" is so widely and so thoughtlessly used that a great many people have come to think that the law is about making order. That's not how domination works.

Domination sometimes, and briefly, makes or imposes order. True, but most of the time and in most of its manifestations it creates chaos in the lives of people it seeks to control and to exploit. Bangladesh factories making clothes for Nike, Gap, J. C. Penney, et cetera, before they murderously collapse or burn are a useful example of the chaos in people's lives that is so deeply embedded in dominant forms of organization and order. Anthropologists and social historians, often with progressive intent, have invoked the "social organization" of the economy, of production, most generally of social life without dealing with the extent to which the social organization imposes both chaos and the inescapable threat of chaos upon us. All this, as we can see, is highlighted by the deceptive, problem-enhancing responses to the need for change by the U.S. merchants who make their clothes in places like Bangladesh; who make their high-priced oh so fancy electronics in Chinese factories like Foxconn: all the places that produce order and chaos simultaneously, but for "foreigners."

Any one of a huge range of instances can be used to make the identical point. "Stop and frisk" may seem to those well within civil society to make order, but that is not at all its effect upon the Black families whose children are stopped and frisked. Black and Latino youth for long could not walk in peace in New York City, or Florida, or Missouri, or Illinois, or many other places—the epitome of what civil society would call making orderliness.

New York City parents have told me about the fear they have, whenever their children go out, that the police will do something more than just grab them, as they regularly do.

But all this is also, I suggest, our opening. If the dominant work their "magic" upon us, transforming us from people to victims, from human beings to foreigners and abusable ethnics, races, religions, and/or women, making us live much of those statuses by the chaos they make in our lives, we can turn that chaos back upon them, making their lives as chaotic as possible, and by so doing win at least some of our claims for justice that we have small chance of winning any other way. At the same time, and at least as crucially important, we can oppose the chaos that domination brings to our lives by working to develop our own orderliness, our own peaceful predictability, our own materialized caring in our relations to one another.

In the context both of my work and also of my desire to be with what I think of as my people, I sometimes go to "fundamentalist" churches— Pentecostal, Evangelical, whatever, though I have not yet found the Catholic equivalent. I would like to visit Islamic fundamentalist mosques but think I would not be welcome, and Jewish fundamentalism seems very different—a side effect, perhaps, of Israel's violent relations with Palestinians. I am not at all religious, not in any way, but I am often deeply moved by the intense level of caring that people in such "fundamentalist" churches show for one another, very much also including people who are not members of the congregation. I sit or stand there watching and listening and sometimes joining people praying for one another, and more, mobilizing to help one another, materially, actually, and thinking if only the left, the progressives, had shown so much direct caring for each other, the world would probably now be a very different and better place. That commitment to one another, that caring actively expressed and actually done, I think must be a crucial component of any progressive strategy. I urge those of my readers who have never been to a fundamentalist Protestant church, or who have only been to one, to go to a few, just to listen and look. I well know that many of them are politically ultra–right wing, but a different issue is at stake here. Bertrand Russell, the brilliant philosopher of the twentieth century, reputedly once said that if socialism ever came to America, it would come in the guise of religion. I would not trust this route, considering the so-called Tea Party and its base, but some elements of this point may be worth considering.

The left classically relates to people, especially categories of people such as workers, the unemployed, and the colonized, on the basis of its "knowledge"—this is why capitalism is bad for you—although sometimes, powerfully and effectively doing actual organizing, for rent strikes, store boycotts, minimum wage increases, and so forth. Yet the level and perhaps also the intensity of direct, person-to-person, individualized, and focused caring in many (but of course not all) fundamentalist churches is an example to be emulated.

It is worth a try, to see if it works. We need to find something that works, and in that search I often come back, in my thoughts, to a strangely apolitical, yet deeply socially committed, novel.

To me the most searing line in this important but ultimately conservative book on race, Ralph Ellison's *Invisible Man* ([1952] 1995), is when the young African American man who eventually tries to become invisible is driven out of his college and his homeland down south by his African American college president, whom he saw in a brothel where the young man waited on tables. The very next day he was called into the college president's office and sent north—told he must get out of town by tomorrow—but with a letter of introduction and recommendation from his college president, supposedly to help him get a job. When it always fails to do so, he opens the letter and reads it, and all it says is "Keep This Nigger-Boy Running." That all too powerfully describes the lives of many of the African American victims of racism, in the midst of their wonderfully impressive attempts to make order and tomorrow, to build place and space for themselves and more: for each other.

It worked to keep him running, at least until the young man went underground, not yet politically, in the narrow sense of political; not underground, in the revolutionary and resistance-movement sense of underground, although that may have been a very distant implication, but he went underneath the streets of Harlem to the underground electric tunnels and to a more peaceful and self-contained life that was possible out of sight.

For all the difficulties of doing so, for all the struggles we are bound to lose, now it is our turn to keep them running, or at least start them running.

How? Not by force; they own that. By the contradictions in their position, by the fantasies they live by, by the fragility of their economic and political base, and especially by their inability to heal their own wounds, the wounds they made for and upon each other. And most of all by our wonderful capacity to disrupt, to rattle their chains of orderliness with the theater of our scary and disruptive, although in our terms peaceful, presence in their squares, in their offices, and on their oh so civil landscapes—particularly if we acquire the power that is very likely to come from much further developed commitments to the actual situations of one another.

A bit more precision may be helpful. For this we can return to Barrington Moore Jr. (1966), who pointed out that very few revolutions or mass social movements "from below"—from peoples' needs and concerns—succeeded unless the ruling elites were split, and the uprisings situated themselves within, and used, this split. We have to recognize that one of the factors in the short-term success of the civil rights struggles of the 1950s to 1970s was the fact that a national elite, to simplify drastically, wanted a factory labor force and literate soldiers that segregated schools and blatant racism could not produce, and a better public image in the "third world," and so put the muscle on a declining southern agrarian elite that was helpful for our uprising. The split between a local agrarian elite and a national elite very much helped our struggles.

Although I think, as I have suggested earlier, that neoliberalism is now so intensely driving what is happening that the strategy of trying to use, via alliances, factional splits in the dominant groups is not for now an effective strategy, that does not at all mean it will never again become one.

In this context it may be useful to pay attention to some very much larger-scale processes that might provide new openings for progressive action, with or without alliances with factions of the dominant. There are at least four large-scale current developments that may well change the strategies for, or consequences of, our interventions, but for the worse as likely as for the better.

The first is an intensifying economic stagnation that some have called "stagflation" in the major capitalist states. These states call themselves "the Group of Seven" and for a while "the Group of Eight." These are the wealthiest countries or, because the group excludes China, the countries that claim to be, by their standards, the most industrialized and the wealthiest rather than the most wealth producing: the United States, Germany, France, Italy, Japan, the United Kingdom, and Canada, with Russia brought in and then put out over Crimea.

The point, at first central to Marxist analyses of capital and now very widely accepted, is that capital must expand in order to continue. This is

so for several reasons rooted in the logic of capitalist-organized production and finance. The reason most relevant here is that there has to be
someplace to invest the profits from current production. As corporations
and banks become more powerful, they are more able to shape events in
self-favorable ways such as increasingly moving to areas with lower labor
costs, to shielding their profits from taxes, to creating fantasy invest-
ments knowing that they will be bailed out by taxpayer dollars when these
investments collapse, to knowingly making, with impunity, automobiles
that have a high risk of killing their occupants, and so forth into the rust
belts around our waists if not our necks. The profits from all this have bal-
looned well past what can be productively invested.

At the same time, consumer demand, especially demand that is paid for
by current income, all across these supposedly most wealthy countries, has
declined markedly. This decline has been masked, for a while, by the huge
surge in credit debt. As is finally being realized in current discussions, the
trillion dollars in current aggregate student loan debt in the United States
will severely depress the housing and new automobile markets, while this
same debt continues to substantially transfer wealth upward: upward and
away from effective consumer demand. (Magdoff and Forster [2014] provide an excellent brief overview of these processes.)

Second, the United States and its allies are increasingly having to realize
that they can no longer control the world militarily. They can smash and
destroy, massively, they can sneak in and either capture or murder, but they
can neither conquer nor administer. And that former ability to conquer and
to administer, to their own advantage, provided a substantial part of the
material well-being of their citizenry, particularly when the foot soldiers
who did this were largely drawn from the poor and dispossessed. So much
of the directly experienced costs of these assaults went to one segment of
the populace and so much of the benefits to another.

Third, we are seeing the rise of China not only economically but also
militarily. China's internal problems will keep this from happening very
fast, but it seems inexorable. It was only a bit more than a hundred years between the claims that "the sun never sets on the British Empire" and "Great"
Britain being reduced to a second-rate economy and political power; the
same is very probably happening now in the United States. As it happens,
whether or not it happens conclusively or rapidly, new factions and frag-
mentations in the state emerge. My hunch is that the current increasingly
intense wave of political and economic opportunists and conservatives in

the U.S. Congress is deeply tied to this intensifying transformation in U.S. self-proclaimed exceptionalism, as the elite and segments of the middle class try to maintain their profits and wealth while the basis for it crumbles underneath them.

The resulting political stalemates and simultaneous collapse of major, but not all, elements of the so-called welfare state that paid some small attention to people's needs may give progressives some new opportunities amid, or arising from, the current devastating losses. Right-wing conservatism is surging in the suburbs, the golden oldie neighborhoods, and the boondocks, seemingly driven by some of the same concerns about tomorrow that have driven our struggles, although the sense both of causality and of possibility remains profoundly different.

Fourth, and for the moment last, we are observing, worldwide, a massive intensification of religious fundamentalism. Europe nearly destroyed itself in an earlier wave of Christian fundamentalism that provoked and sustained the Thirty Years' War (1618–48). Catholics and Protestants, butchering each other, killed about a third of the population of Europe and brought ruin upon countless towns, cities, and agricultural areas. The Swedish armies alone destroyed about eighteen thousand towns and villages in Central Europe. Such murderous and limitless destruction, in the name of religious difference, seems to be developing again, mostly between different religions and also different "sects" of what outsiders would regard as the same Muslim religion.

In my childhood, Catholics and Protestants were all goyim (in practice, as opposed to the more innocent dictionary definitions: aliens, often dangerous others) and the differences between them neither understandable nor seemingly important. That perspective was of very limited use for grasping the Thirty Years' War. Similarly now the goyim and the Israelis seem to not much know or care about the increasingly murderous splits between Sunni and Shia Muslims. So long as we can use one sect against the other, we know all we seem to need or want to know. They are all Muslims, in the same way Catholics and Protestants are all goyim. Thus their wars, and our wars against one or another sort of Muslim, float just on top of shallow understandings, like democracy now floats well above our needs and concerns.

From the mid-twentieth century on we seem to be in a period of continuous war, so the whole notion of wars that have a beginning and an end, a notion implicit in the dating of the Thirty Years' War, 1618 to 1648, now seems either quaint or an archaic reference to a world that once was. War, like democracy, now floats: it just drifts, or gets pushed, from one place to another, scarcely now doing anything positive, just hurting and destroying a lot of people. Think of all the destruction the United States wreaked on Vietnam, napalming villages, bombing cities, spraying long-lasting carcinogenic Agent Orange over much of the countryside, all to prevent the "spread of communism," and by thirty years later the "communist" government of Vietnam was guaranteeing labor at US$50 a month to South Korean–owned factories making Nike athletic shoes.

The fact that this floating war scarcely accomplished anything beyond its massively murderous ways, other than to very temporarily help sustain or increase capitalist profits, as is now again happening in central Africa, of course does not diminish the proclivity for war, nor the fact that worldwide the response to the fundamentalist upsurge, which in some areas includes murderous outrages, has not been to ask what is fueling this recurrent and intensifying development but to bomb from above and to hire other people to get on the ground and shoot or be shot. We, however, need to ask about the causes of these fundamentalist upsurges, some violent and some very much not so, for by doing so we may learn very useful lessons for our own struggles, and within our own countries develop some surprising new alliances.


All I can do is guess the outlines of some of the pieces in the puzzle of what is now happening on this larger scale, and what it portends, positively and negatively, for its current victims. This attempt to guess and to grasp is rooted in trying to figure out what and where the contradictions are that we might be able to exploit. I start with two that seem relevant and useful.

The first contradiction emerges from the vast numbers of utterly disposable people who are now outside the caring, but not the attempted control, of the state—"beyond the pale," in the old but still powerful phrase. Colonialism and imperialism have long been comfortable with this situation, but all those disposable people are now increasingly inside the state, and being there create a massive uncertainty about control and continuity. It is a profoundly different situation when the major imperialist powers of the twentieth century exploit, oppress, and brutalize peoples who live in colonies—in places far away—and who stay there. When these folks come inside the major states, or when the state, either running out of foreigners to exploit or just to increase domestic profitability and to lower social costs, starts (again) to increasingly intensely exploit and diminish its own people, a very different political situation is created, with very different potentials.

My guess is that the bankruptcy of a city once as large and as wealthy as Detroit expanded the problems before the national government from the former yawning over a fading Rust Belt, supposedly that could be dealt with by the expansion of the Sun Belt economies, to something that is starting to seem out of control, even though this bankruptcy is being used as a pretext to loot the workers' pensions—and more: the workers' lives—to protect the assets of the wealthy. This is the same strategy imposed on Greece and Italy and Spain by Germany and France, in favor of their banks. But in the long run such strategies cannot work: there is more debt out there than can be covered by looting everything that workers (and students with massive college debt) own. I think one major reason why the bankers who so illegally looted homeowners, corporations, and also the state were not jailed was that there was the hope that they could use their fantasy economics to dig the state out of the hole it was falling into.

I was asked to prove this last statement. I laughed so hard I cried, then I cried so hard I laughed. The point behind this seemingly playful response is crucial. Absolutely central to the ways domination works in states "ruled by law," even laws supposedly upheld by our current Supreme Court's amoral majority that claimed money is speech, like any other kind of talk, and that corporations have the same rights as actual people, is that much of what is done to us, with us, and against us is done in ways that are designed to be unprovable. For example, New York State's high-handed current governor, Andrew Cuomo, seems to have eviscerated state reports critical of fracking by using personal e-mails, rather than official correspondence, for personal e-mails by elected officials are not subject to being revealed by freedom of information laws (Waldman 2014). *Sic transit gloria mundi.* We cannot avoid using logic, rather than unavailable and concealed evidence, to try and get our hands on what is happening just slightly out of our view.

There is a larger issue at stake here, which does not depend on suggestions about why the U.S. government bailed out the banks, while letting the homeowners the banks stole homes from rot in their upset. And that larger issue, which should give us strength, is that all the ways the vulnerable people are now treated, as inequality grows ever more out of control, seem to be undermining the current system of domination and of expanding inequalities. What "they" try to do to "us," to use the simplicities of the dominant, is paralyzing government, breaking down the market for consumer and production goods, and perhaps also fueling a worldwide intensification of armed and militant religious fundamentalism. But there are simpler and more direct indicators of how the squeeze on the poor, which as usual is very much also a squeeze on African American people and neighborhoods, ultimately also rattles the governments that either orchestrate this or just watch it happen.

It is clearly within our power to use the chaos of failed cities such as Detroit as one basis to pursue our claims against the self-styled princes and princesses of civil society, for the failure of a place as big and once as rich as Detroit not only hurts them but also must scare them. I think the scariness, to the elite, of the increasing urban failures in the United States will more intensely shock those who are causing it and seeking to profit by it. Similarly, the "austerity" imposed by Germany on the southern European countries in order to not make the slightest dent in German banks and their stockholders turns out to wreak uncontrollable havoc in southern Europe, and now to very seriously diminish German exports, much to the current consternation of the financial elite in Germany. They can't both own us and destroy us. That was one of the central contradictions of slavery, and that is now again one of the central contradictions of neoliberal capitalism.

That suggests it may be useful to add a further comment on disposable people. It is indeed not a completely new phenomenon. In some sense, for example, slaves were always disposable, since they could almost always be killed, or beaten or worked to death, at the will of their owner. But slaves were costly, and so when one died while he or she still had the capacity for useful work, or income-earning baby making, the owner was out of pocket, substantially. That provided some constraint, surprisingly more than now, on the essentially murderous treatment of Blacks. You don't lynch slaves, however popular it was to do this to Blacks once they were no longer owned as property and no one "that mattered" lost money when they died.

Further, we might note that Native Americans, in and beyond the colonial period, were also disposable. Yes, but. But they were very much necessary to the way U.S. expansion and trade wealth were organized, so their deaths in this process also had some few constraints, at least for some kinds of Native American societies. (This is spelled out in Sider [2003b, chaps. 10 and 11].)

Second, we have on our side the increasing impossibility of continued dominance based on either force or economic control. The continuing unstoppable defeats of colonial interventions, from Vietnam to Iraq to Afghanistan, not even counting the slipping control over places like Venezuela, Bolivia, and even, in other terms, Greece, and the increasing disintegration of states as large and populous as Nigeria and perhaps also Brazil, plus the continuing loss of production to China, Southeast Asia, and other transient hot spots of easily abusable people seem to have substantially intensified the desire—or more: the need—to abuse the vulnerable at home. The profits from doing this have, for a while, helped to partially replace what is being lost to foreign competition and foreign restrictions on overseas investment.

But this abuse of the already poor and marginal within the homeland has reached its economic limits. The recession of 2008, from which we and the European Economic Community show no realistic signs of recovering at the level of ordinary people's living standards, is in substantial part produced by the collapse of consumer demand. This collapse of consumer demand is, of course, the direct product of the political maintenance of an unlivable minimum wage, the enormous debt burden of the populace, and the almost completely unregulated predations on the populace, from health care to housing. Even extortion has its economic limits, when there are no political or legal controls.

The term "economic limits" is precise. Politically, with a purchased Congress, more can be done to hurt the poor and the marginal, and there will indeed be some savings to the national budget from so doing. But there is scarcely more profit that can be wrung from the necks of the poor. Stealing their homes with fake mortgage recalls, as the banks have done and still do, and then renting these homes—until eventual resale at a profit—might well be the last possible squeeze on a credit-soaked populace. And keep in mind that it has recently been the ballooning of personal credit that has kept domestic capitalism alive. But such debts are now, or very soon will become, unpayable, no matter how tight the grip on vulnerable peoples' throats. That is, I think, the lesson of Mexico. Foreign capital and predatory states, mostly in and from the United States and Western Europe, bled Mexico dry, and then in large sectors of production a great many former workers (including former farmers, ruined by NAFTA) necessarily turned to a different kind of economy, an illegal economy, much less controllable from either within or without.

What is happening here in the United States is that the squeeze on foreign countries that once returned very high average profits—in the 1960s about double the profits that corporations could make with their invest-ments within the United States—became substantially reduced as places like Mexico got bled dry, and places like Venezuela and Bolivia figured out how to keep more of their wealth production both in their own borders and for more of their own people

After years of telling the public employee unions in Detroit that they can save the city, and their own jobs, by spending their workers' pension funds to buy city bonds, so that the public employees became by the summer of 2013 the largest single holders of Detroit's debt, the city declared bank-ruptcy, which allows it to "legally" settle this debt obligation for pennies on the dollar, pennies that can now be spent by the predominantly African American city employee retirees to feed and house themselves and their families for the rest of their lives, lives now without much rest. What can no longer be so easily and routinely extracted from others abroad now must be gotten from the others within.

But such abuse has its limits, different from abusing people outside one's borders, even when the abuse falls most heavily upon the lives of the other within—Mexicans, Blacks, women, whatever. Many of these folks seemingly available for increasingly totalizing abuse are actually citizens, and doing things to them, like grinding down their Social Security benefits, is very widely scary and provokes quite intense pushback.

The collapse of Detroit became all the more predictable when people stopped buying the junk that the Detroit carmakers foisted off on us, so that there was less and less profit that could be made from production. I remember in the 1970s seeing Detroit cars with solid rear axles and leaf springs, when Europe and Japan were selling cars with independent tor-sion bar suspensions on jointed axles, not only far more comfortable but also much more controllable in turns; and I remember a bit earlier, when Detroit carmakers started equipping their cars with tires marked "two-ply, four-ply rating." And at the same time they shifted to a softer and cheaper tire cordage material, polyester as opposed to nylon. The number of layers of cording within the layers of rubber is what gives the tire its body and shape, which controls the car in stops and turns. General Motors, it was said, saved twenty-five cents a tire, five tires on each of eight million vehi-cles, $10 million more profit a year. A person had to value flag-waving over their own comfort and safety, or be mechanically illiterate, to not buy a Japanese or European or later a Korean car—the key to your future, to hav-ing a future, to make another horrible pun about a continuing situation.

This is one part of the background to Detroit now robbing the pension plans of its public employees, the major body of reasonably paid employees left, nationwide—who are also being increasingly privatized out of existence. A for-profit corporation can only do a municipal job—from collecting trash to housing prisoners—if it squeezes down the lives of its workers with very substantial pay and benefit restrictions, and then steals their future, their pensions and a livable income, to benefit corporate management and stockholders.

But not everyone wants to squeeze or loot the U.S. worker or consumer, or more to the point, deny the people who have come to need state-sponsored aid with old-age security, medical access, food, housing, decent education, and so forth; if everyone wanted to deny all this, there would be no struggles in Congress. Some of the elite, and even some of the corporations and the superwealthy who, like ventriloquist puppeteers, have their hands under the clothes of our representatives, to actually make the moves the puppets seem to make, and provide the words that the puppets seem to speak, seem to know that you can't have an economy unless people buy things, pay mortgages, and so forth. For a while all this realization was lost in the enormous credit bubble that made it seem we could have consumption without adequate income, but that strategy has reached its foreseeable end, first with homes and soon with credit cards and college loans.

And not just for the people on the bottom. The strategy of trying to run a high-tech economy with people priced out of the university education it usually takes to work in this economy for the moment has been masked by importing people trained in India and elsewhere in Asia, but that will soon run into substantial opposition. As the credit bill for student loans is now larger than the personal credit bills of families, and as Congress is unwilling to significantly lower the interest rates on these nationally necessary loans, or to subsidize education more realistically, we are increasingly restricting the crucial training to those from already wealthy families. And, of course, we are increasingly dependent upon foreign-trained technologists, who increasingly perhaps realize they will be better treated in a more welcoming Canada than in the United States. Germany, in the fall of 2014, announced that starting the next year a university education would be free—no tuition at all. If a modern economy does indeed depend in good part on a highly educated workforce, places like the United States, which are squeezing down long-term higher education with uncontrollable rising costs, are now in even more trouble.

All this too-lengthy invocation of the impending, intensifying troubles in the U.S. politically constructed economy is designed to say that domination is not just there, it doesn't just happen. It has to have a basis, a fulcrum on which to place the lever it tries to move us with. And that basis is changing now in important ways, ways that call to us to change our strategies, our pathways to tomorrow.

The Republican elite, along with very substantial segments of the Democratic elite, who hire noncitizens and simultaneously call for their deportation, can't eat their cake and shit on it too—much as we might enjoy the spectacle of watching them try. Making life miserable for undocumented workers, as the state of Georgia recently did, who then move away, leaving the crops they once picked to rot, was probably just the beginning of something that will likely expand up the status hierarchies.

Our struggles might well be advanced by focusing on such contradictions, a strategy that will include movements of dis-occupation, of leaving, rather than just occupation. It has worked well for migrant farmworkers, and even, to press the reader's memories, for working-class strikers. It is interesting that in the early nineteenth century the French term that became the name for striking, a central weapon in labor's arsenal—*faire grève*—originally meant to go and look for work someplace else, as William Sewell (1980) has pointed out. There are other ways to withdraw labor than a strike, even though when jobs are made so few, in terms of need, they can be hard to implement. The creativity of labor did not end with the Great Depression and the development of the sit-down strike, the work-to-rule slowdowns, and then the national boycotts.

Are these all the useful contradictions in domination, or even the most useful? Of course not. Each collective entrant onto the terrain of struggle will have particularly relevant contradictions among the dominant to engage. Often these contradictions will be only a small part of the confrontation, if any part at all. There are times when they might help, and there are times when we just have to fall back on the realities of confrontation, and enjoy kicking ass from our stance on just one leg—but it is our own leg, and that matters greatly.

The more we can kick, the merrier, as the old one-legged man points out, on the way to building enjoyable, if deadly serious, struggles. Liberace, a flamboyantly gay, very financially successful piano-playing entertainer from the 1950s and 1960s, when it was not considered at all proper to be or to seem gay, when asked what he thought about being insultingly called gay, replied that he laughed all the way to the bank. With a different goal in mind, and a different purpose for the trip to the banks that rip people off, particularly by stealing their homes with fake signed documents, that laughter on the journey may still be one useful response.

I have been asked who in particular "we" should struggle against—the enemy needs a name and an identity to give our struggles focus. I don't think that is ultimately a useful perspective. The point is that different clusters of us, with different angers and different needs, need to go after different components of those who *actually* make our lives less productively livable. The word "actually" is crucial: those who think that women having rights is part of our problem, or that global warming is, like evolution, unprovable, are more a danger, used against us, than a route to betterment. Our struggles will be more charged with energy and optimism if I leave you to figure out what "actually" means. A good struggle must be rooted in our trust of each other, and our pleasure with, and the rewards of, our capacities to generate multiple and diverse struggles.

Such high-spirited optimism is useful and important, as the Occupy movements showed, but it has to be tempered with realism, as the same Occupy movements also demonstrated. Thus:

___

# TEN

## "We Dies in Harness . . ."

The Tomorrows of Vulnerable People

To both raise again and now continue from the point made in the introduction, by way of building a conclusion, I retell this story here.

In the late 1950s I went to college in Philadelphia and mostly supported myself by washing dishes at night in a coffeehouse restaurant. Weekday nights I was alone at this task; weekends I was joined by an elderly Black man.

One Friday evening he came to work clearly sick and hurting. He was pale, and he leaned hard against the sink while he worked, ignoring the water that splashed down his front. I urged him to go home and rest, telling him that for an evening or two I could work fast enough and hard enough to cover for him. He just shook his head no. When I repeated my urging, he looked at me and just said, "We dies in harness. That's what it is to be colored."

Not that's what it means, but that's what it is.

There are two huge tragedies being made here, around and beyond the specific life of this elderly man, who shortly after did not ever show up again. Nor could I find him, to find out how he was. We were both on a first-name/nickname basis, and the owner paid us at the end of every evening, in cash and stale food, so there were no records of anything.

The first tragedy was what the state did, and in new ways still tries to do, for that is the incident that led me to find out that the laws that established Social Security in the 1930s excluded the majority of Black workers by exempting farm labor and domestic service, the two largest categories of African American employment. When Social Security was expanded, sometime in the 1950s, the requirement that you had to be covered for forty quarter years—ten calendar years at a minimum—continued this policy into the future. And the intensity with which Social Security payments are chained to average income over the last five years of a person's wage earnings further denies a livable old age to the already poor.

We must of course confront, as fully as we can, the current attempts by the state to diminish Social Security, for this attempt, based on a claim that the program will soon run out of funds, is completely based on elite self-interest. All that has to be done is raise the income limits from which Social Security contributions are taken, and the program could continue and even expand forever. But in addition to this we have important work to do.

The second tragedy, the one that we might be able to more readily do something about, in a political climate where Congress is trying to diminish the inadequate Social Security benefits and privatize the program, is far more complexly contained in the same utterance: "We dies in harness. That's what it is to be colored." The tragedy here is my colleague's isolation from a substantial number of at least reasonably prosperous African Americans, who were very far from dying in the sorts of harness to which he referred.

I'm sure he knew that such people existed, but they lived in another world. And I don't think it mattered at all that some of the people in that other world, some of the African American people in particular, cared greatly about what was happening to the poorer and more hard-pressed people in their communities—wrote movingly about them, preached stirring religious and political sermons, painted deeply moving pictures, and tended the ill and injured with brilliance and deep caring. His world, defined by the vulnerabilities that allowed him to be perpetually harnessed, gave him an everyday life utterly separate from that reality, and that reality, for reasons I do not understand very much at all, was largely separate from him, despite the widespread caring in that more elite world.

At issue here, perhaps, is our need to understand what we call class in more complex ways, and to see it as it emerges among folks far down in the multiple hierarchies of domination. To just begin to illustrate the problem now before us, suppose I suggest that the very limited reach of caring by the better-off into the lives of the truly oppressed is part of the attraction of fundamentalism, of Black Muslims, of religious intensification, for they do pay attention to the most oppressed and the most vulnerable. Yet even the fundamentalists only reach so far down into the recesses of domination, into the lives of the most vulnerable, into the most uncertain tomorrows, for it is crucial for grasping what is happening that they usually continue, or intensify, the oppression of women, while at the same time offering them dignity in the church.

The world that people living in the recesses and the abysses that domination creates and they inhabit is, often in very surprising ways, a deeply closed world, a world that the people within it *themselves* wall off from what is beyond them, consciously or unconsciously. The following story begins to illustrate the problem.

My grandfather, the one who lived so assertively with the pie plates under the legs of the tables and beds, never as far as I knew wrote a single word. Nor did I ever see him read, although I think he could read the Hebrew script that is used for writing Yiddish. He spoke five languages, a heritage of his hard childhood and youth, and his travels from one peasant village to another, fixing things. In those days of wood and coal cookstoves, pots occasionally burned through on the bottom; he could rivet on them a completely leak-proof patch. I admired him greatly; his was, in many ways, my ideal of an autonomous and in that sense a successful life. Because of my feelings about him, his wife, my grandmother, was also especially dear to me.

She was, in the fullest sense, a peasant. She came from the Austro-Hungarian Empire. She must have told me more than a dozen times that when she was a little girl she saw the emperor Franz Joseph, on his white horse, and he waved to her. It was one of the high points of her life, and although I thought her focus on this wave from the emperor was strangely simple, I cherished her. She could write, barely—she wrote phonetically, spelling words as they sounded to her, often differently in the same sentence, with no punctuation beyond an occasional period or just a space.

I was a senior in college when I became close to a person whose grandmother wrote letters to us in flawless English, with a full range of punctuation, commas, semicolons, the lot. I was stunned, truly. Some people in my world—in my world—had grandparents who could write. I don't know what I was thinking all through high school and an Ivy League college—all the literature I read, all the histories—almost all were about or by people who could read and write. And I did both well enough in school to learn some of that world, and to have some access to it, but the point I am trying to make so intensely here is that it was not my world, not at all. It was a world out there, important and useful to know, but it had nothing to do with me, even though I went to their classes and washed their dishes. That is the sense of class and race—and race differentiated within its victims into elites and nonelites, and the many kinds of strivers in the middle—that I am trying to illuminate: a perspective that also defines a sense of race in the deeply poignant assertion that *we* dies in harness. But in one of the many realities we live within and against, "we" African Americans don't all die in harness, and even then "we" didn't.

But in some fundamental way, for my colleague at the kitchen sink, "we" did, for him and for many in the same sort of situation. That's how his people lived, the people he lived with, and among, and against. They all died in harness. And that is one of the realities of class and race and gender and citizenship that we have to get our hands and our minds around if we are going to make, or force, change. The felt isolation and the separation of the worlds of the most dominated that we have helped to create in our distance from each other must be accepted and dealt with, for our struggles to accomplish any of their tasks. It is of course not real isolation; the shape of their lives and their situations are deeply influenced, but not controlled, by domination and the daily maintenance of inequalities. But it is very real as a felt isolation, even when such feelings are not at all rational. For one of the clearest lessons of the history of struggle is that those of us who are a rung or a few rungs up one of the ladders cannot do much for those who are not, unless they are a full part of the struggle, unless we find ways of transcending their and our felt separations and isolations.

This situation is even more complex, but in ways that provide openings for our confrontations with domination. Not only do we compress our lives within a familiar and understood "we," but so also does domination. It is stunning how so many representatives in state and national legislatures, and also governors, have no idea about, or seem to think they can pay no attention to, what is happening "out there" in the lived world. They seem to know the world only in terms of their beliefs, not by getting close enough to look and to listen. We close ourselves off within our "we," but they do also, and that inward turning on the part of the dominant—that imperial ignorance of our representatives about the world they supposedly represent, which increasingly takes over whole political parties, opens up a space for us to catch them off guard. Or maybe they know, at least partially, but just don't care, which has the same effects.

We progressives, in our struggles against domination and injustice, may stand on one leg, lacking power, resources, access to media, ownership of elected representatives, and so forth, but we are not necessarily doomed on that basis, not at all. For domination scarcely is able to stand upright at all. The continual and intensifying collapse of contemporary capitalism keeps domination bent over, trying unsuccessfully to vomit out its unworkable strategies, such as printing money—strategies that mostly both perpetuate and intensify existing inequalities. But capitalism has not yet been able to eliminate its illusory fixes, such as just printing more money, so its continual decline provides our opportunity to create new strategies (see Streeck [2011, 2014] on this intensifying decline).

So we start from the constructed isolation—the we—that develops among ourselves in the context of the kinds of oppression that help us to realize that "we dies in harness." To this we add the realization that domination is no less turned in on itself than are we, and that gives us more potential than we might have realized.

After these last two stories about the collective isolation of those of us at the fuzzy end of the lollipop stick, as well as the ones with the sugar, making race can be more clearly seen as also occurring within each race. That is what the stories, which hopefully will come to have lives of their own, sought to accomplish: to broaden, and not at all just in this last instance, our sense both of struggle and of strategy by broadening our sense of what has been and is now happening while tomorrow comes closer.

One thing to mention here, which makes the resources for our struggles more clear, and more graspable. When I wrote, just above, that I could not find my coworker, when he stopped coming to the restaurant after that night when he came in sick, it was because both of us knew each other mostly by our nicknames. His was "Pop," my simple-minded deference to his age. My nickname that he gave me was "Snowflake." Snowflake in those days in the

1950s was what you called the blackest guy in a work crew. I learned that the summer I worked clearing brush under high-voltage power lines. I am visibly White, but the combination of that and the intensity of my racial justice commitments (I refused to say or stand for the pledge of allegiance to the flag when I was in high school in the early 1950s, because there was no liberty or justice for Blacks) made the nickname he pinned on me, Snowflake, a stroke of joyful brilliance. That is the central point here. Even the most oppressed, the hardest squeezed, have their wisdom and their dignity and their joys, and these qualities are crucial for struggle.

## WELL DONE

One further story, and one comment, to tie this book together. This story is likely to be apocryphal, to be something that people wanted to happen that way, or it could be true, for I heard it from one of the organizers of the event. In either case it teaches, very well, a crucial lesson.

The sit-ins at the Woolworth lunch counter in Greensboro, North Carolina, in 1964, were wonderfully successful, for they precipitated a national change. Woolworth, the so-called five-and-dime, was a nationwide chain of stores, mostly quite large stores, that sold a wide range of low-price goods. They almost all had lunch counters, at which the African American patrons of the store could neither sit nor eat. The fact that Woolworth's was a national chain made a national boycott of its stores both possible and effective (although there is clearly more to it than that, for the national chains of McDonald's and Walmart now deeply abuse their workers, if not their patrons, with what seems to be, at least for the moment, assured impunity). But the four young college students from the University of North Carolina at Greensboro, who started the sit-in at the lunch counter to protest their exclusion, suffered a lot of violence for introducing us to the then effectiveness of boycotts in the struggle against segregated public eating.

They went into the Woolworth store, sat down at the lunch counter, and were ignored. Now African Americans spent a lot of money in this store, collectively, but could neither work there nor eat there. As they sat there, a fairly substantial crowd of White racists and curiosity seekers gathered outside and inside, and the manager of the store became concerned that his store might be trashed were there a melee. So he told the waitress to get rid of the four students. The waitress, as the story goes, went to them and said, "We don't serve niggers." One young man replied, "I don't want a nigger, I want a hamburger, well done."

Wonderful beyond wonderful, for it teaches the lesson that we must never play by their rules. And that is crucial for confronting domination. That young man paid a high price for teaching us that lesson, and to honor his gift we must keep firmly in mind that we cannot confront domination if we play by their rules. Those rules are written so they win.

## MAKING OUR OWN "WE"

If we are not going to play by their rules, and if our struggle has to be based on "we," not "I," it might help to return to discuss my use of "we" or "us" and "they" or "them" throughout this book. I imagine that there is a long list of readers who want very much to take me to task for these generalizations, to claim that only lefties make such outrageous groupings of phenomena that are best deconstructed into their minutely different particulars, whatever. The attack on this usage should be organized like a busy deli counter at a store—the critics of this point should take a number, stand in line, and wait their turn. For a crucial political action point is at stake in what I am doing, in what I am trying to teach to a new generation of activists, and in this context the criticisms are baloney: all grease, salt, and filler.

For one of the most crucial lessons of the struggle for rights and justice is that when any of the victims ask, "What can I do about this?" the answer is almost always nothing. It is only when people ask, "What can we do about this?" and *start working to build their own, and an effective "we" that we have a chance.* So this book on the production of race and inequality, and how we might effectively struggle against such continuing developments, must use a perspective rooted in "we" and "them." Whatever simplicities it introduces, and there are many, they are nowhere nearly as harmful as the simplicities of individuation, or the small-group version of individuation, or separating race from gender from class from citizenship from locality, or any other category of inequality, even though each individual and each category of the dominated has its own causal history and its own inescapable struggles, whether or not the victims want this. So it's we and them, in the most inclusive sense of "we."

This is not a novel claim, not at all. Community Organizing 101 has for decades insisted on the "we," as the effective replacement for "I." All I am adding here is a seemingly minor but crucial point. We each need to make our own oppositional and creative "we." There are few if any standards or preconditions, so long as we are centered, more or less directly, on the struggles for social justice. In this context it seems to me crucial to have an enormous range of "we," for when we try to make our struggles and our ideas uniform, we become more vulnerable to attack. Our fluidity and our multiplicity are our protection and our strength. Think of what the pre-Socratic Greek philosopher Heraclitus said: "You cannot step twice in the same river." Think of it as a suggestion for constructing the opposition to domination and exploitation, which would gladly step on us, on "we," if we stood still long enough to let them.

This is what I am invoking when I, a White Jew boy, use "we" in the context of the struggles of African Americans, and even when I discuss the struggles of Palestinians and, more generally, Muslims, for something that even resembles justice, dignity, and equality. For all the self-deception and self-aggrandizement such "we" makes possible, for all the minimization of brutally different privileges and access that "we" conceals, if we don't say "we," the struggle is more likely lost. So we invoke "we" and "them" with our eyes necessarily open to the possibility of our own self-deception. It has to be done, in the midst of its dangers and in the midst of its potential.

And keep in mind that "we" is not in the slightest an invitation to a love-fest. Decades ago there was an off-Broadway play (whose name and author I forget) about the brutally suppressed strike in the Colorado hard coal (anthracite) mines. At the urging of John D. Rockefeller, who owned the mines, the state National Guard was called in, and burned the tent village where the miners and their families were living, in a Colorado winter, after they were driven from the mine-owned houses. More than burned the tents, they shot many people trying to escape the fires. At the end of the play there are three main people onstage, along with the police: one of the organizers of the strike; a tough miner who was also nasty and contemptuous; and an angelic soul who had been a friend of the organizer. It became clear that this angelic soul was the one who pointed out the strike leader to the police, and as they were taking the leader offstage to his predictable fate, the rough and somewhat contemptuous miner tried, at great personal risk, to intervene to free him. The strike organizer turned to the audience, as the curtain came down, and said: "We don't pick our friends and we don't pick our enemies. History does that for us."

While this ending is a mixture of simplicity and romanticism, it also contains a crucial warning. All that I have said about the importance of direct and focused caring and concern, and all that I have said about the political significance of constructing "we," does not for a moment mean you have to like the people you work with. Respect and concern in this context are political acts, not necessarily personal.

Good luck. Enjoy the struggles. Keep believing that "history," that most abstract of categories, "is on our side," as we once said in the sixties, even when it is clear that it could not possibly take sides or, if it did, it would now not be too likely to be very much on our side—when we can't even afford to buy a single congressperson and are struggling against folks who buy them by the dozens or more, and when we must struggle to learn against an education system that is either nonexistent, denied to the poor so it also denies their children, or designed to deny us all an education with classes in memorization, media simplicities, stereotypes, and taking exams. All this very much plus a world that is increasingly uncertain, particularly about what our almost inescapable increasingly totalitarian states can do to us— from a distance, so we have vanishingly little opportunity for dialogue or appeal. All that seems to remain for increasingly many is to fall back on the imaginary certainties of religious texts. Other possibilities remain within our grasp.

The notion that history is on our side helps make it so. History is not just about yesterday but also about the multiple ways that we live and act, on or against, our historically soaked todays, as we reach toward tomorrow. Thus history must also be as much about the impending, uncertain tomorrows as about the half-remembered yesterdays. So all we have to do to start is to realize that tomorrow is just as uncertain for them as it is for us, and that we who actively and consciously live both within and against our histories must already have our hands on some of our tomorrows. That's a good start for the tasks before us. That and a well-done hamburger, now maybe even a vegetarian one.

# DEMOGRAPHIC POST–CIVIL RIGHTS HISTORY OF
## AFRICAN AMERICAN TOWNS IN ROBESON COUNTY

The following is a historical demography of the four now predominantly African American towns in Robeson County, North Carolina, and one town with a slight White majority.

## Population Composition

Fairmont and Rowland were centers of the tobacco production and warehouse business, which declined massively after the 1970s. The large proportion of African Americans in these villages during the 1960s was related to their employment in the warehouses and as day laborers brought out to work on the surrounding farms. Red Springs and St. Pauls had the well-earned reputation of being particularly hostile to African Americans and Native Americans, hence few would try to live there.

Red Springs, Fairmont, Rowland, and St. Pauls—all but Maxton—annexed part of their surrounding townships in the 1950s, which kept the total population stable or slightly expanding. This was largely related to bringing surrounding White populations within the town boundaries so the children could attend the all-White schools in the towns. As soon as you traveled past the actual town of Maxton in the 1950s and 1960s (as opposed to the legally defined town), the countryside was inhabited largely by Native Americans, who did not want to be in the town of Maxton, nor were they wanted, so Maxton did not then expand.

Red Springs had, until quite recently, the reputation that it was unsafe for Native Americans "to be in the town after dark." St. Pauls had, and still has, a reputation of active hostility to non-Whites.

## TABLE A.1. CHANGING POPULATION COMPOSITION, 1960–2010

| Town | Total | White | % | Black | % | Indian | % |
|---|---|---|---|---|---|---|---|
| Maxton | | | | | | | |
| 1960 | 1,755 | 1,089 | 62.1 | 663 | 37.8 | 3 | .2 |
| 1980 | 2,711 | 1,119 | 41.3 | 1,140 | 42.1 | 441 | 16.3 |
| 2010 | 2,426 | 466 | 19.2 | 1,578 | 65.0 | 336 | 13.8 |
| Rowland | | | | | | | |
| 1960 | 1,408 | 581 | 41.3 | 784 | 55.7 | 43 | 3.1 |
| 1980 | 1,841 | 623 | 33.8 | 1,025 | 55.7 | 192 | 10.4 |
| 2010 | 1,037 | 218 | 21.0 | 729 | 70.3 | 66 | 6.4 |
| Fairmont | | | | | | | |
| 1960 | 2,286 | 1,194 | 52.2 | 967 | 42.3 | 120 | 5.2 |
| 1980 | 2,658 | 1,102 | 41.5 | 1,318 | 49.6 | 235 | 8.8 |
| 2010 | 2,663 | 699 | 26.2 | 1,493 | 56.1 | 358 | 13.4 |
| Red Springs | | | | | | | |
| 1960 | 2,767 | 1827 | 66.0 | 940 | 34.0 | 0 | 0 |
| 1980 | 3,607 | 1,646 | 45.6 | 1,725 | 47.8 | 222 | 6.2 |
| 2010 | 3,428 | 1,104 | 32.2 | 1,673 | 48.8 | 430 | 12.5 |
| St. Pauls | | | | | | | |
| 1960 | 2,249 | 2,078 | 92.4 | 171 | 7.6 | 0 | 0 |
| 1980 | 1,639 | 1,421 | 86.7 | 156 | 9.5 | 2 | .1 |
| 2010* | 2,035 | 1,093 | 53.7 | 389 | 19.1 | 119 | 5.8 |

*Source:* U.S. Census of Population, vol. 1, Chapter B, General Population Characteristics, Part 35, North Carolina.

* In 2010 the census started two new categories: "some other race" and "two or more races." These figures were only reported for St. Pauls. The figure for "some other race" was 359, or 17.6 percent of St. Pauls' population; the figure for "two or more races" was 69, or 3.4 percent.

### Economic Characteristics, 2010

Robeson County is still by far the poorest county in North Carolina. The state publishes statistics on which counties qualify for supplemental aid for their school systems, based on poverty in the county. The following list shows percentage of county above poverty level and dollars of aid per child.

LOW WEALTH ELIGIBLE COUNTIES, FY 2012–2013

| | | |
|---|---|---|
| Robeson County | 55.97% | $737.85 |
| Greene County | 59.99% | $670.48 |
| Hoke County | 62.65% | $625.90 |

| | | |
|---|---|---|
| Richmond County | 64.85% | $589.04 |
| Sampson County | 64.91% | $588.03 |
| Scotland County | 64.91% | $588.03 |
| Anson County | 67.44% | $545.63 |
| Harnett County | 67.98% | $536.58 |
| Stanley County | 79.03% | $351.41 |
| Surry County | 79.32% | $344.37 |
| Montgomery County | 81.05% | $317.56 |
| Rutherford County | 80.09% | $289.94 |
| Northampton County | 83.46% | $277.17 |
| Lee County | 83.62% | $274.49 |
| Wilkes County | 83.78% | $271.81 |
| Burke County | 79.85% | $270.14 |

### Economic Characteristics, 2010–2012

The low number of employed males in Maxton, compared with employed females, is breathtaking. But note that far more women than men are in severe poverty. Also note the small numbers of unemployed, compared with the total "working age" population. The number of unemployed does not count those not working but only those registered with the unemployment office. The ones who have stopped going weekly to register are not even counted as part of the civilian labor force. If you compare the numbers of employed to the total adult population, and even discounting a substantial number of this difference for reasons of disability and not wanting or needing to work, the percentage of people employed is very low, and a shocking number of those work at part-time or seasonal jobs. Note from the figures in table A.2 that there are 1,887 people in Maxton over sixteen years old, and the labor force counts only 946, or 50 percent. It is more than doubtful that a substantial proportion of the 50 percent of adults who are not in the labor force just enjoy staying home and being supported by someone else. Not when the poverty rate is so high, and keep in mind that the official "poverty rate" measures not poverty but very serious need. Fairmont is very similar to Maxton.

Rowland is in worse shape than Maxton. It is about half the size in total population and a decade ago looked completely devastated but now is cleaned up—sidewalks swept, many buildings on the main street painted, few if any barefoot children now playing in mostly deserted streets. But the town is surrounded by very large commercial farms that are almost

## TABLE A.2. MAXTON POPULATION

| | No. in Category | No. Poor | Poor (%) |
|---|---|---|---|
| **Age** | | | |
| Under 18 | 661 | 231 | 34.9 |
| 18–64 | 1,358 | 472 | 34.8 |
| 65 and over | 437 | 87 | 19.9 |
| **Gender** | | | |
| Male | 976 | 314 | 32.2 |
| Female | 1,480 | 476 | 32.2 |
| **Race** | | | |
| White | 280 | 79 | 28.2 |
| Black | 1,790 | 493 | 27.5 |
| Indian | 356 | 209 | 58.7 |
| **Education** | | | |
| Population 25 years and older | 1,660 | 518 | 31.2 |
| Less than high school graduate | 372 | 150 | 40.3 |
| High school grad or equivalency* | 503 | 255 | 50.7 |
| Some college or associate's degree | 613 | 104 | 17.0 |
| Bachelor's degree or higher | 172 | 9 | 5.2 |
| **Employment status** | | | |
| Civilian labor force 16 and over | 946 | 164 | 17.3 |
| Employed | 796 | 120 | 15.1 |
| Male | 226 | 65 | 28.8 |
| Female | 570 | 55 | 9.6 |
| Unemployed | 150 | 44 | 29.3 |
| Male | 97 | 21 | 21.6 |
| Female | 53 | 23 | 43.4 |
| **Work Experience** | | | |
| Population 16 years and over | 1,887 | 580 | 30.7 |
| Worked full-time year-round past 12 months | 410 | 50 | 12.2 |
| Worked part-time or part year past 12 months | 515 | 116 | 22.5 |
| Did not work | 962 | 415 | 43.1 |
| **All individuals below:** | | | |
| 50 percent of poverty level | 441 | | |
| 125 percent of poverty level | 1,049 | | |
| 150 percent of poverty level | 1,106 | | |

|  | No. in Category | No. Poor | Poor (%) |
|---|---|---|---|
| Unrelated individuals for whom poverty status is determined | 504 | 331 | 65.7 |
| Male | 180 | 134 | 74.4 |
| Female | 324 | 197 | 60.8 |
| Mean income deficit for unrelated individuals | $6,102 | | |

*Source*: U.S. Census Bureau, 2008–2012 American Community Survey.

*Note:* Total population 2010: 2,426; Population surveyed (2012): 2,456; Percentage below poverty line: 32.2. The following figures for each of the towns are all estimates, with differing margins of probable error. Since the purpose of this appendix is just to give an introductory overview, and the probable margins of error for each figure are readily available from the online source should they be needed, that information has been dropped from these tables.

* High school does little good for avoiding subsequent poverty. Note that social assistance keeps people below the poverty line, meaning that it is designed explicitly to support life at unlivable levels. It does not matter in terms of chances of being below the poverty line whether or not once you start high school you ever finish.

entirely mechanized, and by farms that have been given over to solar electric generation and large, mechanized commercial chicken houses. Both enterprises, after being built, use little "unskilled" local labor. Because the chicken houses almost all use workers from Central America to do such work as combing through the facility daily to pick up and throw out dead birds, or to load birds on trucks for delivery, "unskilled" has a broad range of unspoken meanings that clearly take precedence over levels of socially defined skill.

St. Pauls has much less poverty than Red Springs: 31 percent of residents are below the official poverty line, as opposed to 52 percent in Red Springs. It is, by reputation, the most hostile place in the county for an African American or Native American to live, so it is the only one of the five towns where African Americans now constitute only about 17 percent of the total population, and about a quarter of the White population. Native Americans constitute only about 10 percent of the White population.

## TABLE A.3. ROWLAND POPULATION

| | No. in Category | No. Poor | Poor (%) |
|---|---|---|---|
| **Age** | | | |
| Under 18 | 173 | 56 | 32.4 |
| 18–64 | 603 | 210 | 34.8 |
| 65 and over | 201 | 74 | 36.8 |
| **Gender** | | | |
| Male | 485 | 149 | 30.7 |
| Female | 492 | 191 | 38.8 |
| **Race*** | | | |
| White | 241 | 47 | 19.5 |
| Black | 616 | 269 | 43.7 |
| Indian | 101 | 12 | 11.9 |
| Two or more races | 17 | 10 | 58.8 |
| **Education** | | | |
| Population 25 years and older | 721 | 236 | 32.7 |
| Less than high school graduate | 208 | 66 | 31.7 |
| High school grad or equivalency[†] | 224 | 100 | 44.6 |
| Some college or associate's degree | 211 | 77 | 33.2 |
| Bachelor's degree or higher | 78 | 0 | 0 |
| **Employment status** | | | |
| Civilian labor force 16 and over | 400 | 64 | 16 |
| Employed | 312 | 20 | 6.4 |
| Male | 158 | 3 | 1.9 |
| Female | 154 | 17 | 11.0 |
| Unemployed | 88 | 44 | 50 |
| Male | 45 | 22 | 48.9 |
| Female | 43 | 22 | 51.2 |
| **Work experience** | | | |
| Population 16 years and over | 823 | 290 | 35.2 |
| Worked full-time year-round past 12 months | 201 | 5 | 2.5 |
| Worked part-time or part year past 12 months | 177 | 31 | 17.5 |
| Did not work | 445 | 245 | 57.1 |
| **All individuals below:** | | | |
| 50 percent of poverty level | 127 | | |
| 125 percent of poverty level | 423 | | |
| 150 percent of poverty level | 528 | | |

| | No. in Category | No. Poor | Poor (%) |
|---|---|---|---|
| Unrelated individuals for whom poverty status is determined | 191 | 78 | 40.8 |
| Male | 93 | 38 | 40.9 |
| Female | 98 | 40 | 40.8 |
| Mean income deficit for unrelated individuals | $5,312 | | |

*Source:* U.S. Census Bureau, 2008–2012 American Community Survey.

*Note:* Total population 2010: 1,037; Population surveyed (2012): 977; Percentage below poverty line: 34.8.

* If I were to hunch what is behind the exceptionally high poverty rate of the multiracial population, in addition to the fact that very poor people seem to be either less bound to, or less free to, follow such social conventions as what are regarded as appropriate marriage or intimacy partners, I would suggest that a lack of kin connections and kin support keeps them in this difficult situation, made more difficult by social stigma.

† High school does little good for avoiding subsequent poverty.

## TABLE A.4. RED SPRINGS POPULATION

|  | No. in Category | No. Poor | Poor (%) |
|---|---|---|---|
| **Age** |  |  |  |
| Under 18 | 1,045 | 853 | 81.6 |
| 18–64 | 1,818 | 688 | 37.8 |
| 65 and over | 503 | 186 | 37.0 |
| **Gender** |  |  |  |
| Male | 1,584 | 755 | 47.7 |
| Female | 1,782 | 972 | 54.5 |
| **Race** |  |  |  |
| White | 1,219 | 429 | 35.2 |
| Black | 1,549 | 891 | 57.5 |
| Indian | 265 | 102 | 38.5 |
| Two or more races | 101 | 73 | 72.3 |
| Some other race [= Latino/a] | 219 | 219 | 100 |
| Hispanic or Latino origin* | 357 | 319 | 89.4 |
| **Education** |  |  |  |
| Population 25 years and older | 2,056 | 736 | 35.8 |
| Less than high school graduate | 416 | 205 | 49.3 |
| High school grad or equivalency[†] | 821 | 410 | 49.9 |
| Some college or associate's degree | 437 | 121 | 27.7 |
| Bachelor's degree or higher | 382 | 0 | 0 |
| **Employment status** |  |  |  |
| Civilian labor force 16 and over | 1,299 | 467 | 36.0 |
| Employed | 1,128 | 341 | 30.2 |
| Male | 631 | 169 | 26.8 |
| Female | 497 | 172 | 34.6 |
| Unemployed | 171 | 126 | 73.7 |
| Male | 29 | 0 | 0 |
| Female | 142 | 126 | 88.7 |
| **Work experience** |  |  |  |
| Population 16 years and over | 2,446 | 947 | 38.7 |
| Worked full-time year-round past 12 months | 897 | 187 | 20.8 |
| Worked part-time or part year past 12 months | 369 | 201 | 54.5 |
| Did not work | 1,180 | 559 | 47.4 |

|  | No. in Category | No. Poor | Poor (%) |
|---|---|---|---|
| All individuals below: |  |  |  |
| 50 percent of poverty level | 258 |  |  |
| 125 percent of poverty level | 1,869 |  |  |
| 150 percent of poverty level | 1,996 |  |  |
| Unrelated individuals for whom poverty status is determined | 649 | 266 | 41.0 |
| Male | 217 | 78 | 35.9 |
| Female | 432 | 188 | 43.5 |
| Mean income deficit for unrelated individuals‡ | $7,280 |  |  |

*Source*: U.S. Census Bureau, 2008–2012 American Community Survey.

Note: Total population 2010: 3,428; Population surveyed (2012): 3,326; Percentage below poverty line: 51.3.

* This seems an undercount of the Hispanic population in Red Springs. It is widely regarded as the central residence for Hispanics in the region, and one quite large supermarket in town focuses on "Mexican" foods. The number 219 for "Some other race" probably represents the Hispanic population who do not want to self-identify. It is notable that 100 percent are below the poverty line.

† High school does little good for avoiding subsequent poverty.

‡ Note the income deficit in Red Springs is extreme. There is a comparatively low percentage of unrelated people in poverty, probably reflecting the fact that many Hispanics in town are there as laborers who do not or will not be allowed to settle with their families.

# REFERENCES

Baldwin, James. (1963) 1995. *The Fire Next Time*. New York: Modern Library.

Bauman, Zygmunt. 1989. *Modernity and the Holocaust*. Ithaca, NY: Cornell University Press.

Bauman, Zygmunt. 2007. *Liquid Times: Living in an Age of Uncertainty*. Cambridge: Polity.

Berger, John. (1983) 2011. "The Time of the Cosmonauts." In *Once in Europa*, 74–108. New York: Vintage.

Berger, John. (1985) 2011. "The Storyteller." In *Sense of Sight*, 13–18. New York: Knopf Doubleday.

Berger, John. (1991) 1992. *Keeping a Rendezvous*. New York: Vintage.

Berger, John. 2005. *Here Is Where We Meet*. New York: Vintage.

Blu, Karen I. 1980. *The Lumbee Problem: The Making of an American Indian People*. New York: Cambridge University Press.

Boerma, Lindsey. 2013. "Republicans' Belief in Evolution Plummets, Poll Reveals." CBS *News*, December 30. http://www.cbsnews.com/news/republicans-belief-in-evolution-plummets-poll-reveals/.

Charles, Dan. 2013. "Pig Manure Reveals More Reason to Worry about Antibiotics." The Salt (blog). NPR, February 11. http://www.npr.org/blogs/thesalt/2013/02/11/171690001/pig-manure-reveals-more-reason-to-worry-about-antibiotics.

Christensen, Rob. 2010. *The Paradox of Tar Heel Politics: The Personalities, Elections, and Events That Shaped Modern North Carolina*. Chapel Hill: University of North Carolina Press.

Daniel, Pete. (1972) 1990. *The Shadow of Slavery: Peonage in the South, 1901–1969*. Urbana: University of Illinois Press.

Daniel, Pete. 2013. *Dispossession: Discrimination against African American Farmers in the Age of Civil Rights*. Chapel Hill: University of North Carolina Press.

Downs, Jim. 2012. *Sick from Freedom: African-American Illness and Suffering during the Civil War and Reconstruction*. New York: Oxford University Press.

Du Bois, W. E. B. (1920) 2007. *Darkwater: Voices from Within the Veil*. New York: Oxford University Press.

DW. 2013. "UN: World Trouble Spots Push Refugee Count to 19-Year High." June 19. http://www.dw.de/un-world-trouble-spots-push-refugee-count-to-19 -year-high/a-16893111.

Eagleton, Terry. 2000. *The Idea of Culture*. Malden, MA: Blackwell.

Ellison, Ralph. (1952) 1995. *The Invisible Man*. New York: Vintage.

Fleegler, Robert L. 2006. "Theodore G. Bilbo and the Decline of Public Racism, 1938–1947." *Journal of Mississippi History*, Spring, 1–27. http://mdah.state.ms.us /new/wp-content/uploads/2013/07/bilbo.pdf.

Foucault, Michel. 1977. *Discipline and Punish: The Birth of the Prison*. New York: Pantheon.

Fredrickson, George M. 1989. *The Arrogance of Race: Historical Perspectives on Slavery*. Middletown, CT: Wesleyan University Press.

Geertz, Clifford. 1973. *The Interpretation of Cultures*. New York: Basic Books.

Gill, Lesley. 2004. *The School of the Americas: Military Training and Political Violence in the Americas*. Durham, NC: Duke University Press.

Gould, Stephen Jay. 1977. *Ever since Darwin: Reflections in Natural History*. New York: Norton.

Green, Linda. 2009. "The Fear of No Future: Guatemala Migrants, Dispossession and Dislocation." *Anthropologia* 51:327–41.

Green, Linda. 2011. "The Nobodies: Neoliberalism, Violence and Migration." *Medical Anthropology* 30:366–85.

Hall, Stuart. 1997. "Race, the Floating Signifier." Lecture delivered at Goldsmith's College, London. YouTube. Uploaded November 2, 2014. https://www.youtube .com/watch?v=bRk9MZvOd2c.

Hannerz, Ulf. 1969. *Soulside: Inquiries into Ghetto Culture and Community*. New York: Columbia University Press.

Hobsbawm, Eric. 1994. *The Age of Extremes: A History of the World, 1914–1991*. New York: Pantheon.

Holley, Donald. 2003. "Mechanical Cotton Picker." EH.Net Encyclopedia, edited by Robert Whaples. June 16. http://eh.net/encyclopedia/mechanical-cotton -picker/.

Howell, Joseph T. 1973. *Hard Living on Clay Street: Portraits of Blue Collar Families*. Garden City, NY: Anchor Press.

Hunt, Eleanor P., and Stanley M. Goldstein. 1964. *Trends in Infant and Child Mortality, 1961*. Children's Bureau Statistical Series 76. Washington, DC: U.S. Department of Health, Education, and Welfare, Welfare Administration, Children's Bureau. Provided by the Maternal and Child Health Library, Georgetown University. http://www.mchlibrary.info/history/chbu/2371.pdf.

Iliffe, John. 1987. *African Poor: A History*. Cambridge: Cambridge University Press.

Johnson, Thomas L., and Nina J. Root, eds. 2002. *Camera Man's Journey: Julian Dimock's South*. Athens: University of Georgia Press.

Joint Center's Health Policy Institute—Infant Mortality Commission. 2014. *African American Infant Mortality*. The Community Foundation for Greater New Haven. Accessed October 1. http://www.cfgnh.org/Portals/0/Uploads /Documents/Public/AAInfantMortality_Joint%20Center.pdf.

Lavere, Jane. 2013. "New Ad Campaign Targets Childhood Hunger." *New York Times*, September 5.

Le Blanc, Paul, and Helen C. Scott, eds. 2010. *Rosa Luxemburg: Socialism or Barbarism: Selected Writings*. London: Pluto.

Levi, Carlo. 1989. *Christ Stopped at Eboli: The Story of a Year*. New York: Farrar, Straus and Giroux.

Litwack, Leon F. 1999. *Trouble in Mind: Black Southerners in the Age of Jim Crow*. New York, Vintage.

Lorde, Audre. 1984. "The Master's Tools Will Never Dismantle the Master's House." In *Sister Outsider: Essays and Speeches*, 110–14. Berkeley, CA: Crossing Press.

Lowery, Melinda Maynor. 2010. *Lumbee Indians in the Jim Crow South: Race, Identity and the Making of a Nation*. Chapel Hill: University of North Carolina Press.

Magdoff, Fred, and John B. Forster. 2014. "Stagnation and Financialization." *Monthly Review*, May, 1–24.

Moore, Barrington, Jr. 1966. *Social Origins of Dictatorship and Democracy: Lord and Peasant in the Making of the Modern World*. Boston: Beacon.

Muhammad, Nisa. 2013. "Review of *So Rich, So Poor: Ending Poverty in America*, by Peter Edelman." *Crisis*, Fall, 9.

Piglia, Robert. 2011. "Thesis on the Short Story." *New Left Review*, no. 70: 63–68.

Piven, Frances Fox, and Richard A. Cloward. 1977. *Poor People's Movements: Why They Succeed, How They Fail*. New York: Pantheon.

Robinson, Joan. (1962) 2006. *Economic Philosophy*. New Brunswick, NJ: Aldine Transaction.

Ryssdal, Kai. 2013. "Wealth Gap Grows between Black and White in U.S." Interview with Tom Shapiro. *Marketplace*, February 27. http://www.marketplace.org /topics/wealth-poverty/wealth-gap-grows-between-black-and-white-us.

Scott, James C. 1985. *Weapons of the Weak: Everyday Forms of Resistance*. New Haven, CT: Yale University Press.

Sewell, William Hamilton. 1980. *Work and Revolution in France: The Language of Labor from the Old Regime to 1848*. New York: Cambridge University Press.

Sider, Gerald M. 2003a. *Between History and Tomorrow: Making and Breaking Everyday Life in Rural Newfoundland*. 2nd ed. Toronto: University of Toronto Press. (Substantially expanded and updated edition of *Culture and Class in Anthropology and History*. Peterborough, ON, Canada: Broadview, 2003.)

Sider, Gerald M. 2003b. *Living Indian Histories: Lumbee and Tuscarora People in North Carolina.* 2nd ed. Chapel Hill: University of North Carolina Press.

Sider, Gerald M. 2014a. "Making and Breaking the Aboriginal Remote: Realities, Languages, Tomorrows (A Commentary)." *Oceania* 84, July, 158–68.

Sider, Gerald M. 2014b. *Skin for Skin: Death and Life for Inuit and Innu.* Durham, NC: Duke University Press.

Sider, Gerald. n.d. "The Trajectories of State." Book manuscript.

Stampp, Kenneth M. 1956. *The Peculiar Institution: Slavery in the Anti-bellum South.* New York: Random House.

StateMaster.com. 2004. "Percent of Housing Units That Are Mobile Homes (Most Recent) by State." *American Community Survey 2004.* http://www.statemaster .com/graph/hou_per_of_hou_uni_tha_are_mob_hom-housing-percent-units -mobile-homes.

Streeck, Wolfgang. 2011. "The Crises of Democratic Capitalism." *New Left Review* 71, September–October, 5–29.

Streeck, Wolfgang. 2014. "The Politics of Exit." *New Left Review* 88, July–August, 121–29.

Tolnay, Stewart, and E. M. Beck. 1995. *A Festival of Violence: An Analysis of Southern Lynchings, 1882–1930.* Urbana: University of Illinois Press.

U.S. Congress. 1964. The Civil Rights Act of 1964. Pub. L. 88-352, 78 Stat. 241.

U.S. Congress. 1965. The Voting Rights Act of 1965. 42 U.S.C. §§ 1973–1973bb-1.

U.S. Riot Commission. 1968. *Report of the National Advisory Commission on Civil Disorders.* Washington, DC: U.S. Government Printing Office.

Waldman, Scott. 2014. "Cuomo Administration Edited and Delayed Key Fracking Study." *Capital,* October 6. http://www.capitalnewyork.com/article/albany/2014 /10/8553530/cuomo-administration-edited-and-delayed-key-fracking-study.

Weber, Max. (1905) 2001. *The Protestant Ethic and the Spirit of Capitalism.* New York: Routledge.

Weber, Max. (1919) 1958. "Politics as Vocation." In *From Max Weber: Essays in Sociology,* edited by Hans H. Gerth and C. Wright Mills, 77–128. New York: Oxford University Press.

Williams, Raymond. 1976. *Keywords: A Vocabulary of Culture and Society.* New York: Oxford University Press.

Williams, Raymond. 1985. *Keywords: A Vocabulary of Culture and Society.* Rev. ed. New York: Oxford University Press.

Zola, Émile. (1885) 2004. *Germinal.* Translated by Roger Pearson. New York: Penguin.

Chicago, Illinois, 36
chicken packing. See meatpacking plants
China, 184, 185
Christianity, 147, 168
Chrysler, 123, 161
churches. See congregations
citizens/citizenship, 102, 126, 201; non-,
    176–77; race and, 161–62; rights and
    benefits of, 120, 136, 159
City University of New York (CUNY), 75–76
civilization, 98, 147, 179; wildernesses
    within, 109–10
civil rights: elite society and, 29; indi-
    vidual rights and, 30; laws, 17, 53;
    "Mexican" workers and, 57; peculiar
    consequences of, 61–63; Quaker activ-
    ists, 32; in Robeson County (1970s),
    52–53; role of churches in, 40; role
    of courts in, 180–81; "so-called," 28;
    struggles, 40, 86, 105, 175–80, 184;
    victories, 62, 171
civil society, 132, 133; courts, 180–81;
    Hegel's concept, 28–29, 178–79
class, 50, 78, 102, 142, 198; culture and,
    105; language and, 141; production
    and maintenance of, 123; stability and,
    99; state and, 126; struggles, 86. See
    also middle class; White working class
Clio, South Carolina, 34
coal mines, 166–67, 202
cockroaches: in old-law tenements,
    71–72; people living like, 83; racing,
    78–81, 84
Cold War, 117–18
Colt, Samuel, 121, 162
commodities, 85, 114, 134
communism, 102, 103, 187
congregations, 39–41, 63; fundamental-
    ist, 182–83; Indian/Black differences,
    67–68; Puerto Rican, 73
conk rag, 43–46, 130, 149–50, 177
consent, 136
conspiracy, 30
Constitution of the United States, 61
consumer demand, 185, 190
consumption, 130, 136, 192

corporations, 120, 155, 161, 188, 192; com-
    mercial fishing, 167; profits, 185, 191;
    and state alliance, 97, 177
cotton picker, mechanical, 52–53, 175
credit, 185, 190, 192
Cree Indians, 58
culture: class and, 50; concepts of,
    47–48, 94–97, 104–6, 169–70; local,
    160; modern, 107; problem of, 98;
    shared, 163, 165
Cuomo, Andrew, 188
custom and sorrow, 145, 150–51
cut and stitch factories, 54–55, 62, 153–55

Daly, Maura, 101
Daniel, Pete, 160
Darwin, Charles, 95
Davis, Charles, 113
debt, 185, 188, 190–91; peonage, 109,
    160–61
deconstruction. See meatpacking plants
democracy, 82, 131; floating, 133–35,
    186–87; illusion/fantasy of, 98, 107–8,
    120, 121, 136, 180; voting rights and,
    36, 52
Democratic Party, 134
Detroit, Michigan, 13, 177, 188–89, 191–92
dignity, 28, 46, 200; claiming one's,
    156–59, 164–66; contradiction of,
    80–81; culture and, 48; working class,
    72–73
dishwashing, 3–4, 195
disposable people, 120, 170, 187, 189;
    production of, 7, 140
distance, 137, 141–42
"dog eat dog" expression, 166, 168–70
dominant society, 1, 66, 82, 109, 150;
    values of, 158; wants and needs of,
    176–77
domination: of African Americans,
    24, 32, 35, 68; chaos and, 68, 85, 175,
    181–82; confrontation with, 198,
    200–201; economic control and,
    189–90, 193; elite, 29, 59; government,
    129–30; impunity of, 111–12, 129,
    163, 165; intimacy and distance and,

# For Reference

**Not to be taken from this room**